DIRTY DOZEN 5

DONE AND DUSTED

About the Author

Paul Anderson spent fourteen years as a police reporter with the *Herald Sun* before becoming the newspaper's chief court reporter in 2009. He has won team Walkley and Quill awards for crime coverage. Paul is the author of four other Dirty Dozen true-crime books: *Shocking Australian True Crime Stories*; *Melbourne's Gangland Killings*; *Bodies, Bullets and Betrayal*; and *Reloaded*. He also acted as a researcher for the Channel Seven *Mad Max* and *Manhunt Police under Fire* crime documentaries. In addition to his court-reporting role, he is currently working on other television projects.

DIRTY DOZEN 5

DONE AND DUSTED

True crime stories that shocked Australia

PAUL ANDERSON

hardie grant books
MELBOURNE • LONDON

Published in 2011 by Hardie Grant Books

Hardie Grant Books (Australia)
85 High Street
Prahran, Victoria 3181
www.hardiegrant.com.au

Hardie Grant Books (UK)
Dudley House, North Suite
34–35 Southampton Street
London WC2E 7HF
www.hardiegrant.co.uk

National Library of Australia Cataloguing-in-Publication Data:

Anderson, Paul, 1971-
Dirty dozen: done and dusted / Paul Anderson.
ISBN: 9781742700267 (pbk.)
Crime--Australia--Case studies.
Criminal investigation--Australia--Case studies.
364.994

Cover design by Black Widow Design
Cover photo Angela Wylie/Fairfaxphotos
Typesetting by Kirby Jones
Typeset in Baskerville Regular
Colour reproduction by Splitting Image Colour Studio
Printed and bound in Australia by Griffin Press

Acknowledgements

As usual, thank you to my sources on both sides of the law. Thanks also to Supreme Court of Victoria media liaison guru Anne Stanford and Sandi Quelch, High Court registrar Rosemary Musolino, Lisa Walker at the Office of Public Prosecutions, Val Buchanan from the Supreme Court of Western Australia, Michael Thompson and staff at the Victorian Government Reporting Service, County Court media liaison Anna Bolger and Commonwealth Office of Public Prosecutions liaison Kathy Medved. Special thanks to my Hardie Grant project manager and commissioning editor Sharon Mullins, senior editor Rose Michael and text editor Sally Moss. Reference material used in this book, as stated, has been obtained from court transcripts, tendered police briefs of evidence, interviews conducted by this author with relevant sources, and published media material.

Contents

1

Death Row

The sticky end of gangland killer Carl Williams

'I've got a funny feeling I'll outlive Carl Williams. He hasn't got enough jail smarts … He'll be frightened to death. He'll have to watch out for low-flying pocket knives.'

CARL ANTHONY WILLIAMS KNEW he was a target on Melbourne's streets but probably never thought he would be killed in Victoria's most secure prison. The nature of his death, like that of the deaths of some of his victims, shocked many—but not all. Having his head beaten by a fellow prisoner, for whatever the reason, proved an inglorious end for the man who had shaped the latest stretch of Melbourne's criminal landscape. It was former underworld toecutter Mark 'Chopper' Read, despite his knack for self-promotional hype, who foresaw and foreshadowed what others thought could never happen to the suburban gangster who referred to himself as 'The Premier'. On the steps of Melbourne Magistrates' Court after an appearance inside in mid-2007, Read prophesied Williams's doom some three years before 'Big Carl' was to cop it in the head. 'I've got a funny feeling I'll outlive Carl Williams,' Read said. 'He hasn't got enough jail smarts … He'll be frightened to death. He'll have to watch out for low-flying pocket knives.'

It wasn't a low-flying pocket knife that got Carl Williams in the end. But Chopper was broadly on the money.

While the crimes of Carl Williams—a plump drug kingpin with a cocky strut—shocked not only Victoria but the nation, his bashing death inside the Acacia Unit at Barwon Prison had politicians, prison bosses, police officers, journalists and members of the solid citizenry shaking heads in amazement. How the hell could one of the state's worst murderers be bashed to death inside the high-security Acacia Unit with its round-the-clock surveillance and extreme protection regime? And why? Lax security or a conspiracy, some interested parties suggested. Summary justice, or karma, said others. The man charged with the murder, Matthew Charles Johnson, flagged defensive homicide as a possible reason during a preliminary court appearance in April 2010.

Williams, living a mostly solitary existence in the Acacia Unit—apart from time spent with two other prisoners: Johnson and convicted murderer Tommy Ivanovic—had deflated into an insipid version of his former self. His baleful olive eyes had glazed over and his shit-eating smirk had all but disappeared. Everyday was 'groundhog day' for the drug trafficker turned mass murderer. It had been that way since the Purana Taskforce arrested him in June 2004. Acacia, referred to in some quarters as 'The Slot', is a formidable jail unit built to house the state's most notorious inmates. It is designed to break their spirit.

'That's the neighbourhood for guys like Carl Williams,' a prison insider once told this author. 'And it ain't Sesame Street.' A lawyer said of the place in court: 'It takes the sting out of everyone who is in there, whether it's right or not.'

To pass the time, Williams scribbled hollow justification for his crimes in letters written to his mother in the months before his extraordinary death.

Dear Mum,

I must say I'm extremely pleased that Underbelly won't be shown in Victoria for at least the next three months—after that I can only hope it gets put off again. I don't mind them telling the truth about me, but telling lies and painting me out like some dickhead who is brain dead—well that's just bullshit. They have me associating with people I never met before, such as Alphonse [Gangitano]. They also have me committing crimes that I've never even been suspected of. What a load of crap.

Yes, I did what I did. I am guilty of defending myself and my loved ones from being killed. That I am. And I'm the first to admit that. But please try putting yourself in my shoes just for a moment.

Whether you loathe him, quite like him or couldn't give two hoots about him, one fact is undeniable: unlike most crooks, who become a product of their environment, Carl Williams laid Melbourne's underworld to waste. In an unprecedented crime spree—fuelled by vengeance, paranoia, avarice and fear—the fledgling drug trafficker transformed himself into a kingpin by making fast money and recruiting willing hitmen to do his bidding. But while he promised big money, he rarely delivered.

From humble beginnings as an errand boy for established names connected to the once-powerful Carlton Crew faction, Williams enjoyed a meteoric rise on the crime pop charts as a rogue trader. To coin a rock'n'roll phrase, he went to the top 'with a bullet'. With foolhardy nonchalance he gunned down and orchestrated the shooting deaths of enemies and drug competitors, genuine and perceived. Comfortable in street shirts, cargo pants and flip-flops, he graduated to traditional black gangster couture as he went about wiping out an entire opposing family dynasty—and other individuals of whom he wanted to dispose. Convicted of four murders and suspected of involvement in up to six others, he was known to refer to himself as 'The Premier' at the height of his reign; such was his delusion of grandeur. 'Carl said he was the president, or something like that, and that he wanted to run for parliament,' a relative once told police.

Veteran Crown prosecutor Geoff Horgan, SC, once aired his view of Williams in the *Herald Sun* newspaper: 'He is such an odd character. He has got the maturity of a child but the power of a dangerous adult, and [he has] people willing to do his bidding for no reason at all.' Those people included notorious gunman Andrew 'Benji' Veniamin and a host of others who cannot be named for legal reasons.

Carl Williams started out as a cherubic boy with a cheeky smile and softened into a podgy but popular blancmange. He came from a family of battlers low on the socioeconomic food chain. His father, George, was regarded as a low-level hustler. Williams—who made it to Year 11 at school—reportedly had dreams of joining the police force, until some local jacks roughed him up. He tried part-time jobs and an apprenticeship and ran money at racetracks before testing his hand as a semi-professional gambler. He was banned from the casino and turned to the drug trade. His first girlfriend's father was allegedly a small-time trafficker. After racking up minor criminal convictions, including handling stolen goods and failing to answer bail, 'Big Carl' was convicted and sentenced in 1994 for attempting to traffic methylamphetamine. It was a sign of bigger things to come.

Williams went on to become the undisputed instigator and aggressor during Melbourne's gangland war between 2000 and 2005 after the actions of half brothers Mark and Jason Moran stirred a monster within. Their gambit of shooting Williams in the stomach over a drug dispute backfired horribly.

> *It was my 29th birthday. As far as I was concerned I didn't have a worry in the world. Life was good. That is until I went and met someone whom I thought was a friend of mine, Mark Moran, only to end up getting shot by him and his brother. What for you probably ask—because they were money-hungry, greedy control freaks who I would not bow down too [sic].*

For those new to this story, the Moran half brothers were quite different from one another in their approaches to drug trafficking and intimidation. Jason—son of Lewis and Judy Moran—had forged a fierce reputation as a violent loose cannon. A coroner implicated him in the shooting death of one-time crime partner Alphonse Gangitano—who died ingloriously in his nightgown and underpants—in January 1998 after the pair had a falling-out. 'He was a hot head,' a former Carlton police officer has said of Jason Moran. Mark—son of Leslie Cole and Judy Moran—was the older and less overt, but by no means less intimidating, of the two. He preferred to work under the radar. Mark had links with notorious bandits and at least one corrupt detective. His reputation carried more weight in the circles that mattered.

'If it wasn't for the Morans, Carl probably wouldn't have stumbled into his position in the drug world in the first place,' a former Purana Taskforce detective told this author. 'Carl was just a shitbag who stumbled onto a big pot of gold by selling cheap drugs.'

As was widely documented and explored in *Dirty Dozen 4—Reloaded*, Jason and Mark met Williams in a Gladstone Park reserve on 13 October 1999 while tension buzzed over drugs and money. The 'fat boy' was underselling the competition. Jason pulled a small-calibre pistol and shot Williams in his flabby guts. Mark urged his little brother to shoot the upstart in the head. If Jason had listened, a dozen or more men would not have died in Melbourne's subsequent gangland war. Williams would say of his wounding:

> There was quite a few things said at the time I was shot. One of them was, 'You don't fuck with us. You know what we've done to other people. Look what we've done to Alphonse [Gangitano] and got away with. We're working with the police. We've virtually got a licence to do anything.'
>
> *They not only shot me. They threatened to kill my family and me.*

According to Williams, a corrupt Drug Squad detective was supplying the Moran boys with pseudoephedrine—the main precursor ingredient needed for the production of methylamphetamine. Williams therefore did not report the Gladstone Park shooting to police. He says Jason Moran rang him in hospital and told him, 'Next time you won't be so lucky.' 'I didn't think the police would investigate it properly,' he would claim in court.

Supreme Court Justice Betty King would say:

> You maintain [you did not inform the police of the shooting] because the Morans had told you that they had a police officer in their pocket. I do not accept that was your reason for refusing to co-operate with police investigators, but rather that your reasons related to the supposed code of silence of the criminal milieu in which you lived.

To his mum Williams wrote:

> *On one occasion after I was shot, Jason and Mark Moran went down to a hotel where my dad had drank at for thirty-five years and they tried to lure him outside to shoot him. The only reason he wasn't shot was simply because he seen a gun in Jason's pocket and refused to go outside with him and his brother. From the day I was shot my life changed forever.*

After he healed, Williams turned on the Moran clan, their allies and their associates with a vengeance, employing a wheelman for more than one hit. In a police statement, this man (whom we shall call 'The Wheelman' as his name is the subject of a suppression order) said: 'Since being shot in the stomach, Carl became obsessive about the Moran family. Whenever he was drunk and the conversation came up, he would start saying things like, "I want every one of them dead and every one of their crew dead."'

Police are certain it was Williams who lay in wait outside Mark Moran's plush home and blasted him with a shotgun on the night of 15 June 2000. At the time Williams was on bail facing charges in relation to a $20 million amphetamine operation.

'I have firsthand knowledge that Carl committed this murder,' The Wheelman said in his police statement.

> After this [shooting] incident it was well known in Melbourne criminal circles that Carl Williams was responsible for Mark's death. It was also assumed that Jason would want to seek revenge. In fact, it was well known that Jason had put a price on Carl's head. That is, he was offering money to have him killed. Carl was well aware of this also.

Williams would say: 'One hundred per cent I had a belief that they were serious. It was [a matter of] who gets who first.'

The Wheelman again:

> I remember discussing Carl's obsession with the Moran family with Tommy Ivanovic. We were both worried about Carl killing people like Judy Moran. We were both of the belief that this could send things out of control. Tommy and I spoke to Carl and told him if he went after Judy Moran then people could just as easily get to his family. He seemed to take some notice of this.

Williams met a local girl named Roberta and they were married on 14 January 2001. As well as a new missus, he also had a covert copper in his midst. Narcotics investigators had injected an undercover cop into the arteries of his drug world. The cop—or UC in police parlance—posed as a buyer named Jimmy. The meetings between Jimmy and a main dealer for Williams took place between April and May 2001, always at a specific McDonald's car park. Jimmy first purchased 500 ecstasy tablets for $8500. As a bonus offer, he received a sample of high-purity cocaine. Williams's dealer told Jimmy that he could supply up to 50,000 ecstasy tablets, along with speed and cocaine.

More meetings and drug transactions followed, with the dealer telling Jimmy that Williams was expecting another shipment of imported MDMA ecstasy pills. Wholesale cost would be $13 a tablet for a bulk minimum purchase of 25,000 tablets. Costs were reduced to as much as $8 a tablet as transactions continued. The dealer loved telling Jimmy the pills were 'the best ecstasy available'. During one meeting, the dealer rang Williams at his home to organise more pills. On another occasion, Jimmy asked for two ounces of cocaine. The dealer rang Williams and ordered two 'soccer balls'. They cost Jimmy $8600. Over five weeks, the undercover cop bought 10,500 ecstasy tablets for $134,500. A further 19,500 pills were stored and ready for sale for $218,000. Police swooped and arrested Williams. While on remand in prison in 2002, before being bailed due to police corruption allegations, Williams befriended a career criminal he would later employ to murder Jason Moran and another victim named Michael Marshall.

Williams obsessed over the plan to murder Jason Moran and decided to have him killed when he least expected it. The time: early Saturday morning. The venue: playing fields at the Cross Keys Reserve in Melbourne's north-west. The setting: a kids' footy clinic. The hit team was to be The Wheelman and the career criminal Williams met while on remand in jail thanks to the undercover drug bust. (Like The Wheelman, the career criminal cannot be named due to a court suppression order, so we shall call him 'The Shooter'.)

According to prosecutor Geoff Horgan: 'At one point Andrew Veniamin was engaged by [Williams] to kill [Jason Moran]. When it was apparent to Williams that Veniamin was not proving to be reliable, [The Wheelman] and [The Shooter] were recruited together to carry out the murder.'

The Wheelman said in his statement:

> About four to six weeks prior to Jason's murder, Carl took [The Shooter] and I to the Cross Keys Reserve. Carl told us that Jason brought his kids to Auskick every Saturday and that he thought it would be a perfect place to kill him as Jason would think that he was safe there.

I killed or played a role in killing people who were planning to kill me … Every day soldiers have to kill the enemy, otherwise the enemy will kill them—and no one calls soldiers murderers. I am no saint and

> *I have never portrayed* [sic] *to be one, but the people I killed were far worse people than I will ever be.*

As has been well publicised, the murder of Jason Moran and family friend Pasquale 'Paddy' Barbaro in a van in front of children on the morning of 21 June 2003 took Melbourne's gangland war to a whole new level. Even old-school criminal identities like Kath Pettingill and Billy 'The Texan' Longley said at the time that the act of murdering someone in front of children was 'not on'. Longley did, however, add that it was a hitman's prerogative to carry out a hit when it best suited him.

Justice Betty King would have her say:

> There were many young children present at that park, including the children of the victim, who would have all watched with horror as the murder was played out in front of them. Equally, the parents of those children who were also present will undoubtedly remember the horror of what occurred for a long time.

The Moran/Barbaro hit came the weekend after an initial plan to knock Jason at the footy ground, his half brother's grave at Fawkner cemetery, the Laurel Hotel in Ascot Vale or the Flemington Racecourse pokies venue. Williams had wanted the shooting to occur on the anniversary of Mark's death—but Jason failed to show.

'We all decided that we would try again the next week,' The Wheelman told police. 'I was happy that he wasn't there because we were underprepared.'

In quick review, the hired killers parked where they could see the football oval on the day Jason was to go down. The Shooter sat watching through a set of binoculars. He first saw Jason at 9.20 am on the oval.

'[The Shooter] wanted to go and shoot him there and then,' The Wheelman said. 'I managed to talk him out of that because I was worried about there being kids everywhere.'

About an hour later the hit team moved in. Like a modern-day Terminator, The Shooter went gun crazy—first with a shotgun and then a handgun—as Jason and Barbaro sat in the front seats of the family van. Children in the back were splashed with blood.

'We committed these murders on behalf of Carl Williams,' The Wheelman said in his statement. 'Jason Moran was killed because Carl wanted him dead. Unfortunately Pasquale Barbaro was a victim of [The Shooter's] overzealousness. He was simply in the wrong place at the wrong time.'

> *I accept that no one has the right to go around killing people, but thirty-five years for killing scum like the Morans when my own life was in danger—that's ridiculous.*

Williams and the hit team met for a debriefing, having turned the footy oval into a killing field. 'There was a sense of a job well done,' The Wheelman said. 'However, I still have never been paid.'

Jason's demise had come two months after major drug trafficker Nik 'The Russian' Radev was gunned down in a street in Coburg, north of Melbourne. Andrew Veniamin, a former trigger man for the Carlton Crew before he moved to the Williams camp, shot The Russian with the help of The Shooter. Radev was a ruthless drug competitor so Williams had him liquidated.

'When Radev was killed he had an outstanding debt of about $100,000 which he owed Williams,' a man Carl would later pay to kill Lewis Moran told police. 'This debt was, I believe, drug related.'

Radev's death left his right-hand man, a wannabe drug baron from the western suburbs by the name of Mark Mallia, exposed and under threat. According to Justice Betty King:

> There was, by this time, a climate of fear amongst those involved in illegal drug trafficking as there had been at least fifteen murders that would be described as 'gangland war' murders. Not surprisingly, Mallia had become increasingly

concerned that he too might be murdered because of his associations—particularly his association with Radev.

Williams, on the other hand, told a close associate that he believed Mallia had put out a contract on him and Veniamin. A meeting was organised to smoke the peace pipe, so to speak, at a Southbank restaurant. It was now about six weeks after the Jason Moran/Barbaro hit. At the restaurant meeting, Mallia said word on the street was that Williams had lured Radev to his death. Both Williams and Veniamin denied any involvement. They lied. Veniamin, being Veniamin, told Mallia that he would kill him and his family if the rumours continued. As a safeguard, Mallia had associates watching from a distance.

'If not before it, then at least from this meeting, Williams regarded Mallia as a serious threat to his own safety whilst he lived,' prosecutor Geoff Horgan would say in court. 'In turn, Mallia was fearful for his safety and wary of any traps that might be set for him.' Justice King summed it up when she told Williams in court: 'It was clear from that meeting that both you and Mallia considered each other to be serious mutual threats.'

Mallia called a traitorous friend and told him he was going to Queensland to escape the gangland hotbed, adding: 'They can't kill what they can't catch.' But he was too slow to book his flight. On the order of Williams, Mallia was murdered on 18 August 2003. His body was then burned and dumped. In court, Williams said he 'advised' Veniamin to do the job because it was in their interests that Mallia be eradicated.

Horgan said Mallia was taken to a garage where he was gagged and bound to a chair. 'Williams was then taken to the garage to view Mallia. He was alive at that time. There was a rope around his neck. According to [The Shooter], Williams wanted information obtained from Mallia as to the whereabouts of drug money he was believed to have hidden.' It is thought Mallia was tortured with a soldering iron before he was killed.

To continue the chronology leading to Williams's incarceration in Acacia, it was in September 2003, according to associates, when he received an offer too good to refuse from a major crime figure. The offer was to organise a hit on Michael Marshall, a man who listed his occupation as hot-dog vendor.

According to a member of his team, Williams ordered Marshall's death to placate the major crime figure who wrongly believed Marshall had killed underworld identity Willie Thompson. (Thompson, as gangland war victim number eighteen, was gunned down in Chadstone on 21 July 2003.) The major crime figure, who cannot be named for legal reasons, was alleged to have offered Williams $300,000 for Marshall's head in revenge for Thompson's death. Ironically, according to The Shooter, it was Williams who had actually orchestrated the Thompson killing. King would say to The Shooter: 'There was another meeting and you were allegedly told by [the major crime figure] that all further information and the guns would be passed to you through Carl Williams.' (A murder charge would be laid and later dropped against the major crime figure in relation to Marshall's eventual slaying.)

Whatever the motive, Williams recruited The Wheelman to help The Shooter carry out the hit on Marshall. The Wheelman/Shooter duo had, after all, already put a score on the board. The Wheelman said in his statement:

> Carl gave me one square yellow Post-it note with the name 'Marshall' and 'the corner of Williams and Joy Street, South Yarra' written on it. He told me to have a look at this bloke and that there was two hundred grand to get there. He said that [The Shooter] had already done some [surveillance] work but Carl wanted someone to give him a hand. Carl did not specifically tell me that Marshall was going to be murdered. The only conversation I had with him was that it was going to be a debt collection for monies owed to Carl for drugs; however, it did cross my mind that something further was going to occur.

When you are doing a job like this in the presence of [The Shooter] you have to expect the worst.

It is clear Williams and The Shooter allowed their overzealous desire for bloodshed and revenge to override any ounce of commonsense they may have shared between them. While carrying out surveillance on Marshall, The Wheelman took some photos of what he believed to be an Australian Federal Police car in front of the target's home. He promptly showed the pictures to Williams and The Shooter.

'They both showed no concern over this,' The Wheelman told police in amazement. He said another reason he showed Williams the photos was to prove he had been working surveillance 'so in return I could get … petrol money from Carl for the Marshall job'. The Wheelman was obviously happy to work for peanuts amid the promise of a fortune.

An apparent disregard for possible police surveillance on the part of Williams and The Shooter rose to even more staggering levels of arrogant stupidity after The Wheelman found a Victoria Police tracking device hidden in the vehicle he had chosen for the Marshall murder. The Purana Taskforce, through some good work tracing phone calls, had nominated The Wheelman as a person of interest for the Jason Moran/Pasquale Barbaro shooting four months earlier. The Wheelman told The Shooter about the tracking device in the vehicle. 'His reaction was dismissive and he acted as though it wasn't very important. I told him I would drive him to do the job in my own car. I assumed that if a tracking device was not an issue, there would be no issue in taking my own car to the job.'

The Wheelman was wrong. There would be big issues. Police were listening in, thanks to hidden bugs and telephone intercepts, but still did not know the details of what was to happen—or where it was planned to take place.

It was D-day for Michael Marshall (and in some respects his young son also) on 25 October 2003, when The Shooter gunned him down in front of the boy. Again, as has been well publicised, it was a hit that shocked many. 'I knew by [The Shooter's] attitude and the weapons that he had brought with him that this was not going to be just a debt collection … but it was too late for me to pull out,' said The Wheelman. Much to the chagrin of the Purana Taskforce, their tracking device in The Wheelman's van had cut out, leaving them blind. The detectives had only heard *what* happened, without knowing where.

The Wheelman asked if he should ring 'the big bloke'. 'I was referring to Carl Williams,' he confirms in his statement. 'This job was organised by Carl and I felt that it was an appropriate time to let him know of the result.'

In a later phone conversation with Williams, The Shooter said: 'How are ya, little cunt? Listen, I think that horse got scratched. The one that … ah, you and George tipped me for. Yeah, I think it got scratched.' According to The Wheelman: 'When [The Shooter] said the horse got scratched, he was telling Carl that Marshall had been killed.'

I never killed or harmed any innocent people. I simply killed people who were planning to kill me. One could and would say I got in first. There is no doubt that I was in a kill or be killed situation.

Despite the glitch with the tracking device, police swooped and arrested The Shooter and The Wheelman about three and a half kilometres from South Yarra on the night of the Marshall murder. In a squad car, Purana detectives Stuart Bateson and Boris Buick later had a short taped conversation with The Wheelman before he—and The Shooter—would ever decide to make comprehensive statements against Williams.

BUICK: So you can't tell us anything about Carl?

THE WHEELMAN: No. He's got plenty of mates in jail. I know that.

BUICK: Do you think there'll be any more killings?

THE WHEELMAN: Possibly. Yeah.

BATESON: Who might be next to go?

THE WHEELMAN: Oh, I'm guessing Mick Gatto or, ah, old man Moran. It's just a couple. There's probably more.

The conversation continued.

BATESON: So … who should we look out for?

THE WHEELMAN: I'm supposed to tell you now?

BATESON: Who? Yeah.

THE WHEELMAN: But, ah, well I don't know. You're not doing much for me right now. If I'm out of custody I'm sure I could help you with a lot of things.

BATESON: Fair enough.

THE WHEELMAN: Andrew the Greek Cypriot.

BATESON: Yep … And who's he going to look at?

THE WHEELMAN: Um, I'm guessing old man Moran but I'm not a hundred per cent …

BATESON: And who wants that done?

THE WHEELMAN: Oh, can't help you right now with that.

BATESON: Mmm, big Carl.

Purana investigators were onto Williams but at that stage lacked hard evidence to charge him with murder. Williams was living under heavy surveillance, as was his crew mainstay Veniamin. A dangerous combination, the two could have been mistaken for an underworld version of Abbott and Costello—a buffoon with a vapid smile and his silent foil. In November 2003, Purana arrested Williams after he was overheard making death threats against Bateson and the detective sergeant's then girlfriend. Bateson said in a statement made at the time: 'I have taken these threats extremely seriously. I have taken precautions in relation to our security both at home and at work.'

On 2 December that year, Williams was released on bail on the threat to kill charges, despite Detective Sergeant Shane O'Connell telling Melbourne Magistrates' Court that police feared for the safety of Bateson and his partner.

'Criminals who are not in day-to-day communication with the defendant may take it upon themselves to inflict harm, or worse, on Mr Bateson as a way of aligning themselves and elevating themselves within the criminal network,' O'Connell said.

The magistrate was told that Williams was already on bail over two separate drug trafficking allegations. Six days before Christmas—and one week after the murder of Carlton Crew supporter Graham Kinniburgh—a magistrate varied Williams's bail conditions to allow him to travel interstate on a Queensland holiday. Before Williams flew out with Veniamin by his side, he told the *Herald Sun* that he had nothing to do with the Kinniburgh murder.

'I might as well be charged with the Bali bombing,' the thirty-three-year-old quipped.

For those who don't know, Kinniburgh—gangland war victim number twenty-two—was an old-school crook who detested the limelight. He preferred a status quo within the ranks of the underworld. He was killed because of his alignment with the Moran/Carlton Crew faction.

Williams told *The Age* newspaper that he was not behind any push to monopolise Melbourne's drug market by killing opposition.

'I had no problems with Nik [Radev],' he claimed. 'I've only met Lewis [Moran] once. I haven't got a problem with Lewis. If he thinks he has a problem with me I can say he can sleep peacefully ... I don't know how this [gangland war] started and I don't know where it will end.'

Williams was fast learning how to court the media. In particular, he became very chummy with two journalists whose connections were scrutinised by Purana. Williams became the master of gangland quips, even if most weren't his own.

'I used to hate weddings,' he once told one of his pet reporters. 'All the old dears would poke me and say, "You're next." They stopped that crap when I started saying it to them at funerals.'

Justice King would later observe: 'Whilst you were a suspect and being referred to in the media, it was apparent that you were enjoying the game of "being famous". You gave interviews outside court, and appeared prepared to give your views on a variety of matters and unfortunately the media, to a degree, pandered to that.'

On their Queensland holiday, Williams and Veniamin spent time in Port Douglas before they journeyed to the Gold Coast to meet up with Roberta. A *Herald Sun* police rounds reporter at the time, this author travelled to the Gold Coast with a photographer to secretly document their holiday. With a constant smear of zinc cream across his nose, a tubby Williams wallowed in the surf as Veniamin kicked waves roundhouse style as they rolled onto shore. The duo lolled on the beach, lazed by the resort pool and enjoyed time with Williams's toddler daughter. Williams and Roberta strolled and window-shopped, ate fine food and drank exotic cocktails. His holiday annoyed detectives, one saying: 'It appears to get beautiful one day to perfect the next for Carl Williams. For a bloke who doesn't have an official occupation, he's up there sipping on drinks out of pineapples by the pool while we're here sipping on warm cans of Coke in squad cars.' It was quite amazing to watch Williams and Veniamin as they sauntered the resort district seemingly without a care in the world. Both knew they were marked men, yet strolled and lolled about as though they were bullet proof. To steal a line from a film about cocksure pilots all too eager to engage enemy fighters, their egos had written cheques their bodies couldn't cash—and yet they appeared not to have a care. A Carlton Crew hitman or a Radev comrade could have all too easily shot them down as they walked to the beach or sat alfresco at a restaurant. In the end though, the only bloke who shot them, through a Canon 600 telephoto lens, was the *Herald Sun* photographer.

Two months after their return to Melbourne, 'Big Carl' took a big loss the day Mick Gatto shot Veniamin dead in the back corridor of a Carlton pasta house with the little hitman's gun. Veniamin had a long-standing reputation for carrying a .38 revolver.

'And why?' top defence silk Robert Richter, QC, would ask in court. 'Because for a hitman that he is, it's a good gun to use because they don't jam. And he would know. He's had experience.'

'Benji' Veniamin was living fast, screwing around while on cocaine and fully expecting to die young. He was a modern-day kamikaze who told police not to bother investigating his inevitable death, however it may eventuate. He had admitted to associates—Gatto included—that he shot dead his friends and fellow drug enforcers Dino Dibra and Paul Kallipolitis. He shot dead Nik Radev. Police believe he also killed fruiterer and reputed mafia man Frank Benvenuto. In his time, Veniamin had also shot and wounded another suburban drug dealer over a woman, and kneecapped several men as warnings or paybacks. The little guy with the full body tattoos was a maniac. When he arrived at the Carlton restaurant, Gatto was with a group of cronies. But Veniamin wanted to talk. Gatto saw it as an opportunity to learn whether he was on Williams's hit list. Gatto had previously told Williams at the Crown Casino that the gangland drug battle was not his war and to leave him out of it.

'There was these rumours going around that I was going to be next and there was a possibility that he [Veniamin] was going to do it,' Gatto would say in evidence during his own Supreme Court murder trial. 'That's the only reason [I wanted to see him] … He wasn't worried about anybody … He was a Dr Jeckyll and Mr Hyde.'

Gatto was also of the belief that Veniamin had murdered Graham Kinniburgh, his beloved friend and father figure.

'I just wanted to know what Veniamin was doing,' Gatto told the court. 'You know, keep your friends close and your enemies closer.'

In a version of events accepted by a jury, Veniamin pulled a .38 on Gatto, who wrestled for control of the weapon. Veniamin copped rounds in the head and neck. Like a scene from a Godfather film, he bled out in a pasta house corridor lined with boxes of canned tomatoes. 'I've got to be honest,' Gatto would say in evidence, 'I thought I was a dead duck. I thought I was gone … What I done is stopped him from murdering me.'

Williams said he was saddened by Veniamin's death. 'He was one of my best friends. He was a good kid.' When asked if he was worried about his own welfare, he said he never worried. 'I will never get set up,' he told the *Herald Sun*. But his day of incarceration was approaching.

Despite Purana detectives having informed crime patriarch Lewis Moran that he was an endangered species, the drug-trafficking dabbler kept to his routines. Two fresh gunmen and a driver, new at spreading Carl Williams's cheer, caught up with Lewis inside the Brunswick Club on the night of 31 March 2004—one week after Veniamin's death. But the hit was not a direct Williams payback. It had been in the planning well before Gatto shot Veniamin in self-defence.

While Williams may have been a social dullard, he had a scheming brain. He knew police were all over him and his dogs of war, so therefore had to recruit new people to kill for him. One of those new recruits, who cannot be named due to a court suppression order, we shall call 'The Rogue'—because of his lack of loyalty to any criminal camp.

He told police he had a dispute with Gatto over a supposed contract that Radev had accepted to kill the influential and enigmatic businessman. The Rogue said that Williams, having heard about his falling-out with the Carlton Crew, tried to convince him that Lewis Moran 'had it in' for The Rogue over a debt. The Rogue ended up accepting a $150,000 contract to kill Lewis.

'Carl mentioned that we had common enemies—Lewis Moran was one of them,' The Rogue said in his police statement. 'I remember saying to [associates of mine] that I'd rather get paid for doing it [killing Lewis] rather than doing it for nothing, although at the time I had no need for money. I was just dirty on certain people, including Lewis Moran.'

The Rogue employed the services of two close associates who ran into the Brunswick Club with fingers on triggers as he remained outside behind the wheel of the getaway car. With Lewis running down a hallway and into the gaming area, the lead gunman tried to blast him with a shotgun, but the weapon jammed. Lewis continued his desperate escape bid, bumping into duty manager Sandra Sugars. 'I ran straight into the front of Lewis,' Sugars said in her police statement.

> The man in the balaclava was right behind him. There was all this screaming. Lewis pushed me and said, 'Get out of the way.' I remember the man shooting at Lewis. I could hear the sound. It didn't stop and the man kept getting closer and closer to Lewis and just kept shooting ... I really thought I was going to die. I couldn't run. I couldn't move.

A drinking pal of Lewis's, a bloke named Bert Wrout, meanwhile had his own problems. The second gunman had shot and wounded him in the chest and arm. 'They're weak fuckin' cunts,' the sixty-two-year-old Wrout would whisper to an arriving police officer.

The Rogue said he received $140,000—ten grand less than the promised fee. 'I told Carl about the shortfall. He said "bullshit" and that he would fix it up ... I did not receive the outstanding $10,000.'

Justice Bernard Teague would later tell The Rogue that to some people life is cheap and not as sacred as it should be. When it came to Carl Williams, the only life he believed to be sacred was his own.

> *Although I wish what happened never did happen, I still believe I had no choice but to do what I did. As I said earlier, I was in a kill or be killed situation.*

Williams suffered his second loss on 8 May 2004 when mate and supporter Lewis Caine—then boyfriend of glamorous defence lawyer Zarah Garde-Wilson—turned up dead in a Brunswick street. Caine, a killer himself, was shot in the face for floating the idea of shooting Carlton Crew money man Mario Condello. The only problem was, the two blokes he suggested it to—one being The Rogue—had links to both Carl Williams *and* Condello.

Mario Condello knew he had to get on the front foot and try to put an end to Carl Williams, before Williams put an end to him and every Moran ally his side of Chinatown. Police allege that Condello met with a police informer—known as 166—on 12 May 2004 and discussed a $150,000 plot to kill Williams, his father George and a bodyguard. It was alleged that 166 was to gun Williams down outside a plush city apartment high-rise and then 'fuck off overseas'.

Carl Williams was about as far away from any cemetery plot as he could possibly get at that stage, living among the clouds in the high-rise. A cousin of his, Michael Thorneycroft, who once visited him in the ivory tower, told police: 'I told him that he was used to being outside prison and that I wasn't. I told him that I was spinning out just being there—in the city in an apartment on the thirtieth floor out of my comfort zone.

'Someone who I did not know arrived and gave Carl some coke [cocaine]. Carl did not pay for the coke.' Williams chased the drug through a pipe. 'He was quiet at that time,' Thorneycroft stated. 'He told me that he had a lot on his mind.'

Later, a handsome, swarthy bloke arrived with a pretty, buxom blonde on his arm. Thorneycroft was told the man was a nightclub manager.

> This guy looked like he was about forty and European, with olive skin. The girl was about twenty, of skinny build, with blonde hair halfway down her back. At first I thought the girl was a prostitute because earlier in the day Carl had discussed getting prostitutes. Carl offered me some more cocaine. Carl grabbed me on the shoulders and pulled me in close to him. He whispered in my ear, 'I've had seven of them killed so far.' I do not know why he told me this. I didn't know what to say.

Purana detectives arrested Williams for the final time on 9 June 2004 after foiling his attempt to have Condello murdered. Police had learned of the kill plot via listening devices. Williams was charged with conspiracy to murder.

Purana was finally on top of the game. Geoff Horgan explained in court:

> Williams was the instigator of the [Condello kill] conspiracy. He was a principal figure in an underworld gang that was at war with another underworld gang led by Dominic Gatto and Mario Condello. Gatto had killed Andrew Veniamin. Veniamin was at that time closely associated with Williams but had previously been in the Condello camp. Lewis Caine, another close associate of Williams, had been murdered. There is reason to suppose that Williams might have blamed this murder on the Gatto/Condello camp. Caine, too, had moved from that camp to Williams. Williams ordered Condello's death as a payback for the deaths of his two associates.

Condello was arrested and charged over the conspiracy to kill Carl and George Williams and their bodyguard. (On 6 February 2006, a gunman would shoot Condello dead in his garage after he returned to his suburban mansion while on bail curfew.)

In October 2004—with The Wheelman, The Shooter and another man we shall call 'The Scout' singing like birds to Purana about the Jason Moran and Michael Marshall hits—Williams pleaded guilty to the trafficking charges relating to the $1.5 million drug case brought about by Jimmy the undercover cop. (Charges laid against Williams in 1999 over a $20 million Broadmeadows drug syndicate had been dropped due to a lingering cloud of police corruption.) Justice Murray Kellam sentenced Williams to seven years' jail with a minimum of five years for his deals with Jimmy.

'There can be no argument but that the trafficking of such substances does enormous harm to the youth of the community,' Kellam said.

> Clearly you were the supplier of drugs. The trafficking of such drugs by you was in cynical disregard [for] the welfare

of those who would finally purchase and use the pernicious goods in which you traded.

A letter from the Commissioner of Corrections dated 28 September 2004 was tendered before me whereby he stated that for the foreseeable future you are likely to be retained in the Acacia high-security unit. I accept that the circumstances under which you will be held in the Acacia Unit are oppressive indeed ... [But] those like you who play for high stakes and are detected conducting the business of trafficking in drugs of addiction for profit can expect condign punishment for their conduct.

In late 2005 a jury found Williams guilty of having ordered and procured the Michael Marshall murder. Justice King sentenced him to twenty-six years' jail with a twenty-one-year minimum. One year of the drug sentence imposed by Justice Kellam was ordered to be served on top of that maximum term. King had a bit to say about Williams's prison setting.

You are currently held in the Acacia high-security unit at Barwon Prison, which is the maximum-security unit of the state penal system. The conditions at Acacia are quite different to those from mainstream prisoners. The visits from family are severely restricted—particularly in terms of contact visits. Access out of cells during the day, mixing with other prisoners, and access to phone calls all are severely restricted. This is not what the average sentenced prisoner has to endure by way of conditions of serving a sentence. It is how you have been held, both as a person on remand and as a sentenced prisoner. It is equally evident that this will be the manner of your incarceration for some substantial time.

There was a recent arrest in relation to another victim of so-called gangland wars, and it becomes really an unknown situation when all prosecutions relating to them will finish. Accordingly, I act upon the basis that you may serve a significant or substantial part of your sentence in that unit or [a] similar unit. Due to the nature of the so-called gangland war with what appears to be groups of different criminals seeking to cause harm to each other, it is not surprising that the authorities need to consider your protection—as well as the protection of others allegedly involved in such a war.

After entering a plea deal that saw murder charges in relation to Mark Moran and Pasquale Barbaro dropped, Williams pleaded guilty to the murders of Jason and Lewis Moran and Mark Mallia and to conspiring to kill Condello. He was to face no other murder charges. Not for Nikolai Radev. Not for Willie Thompson. Not for any links he may have had with the deaths of Graham Kinniburgh or Richard Mladenich. Nevertheless, Carl Williams, the man who once called himself 'The Premier', had lost office.

One former Purana detective told this author that Williams managed to tie up an estimated 90 per cent of the police force's major resources for one or two years, as other drug criminals—including those in Lebanese and Asian syndicates and outlaw motorcycle gangs—continued to operate under the radar.

'Money buys power,' the former Purana member said. 'It was the criminals who joined Carl who built his power, on the promise of easy money. He built his own celebrity and status. As for the suggestion he was the state's greatest ever arch villain—spare me. In reality he was just a dumb-arse from the suburbs with disposable drug income.'

During his pre-sentence plea hearing, Williams presented as a far-from-reliable witness. He came across as smug and supercilious. He enjoyed having the limelight again.

HORGAN: Mr Williams, would you tell the court again please your full name?

WILLIAMS: Carl Anthony Williams.

HORGAN: And your address?

WILLIAMS: Barwon Prison.

HORGAN: And your occupation?

WILLIAMS: Unemployed at the moment.

Before he gave the bulk of his so-called 'evidence', relatives of his victims were given the opportunity to have their say in the Supreme Court. Judy Moran took the witness box and had to be pulled up a couple of times.

JUSTICE KING: Yes. What would you want to say, Mrs Moran?

MORAN: To the Honourable Justice Betty King and court. Carl Williams, the evil person that you are …

KING: No, Mrs Moran … This is not the purpose of what you are here to say … You are allowed to tell me about the impact that this has had upon you—emotional, financial—but you are not here to vilify anyone.

MORAN: Okay, I am sorry, Your Honour. Killing my baby Jason and his friend Pat, knowing eight children were in that van that day …

KING: Mrs Moran, I will ask you again. You need to refer to the impact on you. It is not for you to go through the actual form of how your son was killed, or how your husband was killed. The prosecutor has done that. You are here to talk about the emotional, financial consequences upon you.

MORAN: The impact it has had on me for my whole family to have been murdered, you have all but destroyed me. Ripped out my heart. But I have the strength to be here today and I will be here to the end. My biggest regret is I never got to say goodbye to my family. Thank you, Your Honour.

Williams told the hearing that after one of his arrests for drug trafficking—just before his daughter's christening—police had passed on some news. 'I was told by members of the Drug Squad that they had saved my life because there was a plan on foot to have me killed at [my daughter] Dakota's christening in front of her,' he said. 'After I was shot [by Jason Moran] my mind was not normal. I was using crack cocaine, drinking alcohol heavily and using sleeping tablets — sometimes all at the same time. [I was feeling] paranoia—when was I going to die?'

Even though he had pleaded guilty, Williams disputed several parts of the prosecution summary. While claiming he did not recommend Jason be killed at the Cross Keys Reserve, he added: 'I didn't care if it happened there, but there weren't no concrete thing that it had to happen there.'

HORGAN: But you discussed it happening there with them [The Wheelman and The Shooter], didn't you.

WILLIAMS: Amongst many other places.

HORGAN: You were happy for it to happen at the Cross Keys Reserve at Auskick?

WILLIAMS: It was sooner the better. As I said, I wanted the murder to happen asap … if Jason Moran was at Hanging Rock sitting there by himself in the car park and we knew he was there, it would have happened there.

HORGAN: Mr Williams, was there a plan that if Jason Moran arrived at Auskick that he would be killed?

WILLIAMS: Hopefully, but …

HORGAN: And Mr Williams, the next part of that question is, you knew, didn't you, that it was going to happen there that morning.

WILLIAMS: I didn't know. How did I know he was going to turn up?

HORGAN: If he did turn up, was he going to be killed that morning at Auskick?

WILLIAMS: If my aunty had a what's-his-name, she'd be my uncle.

HORGAN: You were hopeful that if he did turn up at Auskick that morning that he would be killed, is that your position?

WILLIAMS: It was in all of our best interests for it to happen asap.

HORGAN: You, I am asking about. You were hopeful that if he did turn up that morning at Auskick he would be killed by [The Shooter] and [The Wheelman]. Yes or no?

JUSTICE KING: You need to answer it, Mr Williams.

WILLIAMS: Yes.

Williams disputed ever going to the place where Mark Mallia was tied up and tortured before his death. He also denied paying money for that killing but admitted telling Veniamin to kill Mallia because he was a perceived threat. Once again, his denials were dubious and lacked substance—although he did tell the truth when agreeing that he was overweight at the time.

JUSTICE KING: Why would Mallia be coming after you? On the scenario you have just given me, you had no involvement.

WILLIAMS: In what murder?

KING: In any of those. Radev. Thompson.

WILLIAMS: I had no involvement in Thompson.

KING: Would you agree that people seemed to refer to you as the leader of the group?

HORGAN: The Big Boy?

WILLIAMS: That is because I was carrying weight at the time.

KING: Can you just answer my question. Did people appear to defer to you as the equivalent of the leader of the group?

WILLIAMS: I didn't think of myself as the leader of the group.

KING: Were you the person who was in control of the drugs?

WILLIAMS: More or less in the drug part. I was, yes.

According to Williams, it was Veniamin who confirmed to him that Mallia had been murdered. King would not be satisfied that Williams did pay $50,000 for the killing to occur. Rather, she sentenced him on the basis that Williams was the counsellor and procurer, 'not necessarily concerned with the detail of how or where the murder occurred'.

Williams disputed The Rogue's assertion that he paid money for the Lewis Moran hit.

HORGAN: Mr Williams, you say that what [The Rogue] says about your involvement in this murder is wrong and is a lie?

WILLIAMS: I would say you couldn't trust [The Rogue] as far as you could kick him.

According to Williams, his ally Lewis Caine told him that a hit on Lewis Moran had already been arranged. Williams claimed that he agreed to pay about $120,000 worth of speed—but not cash—for the murder to happen.

Williams said: 'Caine said the murder was going to happen anyway. He was getting money from elsewhere. I said, "That's fair enough. It's in my interest that it happens." He asked if I would give drugs at a wholesale price through him to [The Rogue] if it was to happen.' King disregarded Williams's claims.

In relation to the Condello kill conspiracy, Williams told the Supreme Court:

> Mario Condello put a contract out on me through 166 and I had been called in by the police and told my life was in danger. Two and two together that it was coming from there. And it was not only my life—it was my dad's life and another person. Everyone was smoking cocaine and on pills at that time.

Horgan said:

> You will find the sentencing exercise difficult because all of this demonstrates no remorse; a cavalier disregard for any truth at all ... The question is if it did happen, you have organised it. You want it to happen. You have set it up. You are pleading to that. Were you prepared to pay money to those who did it if they carried it out?

Williams replied: 'There was no talk of any money.'

If Williams had been carved from wood, his nose would have grown twelve inches throughout the plea hearing. King told him in regard to the Condello plot: 'I am satisfied beyond reasonable doubt that you promised to pay the [would-be] shooter in the conspiracy and whoever assisted him a sum of money. I do not accept in any way that all of the persons involved were enthusiastic volunteers, just wishing to help you out.'

Horgan accused Williams of not wanting to testify against other crooks who were still alive and had not been charged.

HORGAN: Is this the situation just generally—that you are prepared to give evidence in relation to matters of corruption if they might involve police?

WILLIAMS: That's correct.

HORGAN: But you are not prepared to give evidence about any of these murders that might implicate another offender?

WILLIAMS: I am not prepared to make up stories.

HORGAN: Just deal with the question. You are not prepared to give evidence in any of these matters that nominate and put in another person?

WILLIAMS: As I said, I am not prepared to make up stories or make up lies for a reduction in sentence.

HORGAN: You say, 'The only person who is involved apart from me in the murder of Lewis Moran is [The Rogue] and [the two gunmen].

WILLIAMS: I don't say that … That is what you say. I say [The Rogue]. I don't know about [the two gunmen].

HORGAN: You say the other person involved was Lewis Caine, who is dead?

WILLIAMS: That's correct.

HORGAN: In relation to the murder of Mallia, you are not prepared to say anyone was involved except Veniamin, who is dead?

WILLIAMS: [The Shooter] and [The Scout].

HORGAN: But they would be, I suppose, your enemies, wouldn't they, since they have given statements against you?

WILLIAMS: Not really. No … I am prepared to give evidence against [The Wheelman] in the murder of Mark Moran. I am prepared to give evidence against [The Shooter] in the murder of Radev …

KING: Are you prepared to give evidence against anyone who has not been dealt with or who has not already indicated that they intend to plead guilty, is my question.

WILLIAMS: No.

King sentenced Williams for the final time on 7 May 2007, describing him as a puppetmaster who decided whether people lived or died.

'You made constant references to the fact that it was in your interests for the murder or murders to happen, as though that was enough to justify the murders,' King said. 'These killings have clearly engendered a level of fear within our community as to potential harm of innocent persons and, equally, a concern relating to the degree of lawlessness into which Victoria, as a community, has been plunged. You were responsible to a very large degree for this fear'

For the three murders and the Condello kill plot, King sentenced an unrepentant Williams to life in jail with a thirty-five-year minimum—to be served from the day of sentence.

> *Some people would say the chances of me remaining fit or sane for that long in prison are slight, but I will do my best to prove them wrong. The system, the authorities, are being aloud [sic] legally and systematically to destroy my body & my mind—and they say this is a civilised society we live in. I beg to differ. Many would say I deserve what I cop; fair enough, they are entitled to their opinion. However, what about those who worked alongside me, who [sic] crimes were every bit as bad as mine. Was it really fair, was it justice that they got away so lightly … in exchange for my liberty? I think not.*

It was Purana's ability to break the legendary code of criminal silence that enabled them to, as one detective likes to say in rhyme, 'bring Carl down in Chinatown'. The Wheelman was the first to talk, causing a domino effect among Williams's crew. Four main killers—who ironically did Big Carl's bidding while either on bail or serving suspended sentences for other crimes—made several statements to Purana implicating Williams as the driving force behind the murders. In return they received more lenient jail sentences. They wanted some chance of walking from prison as old men, rather than being carried out as dead old men in pine boxes.

Williams lodged an appeal against the severity of his sentence, saying it should have been shorter due to his guilty pleas. As the months passed, and the public spotlight swung away, the novelty of his situation in the Acacia Unit wore thin. Comments made by Justice King about his incarceration might have been playing on his mind. They would prove to be pertinent words.

> There are many reasons why persons are in that [Acacia] unit and, in your case, a major part of it is ensuring your safety. You have been in a gang war with other criminals and the issue of revenge being taken by those other persons is not far-fetched. Equally, there are many within the prison system that may have a desire to make a name for themselves by causing you harm. Equally, those persons who have elected to give evidence against you must be protected from you.
>
> I have received five psychological reports which refer to these conditions [in Acacia] and the effect that they are having upon you, which include anxiety, depressed mood and adjustment disorder. None of that is surprising as most persons incarcerated in this manner would have a great deal of difficulty adjusting.

Acacia was doing Carl's head in, metaphorically speaking. Little did he know that, in less than three years' time, he would have his head done in literally in Acacia.

> *Fair enough I have lost my freedom, but should I really have to serve my time in solitary confinement, which I have done since the day of my arrest? To give you a little bit of an insight into what solitary confinement can do to ones [sic] mind; take a look at the likes of Francis Chichester, who, after a year at sea alone on his yacht, could not converse properly on his arrival home. He was suffering a sort of personality disorder brought about by being in total solitude. There is also the case of the Englishman who was arrested in Russia for spying. He was in solitary confinement in a Russian Prison for 18 months and nearly went insane. He wrote a book about his experiences and his fight against insanity. Now, if you compare his 18 months in solitary confinement with a life sentence with a minimum term of 35 years, on top of the 3 years I'd already served prior to receiving the minimum term of 35 years, which was all served in solitary confinement, you will some*

> *[sic] idea of what I am up against. It is one hell of a hill to climb, and one hell of a battle to fight. However, have no doubt I will continue to fight it day by day, month by month, year by year.*

It would be the entire Williams family who would lose the fight Carl had alluded to. In November 2007, Justice King sentenced sixty-one-year-old George Williams to four and a half years' jail with a minimum of twenty months for trafficking 4.79 kilograms of amphetamines with his son between 2002 and 2004. A buyer purchased $351,800 worth of speed during meetings at shopping centres and George's Broadmeadows home. It is astonishing that George and Carl Williams embarked on a drug trafficking career, considering Shane 'Pear' Williams—George's eldest son and Carl's older brother—died of a heroin overdose in 1997. Defence barrister Shane Tyrrell told Justice King that George was merely Carl's 'gofer', and that his heart was a 'ticking time bomb' due to a severe congenital condition. Tyrrell said George would face a 'death sentence' if he was jailed.

King said: '[His heart] didn't stop him from committing the crime. Why should it stop him doing the time?'

When sentencing, she told George: 'You chose to engage in this very serious illegal activity with this heart problem and you managed quite well. Whilst I accept that Carl Williams was the man in charge, I do not accept that the role occupied by you was merely that of a gofer doing only what you were told by Carl.'

Just over a year later, on 22 November 2008, a broken Barbara Williams took her own life by drinking down a fatal mix of medication with cheap champagne at her Essendon home. The sixty-year-old left a simple note written on a mirror: 'I'm sorry.' Williams, who was devastated, ripped off Celine Dion's *Because You Loved Me* for his death notice: 'You were my voice when I couldn't speak and strength when I was weak,' he wrote.

While prison authorities allowed George Williams to attend the funeral under guard, Carl was refused permission to farewell his mum at the church service. 'The issues of security and public safety were key factors in considering this application,' Corrections Victoria said in a statement at the time. A eulogy was read on his behalf at the church: 'There's nothing in the world I would not have done for you. I always looked so forward to ringing you up every morning [from jail] and hearing your voice. You were my pillar of strength. You were my everything and I love you with all my heart.' Roberta, no longer Carl's wife but a close friend nevertheless, described Barbara as 'the mother I never had'. 'She stuck by us even when we did wrong. She stood up to our enemies, the police and even a Supreme Court judge because she thought that loyalty was a lifetime thing.'

> *I know the authorities won't be happy until they've pushed me over the limit. But they are wasting there [sic] time, they wont [sic] succeed—that I assure you.*

Williams was bashed to death in the Acacia Unit just after lunchtime on Monday 19 April 2010. He was pronounced dead at 1.47 pm.

The first official confirmation of the jail death—after off-the-record confirmation had appeared as breaking news on media websites—came via a Victoria Police press release. It read:

> Victoria Police can confirm that Carl Williams has died following an assault at Barwon Prison this afternoon. Homicide Squad detectives are at the scene and are investigating the circumstances surrounding the death of the thirty-nine-year-old … Medical staff at the prison attempted to revive Williams until ambulance officers arrived, however he died at the scene. Police are currently working with Corrections staff to ascertain as much information as possible. A man is in custody and will be spoken to by police as part of the on-going investigation.

Outside the prison, Detective Inspector Bernie Edwards explained to the gathered media that it appeared Williams was bashed with the stem of a prison exercise bike in the combined kitchen and exercise area. There was CCTV footage of the incident, he said.

Deputy Corrections Commissioner Rod Wise said Williams had been 'happy' sharing the unit with the two prisoners. 'Mr Williams was happy with those arrangements. There had been no previous incidents or any problems between them.'

It was later revealed that Williams could have lain in his cell undiscovered by prison guards, bleeding and in possible cardiac arrest, for up to twenty-five minutes. He had been dragged and left there. Corrections Commissioner Bob Hastings did not comment on any delay in Williams's body being found. 'Our staff will be investigated … what they saw and what they did,' Hastings told ABC radio.

Williams's lawyer, Rob Stary, told Channel Nine: 'Being in the state's strictest regime, where he was constantly monitored … we thought he was secure, he thought he was secure and the authorities thought that he was secure. There has obviously been a very, very serious lapse.'

Victoria Police Deputy Commissioner Sir Ken Jones also entered the fray, saying Williams's death could affect on-going police prosecutions. 'It doesn't take a genius to work out that there will be ramifications and impacts,' Jones said. 'As we speak I've got people working on this.'

Then-Premier John Brumby hosed down calls for royal commissions and the like, saying several inquires into the jail killing had swung into action. They were being conducted by the Homicide Squad, the Office of Police Integrity, the Office of Correctional Services Review, and the coroner. Police also created a special taskforce, codenamed Driver, to investigate any possible links between the death and suspected police corruption.

'To be honest, what occurred in the prison was obviously unacceptable but [Carl Williams] was a serial killer,' Brumby said in what was perceived as an ill-advised comment. 'I think it would be quite unnecessary and a quite inappropriate use of taxpayers' money to have a royal commission.'

The comments attracted immediate criticism. Then State Opposition Leader Ted Baillieu led the charge. 'Something has obviously gone horribly wrong down at Barwon Prison if a prisoner like Mr Williams can be [killed] in the middle of the highest security jail we have,' he said.

Away from the police and politicians, the death drew comment from the 'usual suspects'. Chopper Read said he burst into laughter when he first heard the news. 'I spat out my drink,' he told Adelaide's Nova FM breakfast show.

> I laughed my head off. I thought to myself, 'Ha, ha, ha, another one bites the dust.' He was just a big, fat, wobbly-bottom kid. He wasn't much of a man at all. I mean, you know, if you met him in jail you'd bend him over and stick it up him. I mean, he was nothing. There's only me and Mick [Gatto] left. No one is gunna hurt me and no one is gunna hurt Mick.

Gatto, when asked for his thoughts, was a little more reserved. 'I would rather let dead dogs lie,' he told the *Herald Sun*.

Bert Wrout, still kicking despite being wounded at the Brunswick Club back in 2004, wrote a newspaper column. 'Carl, as far as I was concerned, grew up as a gofer for Jason and Mark,' he wrote.

> He ran the messages and bought the cigarettes. He was just a fat bumbling fool. We let him get under our guard when Mark was killed. It's common knowledge in the world I live in that Carl was a gutless, weak coward ... My thoughts on Carl are just a fat rat that was eventually going to get his right whack in the boob [jail]. I felt not the slightest bit of feeling. He'll be consigned to the rubbish tip of history.

George Williams, out of prison and still alive despite his dodgy ticker, described his son as a 'special man' with a 'special smile'. Roberta said their life together had been 'memorable, full of fun and happiness'.

Surely the most comical comments came from Roberta, who told *New Idea* magazine that she was donating Williams's brain to science. 'I believe it's to help with research and might explain why guys like Carl do the violent things they do,' she said. (To which one of my office colleagues responded: 'They'll need a search warrant and a microscope to find his brain.')

On the flip side, Matthew Johnson had very little—if anything—to say during his first court appearance via video link from jail. He appeared in Geelong Magistrates' Court on a television screen. He sat impassively as Magistrate Ron Saines remanded him to reappear at a later date. When asked if he had anything to say, Johnson simply answered, 'Nuh.' At a second committal mention, the accused's lawyer, Christopher Traill, told Saines that he was considering defensive homicide as a defence.

Matthew Johnson's committal hearing, which ran in December 2010, heard that Monday 19 April started as just another day at the office for Barwon Prison guard Suzette Gajic. After the morning parade Gajic was escorted to the Acacia Unit and, after a security clearance, collected her foyer keys and radio.

'Within the Acacia Unit there are four separate units which house fourteen prisoners and I am responsible for the entry and exit to each unit,' Gajic explained in her tendered police statement. About ten minutes before the 8.30 am inmate count, Gajic saw Carl Williams in the Unit One yard talking on the telephone. 'He appeared to be having a normal conversation.'

Acting general manager of Barwon Prison Nicholas Selisky explained the layout and management of Acacia in his statement. 'Under the current system, staff are not required to enter the units unless they have a specific reason and monitoring is done via CCTV. Due to the structure of the Acacia Unit, officers only have direct vision of Unit Three. All other vision is through the camera system and staff interaction when they attend the units.'

At around 11 am Gajic let Williams and an escort guard out of the unit so that the gangland killer could visit with his father. George Williams told police his son appeared agitated. 'Carl was very disappointed [about a press report],' George said in his police statement. 'He also spoke about the way he was being treated ... Carl was unhappy that they were not moving him as he had requested.' The court was told that Williams wanted to be moved to a different unit to be with long-serving prisoners he knew well.

'He did not say there were any problems with [his unit inmates] Matty [Johnson] and Tommy [Ivanovic], but he probably would not tell me if there was,' George said.

Gajic remembered Williams arriving back inside the unit at about 12.40 pm. 'I said to Carl, "It's your lucky day, Carl. Today I'm going to let you [back] in via the tradesman's entrance," which is the airlock,' Gajic told police. 'There was no verbal response which [was] very strange. Carl [was] usually jovial.'

Around 1 pm, while Gajic was having lunch at the unit console, a delivery arrived. She went to fetch a trolley, with no idea that her ordinary Monday was about to be turned on its head.

'As I have approached the airlock I could see Matt Johnson and Tommy Ivanovic cutting laps around Yard One. I then opened the gate and Matt and Tommy began to approach me.' According to Gajic, Johnson said to her, 'Miss Gajic, you need to press your buzzer.' 'I then looked at Tommy and he and Matt had a very startled look on their faces and their eyes were wide open. I then questioned Matt and said, "What are you talking about?" Matt then again said, "Miss, you need to press your buzzer," in a very firm, slow voice.'

Gajic said the following conversation then took place:

GAJIC: What the fuck have you done?

JOHNSON: Carl has been hit in the head.

GAJIC: Where is he?

JOHNSON: He is in his cell.

Prison officer Stuart Drummond, who was with Gajic when the two inmates approached, told police of his memory of the conversation. 'Johnson said to me, "You had better press your alarm. Carl's hit his head." I then said to Johnson, "How bad?" and he then replied, "Don't send any females in there. Miss Gajic, don't go in there".'

Gajic immediately called in reinforcements, yelling 'Carl's down! Carl's down! Respond, Unit One!' She said five officers responded.

The guards entered Unit One. Williams's body was not in the day room, where court documents allege he was struck eight times with a seat pole from an exercise bike. (In his statement Selisky said the day room contained a bike, a pool table, a small kitchenette, a fixed gym, medicine balls, a coffee table and about six chairs.) Officer Glen Fiscilini told police he saw a blood-soaked towel on the day-room floor. 'There was heaps of blood and chunks of human organ on the floor. We went to Cell Two yelling, "Carl! Carl! Carl!" There was no response.'

The guards opened Williams's cell door.

'I saw Carl lying face down on the floor with his arms above his head,' Fiscilini said. 'He was about two feet inside the cell. I could see a lot of Carl's brain hanging out. I thought he was in a lot of trouble.'

A Code Black — the alarm for a serious medical emergency or the death of a prisoner — was called. Johnson and Ivanovic ('pacing up and down' in Yard One, according to Fiscilini) were placed in separate cells while guards checked Williams for signs of life.

'There was no pulse,' Officer Drummond said. 'At the time Carl's eye was open. I then touched his pupil for a reaction and there was no eye movement.'

Selisky later had a short conversation with Johnson. 'Johnson told me that the war was not with the staff and requested that he be given a radio. This was done. Johnson's demeanour was very calm and relaxed and he appeared no different to any other interaction that I have had with him.'

Gajic said, 'I have worked in the Acacia Unit on a regular basis and I know Carl Williams, Matt Johnson and Tommy Ivanovic very well. [On 19 April 2010] there was something not quite right. There was no communication. They were all very quiet.'

In his statement, tendered during the committal hearing, George Williams said that while serving part of his drug sentence at low-security Dhurringile Prison back in December 2008, he was transferred to Barwon Prison on very short notice.

'I [had] asked to be put with Carl a hundred times or so whilst I was in Dhurringile but they would not do it. Carl also asked to be put in with me. Carl and I were very close and wanted to be with one another.

'[After being moved] I was in Unit Four in Acacia for one night and then I was taken out of prison to where Carl was at a location out of jail. Carl was assisting in police corruption. He was with the police. We were out for approximately ten days.'

In court George Williams told Magistrate Rosemary Carlin that he and his son were allowed to spend time with their then-girlfriends on the prison outing. He said that while his time with his partner was spent in a room with a table, chairs and guards, he couldn't say what Carl and his girlfriend got up to in a separate room.

'After this [trip], Carl and I were taken back to Barwon and we were both placed in Melaleuca [Unit] together,' George said in his statement. 'It was Unit Two, I think. It was just the two of us at this time … [Carl] was a bit worried that it might get out that he had spoken to the police.'

The father and son spent two months in Melaleuca before they were moved back to Acacia and into a unit with Matthew Johnson. 'This was the first time I had met Matty,' George said in his statement. 'I got on pretty well with him. Carl was getting along with him good. Carl and Matty talked about the police corruption stuff regularly. There was no disagreement about what Carl was doing and, as time went on, Matty agreed with what Carl was doing.

'When I got out [on 20 June 2009] Matty and Carl were together and they were getting along as good as gold.'

Ivanovic, a close mate of Carl's, later moved in to the unit.

George stayed in daily phone contact with his son. 'A prisoner is usually allowed thirty-two calls a week, providing you pay for them. Carl requested extra each week. Any prisoner could request more. Carl was a phone person.'

George told police that Carl 'was always helping' Johnson: 'Matty did not have much support. Carl would often help out and share things with him.' George said he regularly stocked up Johnson's prison spend account, as a favour, right up until the month of Carl's death.

The committal hearing also heard from Peter Hatziminas, a mate of Ivanovic's, who had visited his friend about a week before the killing. 'I asked after Carl Williams. Tommy told me that Carl had lost the plot. He told me that he was "just gone". I asked Tommy what he meant by that and he explained that [Carl's sentence] was getting to Carl and he was losing it.'

Roberta Williams also gave evidence at the committal. In her tendered statement she said she'd kept in regular contact with her former husband and that the last phone call she'd had with him was on the morning of his death. It was a rushed conversation, according to Roberta.

'We had a small disagreement,' she said. 'I had to go to a photo shoot for a magazine and Carl wanted to keep talking. Carl seemed a bit agitated about something, but he did not mention any problems.'

On the final day of the three-day committal the court heard that Detective Senior Sergeant Peter Harrington — the man in charge of the investigation — wrote several notes in his day book, including one that read 'falling out'.

Johnson pleaded not guilty to murder and was committed to stand trial in the Victoria Supreme Court in 2011.

Carl Williams's jail letters, meanwhile, continue to talk from the grave. They suggest that he did expect to walk from jail one day, albeit as a mere shell of an old—and more than likely unrepentant—fallen criminal.

> *No matter what happens from here on in, I will always be able to see & talk to my loved ones, whether that be on the telephone or face to face, and that is a lot better than the scumbags who shot me can do.*

Like his murdered enemy Nik Radev, Williams was laid to rest in a gold-plated coffin. For a man who had caused so much carnage while chasing gold, Carl Anthony Williams ended up encased in it. At least his criminal career had provided something in the end: protection from the worms underground. 'Sometimes people roll the dice and come up with gold,' a former Purana detective said. 'And other times people get buried in it.'

> *I will always be able to look in the mirror and be very proud of the person I see, unlike a lot of other people who I doubt could even look at themselves in the mirror. But they have to live with that, not me!*
>
> *Lots & lots of love always—Carl—XX*

2

The Dark Side

How multimillionaire Herman Rockefeller lost his head in the secret world of sex swingers

'With his kind of money he could have bought a bloody whore house or whatever and did what he wanted, but yet he chose to come to us.'

In the minds of detectives Peter Towner and Tim Bell, there was still a slim chance of finding missing multimillionaire Herman Rockefeller alive. The company director and God-fearing family man had been missing for several days, presumed murdered, but information from an adjacent Homicide Squad interview room had him lying bashed—and possibly still breathing—in Heathcote scrubland about 110 kilometres north of Melbourne. Any man who ran up to ten kilometres a day to maintain peak physical fitness would have a survivor's constitution, Towner and Bell figured.

Where there is hope there is life, they say, and the two detectives had to get their suspect talking. Mario Schembri, sitting with guilt and consternation etched across his swarthy face, had so far given 'No comment' answers during his record of interview. Visions of a chainsaw grinding through flesh and bone were tormenting his conscience. As Schembri would later tell Towner, no amount of Hail Mary prayers could banish those gruesome images from his mind. Despite Schembri's silence, Towner pressed with a personal touch not found in any police textbook.

> I am appealing to you because you are a family man. You told me you're a Catholic. I have a grieving widow [out there] who has an eighteen-year-old daughter and a sixteen-year-old son who are absolutely beside themselves in grief. Now, whether Mr Rockefeller is or is not dead, I am obliged and it's a duty of care and I am appealing to you as a human being to tell us exactly where that person is so we can get medical [help]. Let's just forget about all the other stuff—how or what happened. You've chosen not to tell us about that. It's on humanitarian grounds that I'm appealing for you [to tell us where Rockefeller is].

Mario John Peter Schembri knew full well where Rockefeller was. In Schembri's eventual words, the married father of two had been 'dismantled' with a chainsaw and incinerated in a mate's backyard—and was now lying scattered in rubbish bins across the northern suburbs of Melbourne.

According to a police document tendered in Melbourne Magistrates' Court, Herman Charles Rockefeller 'had another side to himself which he managed to keep secret from his closest friends and family'. That 'side' was a dark, perverse attraction to having sex with strangers on the salacious 'swinging' circuit. Masquerading as a swinger named Andy Kingston, Rockefeller hawked for interested couples via advertisements in sex magazines.

Born in Akron, Ohio, in the United States of America on 25 January 1958, he was the eldest of three brothers. In July 1990 he married his wife Vicky, who originally hailed from New Zealand. The couple had two teenage children. While he lived in Melbourne, Rockefeller regularly travelled interstate as the director of his family-owned commercial property investment company.

'Herman is mainly the financial director of the company,' Vicky Rockefeller would tell police before his fate was finally known. 'Herman runs the business from home. The main office is in Hobart and he would probably travel there … for two to three days at a time.'

Police investigators determined that Rockefeller was 'highly intelligent' and 'strongly involved with his family and the local church' when not prowling as Andy Kingston.

Mario Schembri was born in Malta on 6 July 1952 into a very large family. He was one of nine children. His clan migrated to Australia in 1954 when he was only two. Eighteen years later, at age twenty, he met the woman who later became his wife. Over their journey they conceived and raised eight children. They lost one child, a daughter, who fell ill to a fatal bout of meningococcal disease in October 1990.

Not unlike Herman Rockefeller, Schembri had an insatiable craving for women other than his wife—and acted on his desires. According to the police summary: 'Throughout his marriage [Schembri] had numerous affairs and cheated on his wife.'

Schembri was also known as a bit of a jack of all trades when it came to earning money. 'Mario does all sorts of work and odd jobs, from towing cars to removing rubbish,' his nephew, James Johns, said in a police statement.

> He also buys and sells cars and deals in scrap metal and parts. He keeps all his vehicles and junk in the backyard of a house in View Street, Glenroy, that is owned by a guy named Jack Gottinger. Jack is a pensioner and Mario has arranged a deal with him to use his backyard as a storage yard.

It was through this relationship with Gottinger that Schembri met a new girlfriend in 2001. Her name was Hellen Battersby. She lived next door to Gottinger.

'I asked Mario to take away some hard rubbish for me, as the council wouldn't do it,' Battersby told police.

> Mario came around to my place and he took the hard rubbish away for me for a fee. When he came around to get his money, we started talking and began a relationship.
>
> Mario told me that he had eight kids. [He and his former wife] were split up when I hooked up with Mario. Our relationship was a sexual relationship and early on Mario asked me if I wanted to have sex with other people while we were having sex. I told him I wasn't interested in that kind of thing and he never asked me again.

Despite Battersby's relatively conservative approach to sex, the two stayed together for several years. Over that time it became evident that Schembri had an overbearing nature, despite his own desire to stray.

'Over time, Mario and I fell apart and I would say that I fell out of love with him,' Battersby said in her police statement. 'We started arguing and he started accusing me of having affairs—which I wasn't. I got sick of him always accusing me of having an affair, so I told him to stop ringing me and we broke up.'

In 2009 Schembri met Bernadette Denny. Born on 11 June 1968 in Victoria, Denny was an alcoholic widowed mother of two. Schembri was living with relatives, including James Johns, in the suburb of Hadfield north of Melbourne when he and Denny crossed paths.

It was a lost dog that strayed from home and the perverse wanderings of the multimillionaire who strayed from his wife that inadvertently led to one of Victoria's most gruesome killings. The three tragic players in this sorry tale of debauchery, death and dismemberment were—according to prominent defence barrister Phil Dunn, QC—star-crossed by coincidence. Had Schembri and Denny not met and bonded over a stray pooch in Hadfield, then Rockefeller might still be alive.

'I had found a stray dog in the street,' Johns said in his police statement.

> I had never seen this dog in the street before. I rang the council ranger and informed them about the dog and then

> I tied it up at the front gate in case the owner was looking for it. Mario and I were out the front with the dog when the woman who lived across the street [Bernadette] and her two daughters walked past. They stopped to have a chat about the dog.
>
> This was how Uncle Mario met Bernadette. Uncle Mario and Bernadette started chatting and they quickly formed a relationship and started going out. Not long after this Mario moved in with Bernadette and her two girls. There were some initial issues between Mario and Bernadette's two daughters. Uncle Mario is very strict and proper in lots of ways and he objected to the way Bernadette's daughters treated her. This caused some real problems as the girls refused to respect his authority. [So] they moved out and started living with their grandparents.

Schembri seemed to enjoy the space, as it allowed him and Denny to start exploring their sexual fantasies. They began by engaging the services of a female prostitute for a threesome in July 2009. The sex session took place at the Formula One hotel in Campbellfield. It lasted two hours and cost the couple $1200. The police summary states:

> The escort worker informed investigators that during the meeting, she and Denny kissed and fondled each other and engaged in sexual intercourse. When Schembri tried to involve himself, Denny got 'really, really angry' and said to the escort that 'this was supposed to be for me'. Schembri and the escort worker did not have sexual intercourse.

The day after the rendezvous with the escort, Denny sent the sex worker a text: 'Hi there, it's Bernadette from last night—F1 Motel. Just want to say thanks 4 a memorable nite. Hope we can do it again soon …' According to the escort, Denny contacted her on a number of occasions trying to arrange another meeting, stating that money 'was no object'. On 29 July Denny sent the sex worker another message: 'How does 300 for 2 hours sound?' On 17 August she sent another: 'U want or able 2 catch up with us—would love 2 c u have fun with him—at what price 4 him.'

Schembri had witnessed Denny tasting forbidden fruit and liked what he had seen. Denny's texts to the prostitute suggested she, too, had enjoyed the experience. The couple decided to delve further. In about October 2009 they visited the Sexyland store in Campbellfield and bought a copy of *Australian Contacts Magazine*. It was time to 'swing'. 'We had this fantasy, I guess,' Denny would tell Homicide Squad detectives Sharyn Bell and Graham Ross.

An advertisement in the magazine caught Denny's eye:

> Melbourne—attractive, sexy uninhibited fun-loving couple who enjoy engaging but safe sex life. Swing together and independently in an open relationship. We are in our late 30s. Can meet during the day times and discretion is assured. No single males please. All replies answered.

It would later be revealed in court that Rockefeller had placed thirty-four similar advertisements since the year 2000.

Denny contacted him via text. 'It was an ad for him and his "wife",' Denny later said. 'They both liked swinging—discreet and clean cut and what have you—and I tried to make contact.'

But all was not as it seemed. Crown prosecutor Chris Beale, SC, would say in the Supreme Court: '[Mr Rockefeller] gave his name as Andrew Kingston and claimed to have a wife named Jenny who would be involved. This was false as his actual wife Vicky knew nothing about it.'

Denny received a call back from Rockefeller, aka Andy Kingston. 'He was saying how they swing—him and his partner—and that she's more into threesomes but she's willing to try the foursome,' Denny said. 'He just spoke about sick stuff that they were into … He sounded like he'd done it all before.'

According to Denny, they 'spoke a bit'.

> I mentioned to him that I had children. He said that he had a child. I can't remember if he said it was a girl or a

> boy. I know he said it was a twelve-year-old. He told me his wife's name was Jenny. I recall that because I had a Barbie doll named Jenny when I was a kid.
>
> Another time we made contact, we spoke about likes and … kinky stuff. When I say kinky stuff—stuff that they were into.

Rockefeller eventually spoke to Schembri. 'Mario got off the phone,' Denny would tell the detectives, '[and] said that he was really keen. He [Rockefeller] wanted to have a three-way with me and my partner and him and then do the swap around. At the time it was a bit of a fantasy. We were both curious.'

According to Denny, Rockefeller kept ringing.

> He kept on saying he wanted to catch up with us … At the beginning it was a bit of a turn-on. He wanted to know if we were still interested. It was a bit like, I guess, someone putting a bone underneath a dog's nose and teasing him. He said something about, 'We can go on holidays. Travel a lot.'

BELL: Did he mention anything personal about himself?

DENNY: [No,] apart from the fact that he had this Jenny—his partner or his wife. But then, I don't know, because one time he said it was his wife and then another time he referred to this Jenny as his sex partner … I think he said he was into stock markets, or something.

Rockefeller first visited Denny and Schembri at Denny's Hadfield home in December 2009. Rockefeller and Denny had sex while Schembri watched. Rockefeller reportedly tried to get Schembri involved but he refused.

DENNY: He came during the day.

BELL: Yeah? Who was home then?

DENNY: Mario was home.

BELL: And what happened?

DENNY: He had sex with me.

BELL: Whereabouts?

DENNY: In the lounge room.

BELL: How did that all come about?

DENNY: 'Cos he said at that time that he wanted Mario to go and meet him and his wife somewhere.

BELL: So was Mario involved when you had sex with him that time?

DENNY: He was trying to feel Mario up.

BELL: How did Mario cope with that?

DENNY: He didn't like it. He just backed off.

Rockefeller stayed for about half an hour. After the lounge room sex with Denny he helped himself to a shower and left as a content man with an ongoing promise. It was one he would never fulfil.

BELL: So what happened after that?

DENNY: He just kept on saying he was going to send a photo [of his sex partner]. There was one day we were meant to catch up and then he sent a text to say that she had bronchitis and we'd have to do it some other time.

BELL: What were you thinking?

DENNY: We'd been taken for a fool and he knew that ... He just kept on coming up with excuses.

On 18 January 2010, Rockefeller flew to New South Wales for a four-day business trip. 'In NSW he met his brother Robert,' the police summary says, 'and over the following days they undertook meetings in connection with their business at various locations in New South Wales.'

Rockefeller telephoned Vicky constantly while he was away. 'Whilst he was up there, I spoke to him every day,' she recalls. 'He was calling a fair bit because he just found out our daughter got in to medicine and he was really excited.'

On his last day interstate, 21 January, Rockefeller visited Maitland, Edgeworth, Glendale and Cameron Park before being dropped off at Newcastle Airport for his 4.50 pm flight out. He flew Virgin Blue to Brisbane for his connecting flight home to Melbourne. While in the Brisbane terminal he made several phone calls. On what police described as his 'secret telephone', he called Denny to confirm a prearranged rendezvous, and scribbled her address on a newspaper page next to a sudoku puzzle he was working on. Using his 'normal' phone he sent a text to his wife at 6.35 pm, in which he lied and also made mention of his daughter: 'Plane is not expected in until 10.30. Sarah accepted into ANU MED course according to paper. Heard she has QLD offer.'

The message about the flight being delayed was a ruse. According to police, 'Investigators allege this was a deliberate lie designed to give Mr Rockefeller a spare hour in which to attend South Street, Hadfield, and have sex with Schembri and Denny.'

Rockefeller arrived at Melbourne Airport at 9.12 pm. He drove his Toyota Prius from the long-term car park at 9.35 pm. From Tullamarine he travelled to Hadfield. He arrived at Denny's house, parking his car around the corner. He knocked and went inside. What followed and led to his death may never be fully known. Police can only rely on the accounts of Schembri and Denny, as dead men tell no tales. Crime scenes talk, but no evidence would be found at the unit to refute the couple's version of events. Rockefeller's remains would prove even less helpful, not even offering a whisper as to his cause of death.

Rockefeller arrived alone and full of lust the night he died.

BELL: Tell me what happened from the start.

DENNY: He came to the door. Came in and wanted sex … Started feeling me up.

BELL: And?

DENNY: I questioned him about this thing with his so-called wife, partner … whatever it was … and he said, 'It's not my wife, it's my sex partner.'

BELL: Then what happened? What were you thinking?

DENNY: I was pissed off. I was upset … He knew we were both pissed off.

BELL: Where was he touching you?

DENNY: Just on my body and my breasts … Just trying to get his hand between my legs.

Denny told Rockefeller that she and Schembri were 'sick of the lies' about his plans to introduce a second woman into the mix. Rockefeller then responded by saying he would show them a photograph of his sex partner—only to fumble around and say he did not have one.

BELL: What did Mario do?

DENNY: He wasn't happy. I wasn't happy either.

BELL: So what happened after that, when he couldn't show you a photo?

DENNY: He said he still wanted to have sex.

BELL: How did that make you feel?

DENNY: Dirty.

Rockefeller continued his groping. Denny slapped him in the face. Schembri told Rockefeller to 'keep his fucking hands off'.

Denny says her slap took Rockefeller by surprise but appeared to excite him. The multimillionaire is said to have smirked and remarked that he liked feisty women. That's when argument came to push. Push then came to shove and an all-in fight ensued.

Schembri would eventually tell detectives that he reacted because Rockefeller 'welshed' on his promise to bring his woman for a foursome. 'We'd had a meeting once before with him,' Schembri would tell detectives Towner and Tim Bell.

> He had it on with Bernie for a bit and I was there and that was all right and then he promised to get his wife involved and he didn't come with it ... He come over [sic] and he didn't bring his missus and there was a bit of a confrontation ... We weren't happy and then it went from not happy to arguments and then it just flared up and I got a little bit—and Bernie got a little bit—upset and ... I don't know, stepped in.

After eventually agreeing to talk to police, Schembri would say that the night started badly thanks to Rockefeller's attitude.

> All he said was, 'Can I have a quickie?' blah, blah, blah, so we sat down and had a drink. We had a talk and I said to

him, 'Where's the wife?' [He said] 'She's sick,' she's this, she's that. I said, 'Come on … You've used my wife. What's happening? [You're] a bit selfish.'

Rockefeller tried to leave but Schembri stopped him. 'No hang on, what's the problem?' Schembri asked. 'Let's work it out. When's she coming?'

Schembri felt Rockefeller had got the better of him. 'He kept saying a few things that annoyed me here and there and the next thing you know we're into it,' Schembri would tell police. '[I was] getting harder and stronger and harder and harder and he got harder and harder. We both banged our heads on the wall and it happened. We were both banging heads together. He was tryin' to protect himself and he just fell and hit his head and that was it.'

Schembri would even liken himself to Muhammad Ali, telling his police questioners that he never hit anyone as hard as he did Rockefeller that night. 'I got a bit heavy handed and he wasn't able to take it.'

TOWNER: Who struck who first?

SCHEMBRI: Anyone's guess … He got angry because—look at his position in life. He's a millionaire … His theory was have three people at once and then we have it with his missus. So we'll have a foursome, but he wanted to go first with my missus … He welshed on it.

Schembri would admit that he could become quite angry when pushed. 'I don't know how to explain anger. It's like you shoot me with a gun and I'll shoot you with a bloody atom bomb. He actually tapped into that and that's not something that is good.'

TOWNER: Was the violence part of the joy? Was it part of the sex?

SCHEMBRI: No, no, no, no. It was [all about] just having someone else. Having two women there and doin' what you want for as long as you want and swappin' over, you know, and enjoying that … I didn't want his money. I only wanted his missus and my own missus to have fun together. Is that a crime?

SCHEMBRI: He kept ringin' up and then he had a good time with Bernie and said he wanted to come back.

BELL: What was the arrangement after that? Was it going to be you and his wife, or … ?

SCHEMBRI: Yeah.

BELL: Bernie and … ?

SCHEMBRI: The two of us.

BELL: The two ladies together, or … ?

SCHEMBRI: Three of us, with him and his wife and then … I don't know—like this guy says one thing and you say another.

TOWNER: At what point did you, you know, make an opinion or form an opinion that he was bullshitting to you?

SCHEMBRI: When he didn't bring his missus … He wanted himself to be happy and I wasn't happy with that. The idea was he was gonna bring his wife, I thought. I was hoping he would, but he come on his own.

Denny told her questioners that during the fight she was trying to fend Rockefeller off Schembri and copped a kick in the leg. 'It was just shit,' she said of the fight.

BELL: Then what happened?

DENNY: It's all a blur.

BELL: Who was fighting?

DENNY: All of us … He was tryin' to fight back.

BELL: When he kicked you, what did you do?

DENNY: I started hitting him too. Then we went into the garage … and then the fighting just started again.

BELL: What would you describe as fighting?

DENNY: It was like wrestling. It was full on.

In Denny's words, Rockefeller 'just fell to the ground' during the assault. But he was breathing, she claimed. 'He didn't say anything but he was breathing … Mario and I just walked into the house. We were in shock. We didn't know what to say to each other. Sort of like, "What's happened. It's gone too far." I was just panicking. Panic, panic, panic stations.'

Schembri's eventual version would be somewhat different.

BELL: So he didn't get up again after he fell and hit his head?

SCHEMBRI: No, he was pretty well dead.

A few hours later, Schembri and Denny loaded Rockefeller's body into the boot of Schembri's car and drove to the semirural town of Heathcote to dump it. They scouted the area for a suitable spot in scrubland but failed to find a dumping ground to their liking. They did a U-turn and drove the dead man—who they had no idea at that stage was a multimillionaire —back to Denny's garage.

Using available cleaning products, the couple scrubbed and cleaned Rockefeller's blood as best they could from the lounge room, garage floor and kitchen tiles. Rockefeller's cooling body lay on the cold garage floor for the rest of the night. The next day Schembri and Denny loaded Rockefeller's Prius onto Schembri's trailer. Schembri drove it away and dumped it.

Police took a statement from Vicky Rockefeller after her husband failed to materialise the following day.

'I have been married to my husband Herman for twenty years in July,' she said.

> I would describe our relationship as good and solid. Normally Herman comes straight home. He would normally call me on his way to the car, or shortly after, but he didn't last night … I am worried sick for Herman. I haven't slept all night. I just feel so helpless. I mean, he's not even the kind of person who would go for a drink on the way home.

On Saturday 23 January, Schembri and Denny visited their local Bunnings Warehouse where they chose a $99 Ozito electric chainsaw. In-store security footage shows Schembri wielding a display model Ozito and moving it in a practice motion to confirm it appropriate for home body dismemberment. Justice Terry Forrest would later say: 'CCTV footage shows you, Mr Schembri, testing a chainsaw for weight and balance, much as a cricketer might sample a bat for pick up and grip.'

Happy with the choice, the couple then gathered up six plastic drop sheets, two pairs of disposable overalls, face masks and a shovel set and paid for the gear in cash.

James Johns received a phone call from his uncle Mario at about 9.45 pm on the Saturday night. The conversation went as follows:

JOHNS: What's wrong?

SCHEMBRI: I'm in a bit of trouble.

JOHNS: With what?

SCHEMBRI: We went a little bit too far.

JOHNS: What do you mean? If it's something about that fucking idiot [Bernadette], keep me out of it.

SCHEMBRI: You're actually right. I'll keep you out of it. It's all cool.

On either the Saturday night or the following evening (investigators are unsure which) Schembri cut Rockefeller into pieces where his body lay in Denny's garage. According to Schembri, he did the gory job after thinking about it for a day. 'We dismembered him in the garage … Me and a chainsaw,' he told the detectives. 'I didn't think I had the balls to cut him, but I did.'

TOWNER: How did that make you feel?

SCHEMBRI: Yeah, well, I don't know. Really horrible.

TOWNER: Were you physically ill?

SCHEMBRI: I wasn't far from it.

TOWNER: Were you ill?

SCHEMBRI: I didn't vomit, but I had to be strong, you know, because it wasn't gonna get done, was it?

TOWNER: Was there much mess in the garage?

SCHEMBRI: There was a fair bit.

TOWNER: And how did you clean that up, or what happened to that?

SCHEMBRI: We cleaned the best we could. You'll be able to find some DNA there, won't you?

BELL: What parts of the body did you cut off and where?

SCHEMBRI: His hands and his legs and his head.

BELL: Was he dressed at the time?

SCHEMBRI: Was, yeah … There's no way I can say one hundred Hail Marys and it'll go away.

The questioning would continue.

BELL: And so, where was Bernie while you were using the chainsaw to dismember him?

SCHEMBRI: She wasn't impressed, no.

BELL: Was she in the garage?

SCHEMBRI: Tried to, but she couldn't.

BELL: Couldn't stomach it?

SCHEMBRI: Neither could I, really.

BELL: But you thought it had to be done?

SCHEMBRI: Well, what choice did I have?

BELL: You mentioned you cut his hands off. Was it at the wrists or … ?

SCHEMBRI: No, a bit higher.

BELL: At the elbow?

SCHEMBRI: A bit higher somewhere.

BELL: Can you tell me about the legs?

SCHEMBRI: Thighs, I suppose.

After cutting up the corpse, Schembri stuffed the pieces into heavy-duty garbage bags. The final step in the disposal plan was to transport the bags to Jack Gottinger's Glenroy backyard and burn them and their contents. It took a couple of trips to transport the body bags. 'Two loads. Three loads,' Schembri would say.

At a police press conference, Vicky Rockefeller described her feelings of dread. It had been three days since anyone had heard from or seen her husband. 'You just can't imagine what it's like. It's unbearable,' she said.

Rockefeller's brother, Robert, said the business trip to New South Wales had been a successful one and that Herman had not hinted at any brewing trouble or distress in his life. 'I spent probably the best four days I've spent with my brother,' he told the media.

It was Monday 25 January—Herman Rockefeller's birthday—when Schembri began to burn the bags containing the 'dismantled' millionaire—and other incriminating items, like parts of the Ozito chainsaw—in a 44-gallon drum. 'He started a fire using petrol, shredded paper and timber,' the police summary suggests. In his record of interview there would be questions about Rockefeller's personal belongings.

TOWNER: Do you know what happened to his ring?

SCHEMBRI: Don't know.

TOWNER: The family tells me that he was wearing a wedding ring.

SCHEMBRI: It wasn't on him.

BELL: What about any personal belongings he might have had in his pockets?'

SCHEMBRI: I didn't want to go through his clothes. Jesus.

On the Monday, Jack Gottinger's next-door neighbour Hellen Battersby travelled home on a bus having visited her father in hospital. When she arrived at her stop, about 200 metres from her home, she immediately smelled putrid smoke.

'I thought someone was burning tyres or something. It stunk!' she said in her police statement. 'As I walked closer to home, the smell was stronger. As I got closer the smell changed. I didn't think it smelt like burnt tyres any more but like something I have never smelt before.'

As the fire burned, Schembri intermittently plucked bones from the drum, put them in bags and drove them around the northern suburbs where he dumped them at various points.

On Australia Day—the 26th—Schembri bought a bag of heat beads and gloves and returned to the Glenroy property. He built up the fire and continued the burning process. One of Gottinger's other neighbours, Robyn O'Brien, could barely stand the stench. 'The smoke that I smelt coming from Jack's backyard on the Monday and Tuesday was disgusting,' she later told police. 'I have never smelt anything like it. It was horrible. It wasn't like rubber burning—it was too strong for that.'

It got so bad that the Metropolitan Fire Brigade was called in to douse the drum fire.

'Mario asked me if I knew who called the fire brigade,' Hellen Battersby says. 'I told him that I didn't know. Mario appeared agitated and nervous.'

Thanks to information provided after the Vicky Rockefeller press conference, police located Rockefeller's dumped car. Investigators checked its GPS system. Its last recorded address: Bernadette Denny's South Street home in Hadfield. In the dumped Prius, police also found the *Daily Telegraph* newspaper page on which Rockefeller had scribbled Denny's address next to the sudoku puzzle while waiting for his Melbourne flight from Brisbane.

After purchasing bottles of bleach at a local Safeway supermarket on Thursday 28 January, Schembri and Denny were arrested. Detectives Towner and Ben Wiseman decided to play good cop/good cop to try to build an early rapport with Schembri.

TOWNER: Okay. We arrived here at the police station and you have been placed in this interview room. Mr Wiseman kindly donated a dollar and bought you a can of drink. A Solo. Is that correct?

SCHEMBRI: Somebody did.

TOWNER: Somebody did.

WISEMAN: Yep. It was my dollar.

TOWNER: Mr Wiseman spent a dollar and bought you a can of drink.

SCHEMBRI: Well, there you go. It was a dollar.

Initially, Schembri was not keen on saying much. He'd asked for a solicitor.

TOWNER: We asked whether you had your own personal solicitor which we did by giving you the Yellow Pages … but you got a bit aggressive there for a bit.

SCHEMBRI: Well, I dispute that … I said to you ad nauseam that I couldn't point out a solicitor, all right?

As the questioning began, Schembri replied with 'No comment' answers. The interview was suspended at 7.15 pm.

In a separate interview room, Denny, meanwhile, was not playing as staunch. She began to talk to detectives Sharyn Bell and Graham Ross during her taped interrogation. She said she knew of millionaire Herman Rockefeller from what she had seen on television after his disappearance.

BELL: Do you know anyone that may be Herman Rockefeller?

DENNY: Well it may be, I dunno … Andy Kingston.

BELL: What can you tell me about Andy Kingston?

DENNY: I bought a contact magazine from a sex shop.

BELL: Yep …

DENNY: And he was in the swingers section …

And so the story went on, with Denny outlining the first contact involving the lounge room sex, the follow-up phone conversations and the doomed second meeting during which Rockefeller was all hands. She spoke of the fight and how Rockefeller fell and hit his head in her garage. But he was breathing when they left him, she said. 'We could hear him … We just walked in the house. We were in shock … Didn't know what to say to each other. Sort of like really, 'What's happened? It's gone too far.'

Denny said she retrieved Rockefeller's mobile phone from his car and later threw it in a bin in the suburb of Broadmeadows.

BELL: Where is he, Bernadette? Can you tell me where he is?

DENNY: I'm stuffed.

BELL: Can you tell me where this man is, Bernadette? Where did you put him?

Detective Sharyn Bell's plea for an answer continued. At that stage it appeared that maybe there was a chance Rockefeller could still be alive.

BELL: You understand we need to find him.

DENNY: Yeah, I know. I know.

BELL: I know this is hard but, as I said, you understand that we need to find him. So can you tell me where he is?

Denny then continued the lie, falsely raising the detectives' hopes. She said she and Schembri drove Rockefeller to a place 'near the freeway in Heathcote' and 'just left him there'.

DENNY: He was still breathing.

BELL: He was still breathing?

DENNY: Yeah.

The lies continued. Denny knew full well that Rockefeller had been chainsawed to pieces in her garage and bagged for burning on a backyard pyre.

BELL: So when he was in the boot, was he still breathing?

DENNY: Yeah. 'Cos every now and then you could hear like banging …

BELL: What do you mean banging?

DENNY: I dunno, like a tapping sound.

BELL: Coming from where?

DENNY: From the boot.

BELL: Was he doing anything other than tapping?

DENNY: You could hear him groaning every now and then.

Denny continued with her fictitious account, saying she and Schembri dragged Rockefeller by both arms and dumped him in an unknown location.

'I couldn't look back,' she lied. 'None of us looked back … Not me or Mario.'

BELL: When you saw it on the telly, what was your reaction to that?

DENNY: Like a shock because then I found out who he was.

BELL: Did you know that beforehand?

DENNY: As I said, until what I saw on the TV, he was … Andy Kingston.

The interview was suspended at 9.30 pm. Upon its recommencement, Bell showed Denny a Google map of north-western Victoria and asked for basic directions to locate Rockefeller. It was decided the detectives would drive Denny to the area and mount a search.

BELL: Let's just hope he's alive, eh? Are you right?

DENNY: Yeah.

BELL: You know he has to be found … He does have to be found because he does have kids.

That night police conducted a vain search of the Heathcote scrubland for a body that was never there.

According to prosecutor Beale: 'Denny's false claim that they dumped the deceased alive led to an extensive search by police in the Heathcote area involving police helicopters, the Dog Squad, the Search and Rescue Squad and State Emergency Service personnel, during which Denny pretended to be assisting police.'

Denny slept in a cell at the nearby Bendigo police station before the search began again at first light on the 29th. With no sign of a body, Denny was driven back to the St Kilda Road police complex.

Just before noon, in the Homicide Squad office, detectives Towner and Tim Bell picked up their 'No Comment' interview with Schembri from where they had left off the previous evening. Based on Denny's false account of how Rockefeller was dumped in scrubland, the two detectives had to believe there could still be a chance of finding the missing millionaire alive. They therefore had to get their suspect talking.

TOWNER: All right. Mario, again, you're here because we believe that you are involved in the disappearance of a person known as Herman Rockefeller that disappeared or was last seen alive last Thursday evening on 21 January at approximately 9.32 pm. Do you understand that?

SCHEMBRI: Yeah. No comment.

TOWNER: No comment?

SCHEMBRI: No comment.

TOWNER: Do you know anything in relation to this missing person?

SCHEMBRI: No comment.

TOWNER: Do you know a person by the name of Bernadette Denny?

SCHEMBRI: No comment.

TOWNER: Mario, so you understand why I am asking you these questions I will give you an opportunity to digest this. Police have arrested Bernadette Denny at her home address last night. She has provided certain information to us which is critical to this investigation, nominating certain persons and certain things. It's obviously no secret to you or anyone else that she has implicated you as being involved in this disappearance of this person. Do you want to comment on any of that information I've just provided to you?

SCHEMBRI: No comment.

Towner then explained:

> Bernadette has told us that Mr Rockefeller was assaulted in her garage by you and her. As a result of that altercation, he fell to the floor and she panicked and he was then conveyed in a car by you to an unknown address at Heathcote. Now why I'm asking you these direct questions is that she has told us that en route in the vehicle both you and her could hear the sounds of this person banging on the boot and making noises and groaning. Now, regardless of how he came to be in that position and those circumstances … I, myself, and every member of the police force have a duty of care, however remote—the possibility may be that Mr Rockefeller is in urgent need of medical assistance and may be alive. Bernadette has currently been with the police all night scouring the countryside where she thinks you—she has told us that you and her—disposed of his body. Not disposed. Placed him.

That was when Towner made his appeal to Schembri, as a family man, to tell them where the victim was. Afterwards, the detectives played Schembri part of Denny's record of interview.

TOWNER: Do you want to watch that again Mario?

SCHEMBRI: Not really.

TOWNER: Is what you have just viewed and what Bernadette Denny has told police last night—are you involved in any of that or is that a pack of lies?

SCHEMBRI: No comment.

Towner showed Schembri a photograph of Rockefeller.

TOWNER: Is that the person that you have known as Andy Kingston?

SCHEMBRI: No comment.

TOWNER: All right. I'm not going to beat about the bush any more. A very in-depth and full-scale search is being conducted. I am hoping that what Bernadette has told me is the truth and that there's a remote, slim chance that we find Herman and he's alive and we can offer him medical assistance. Stranger things have happened because the earthquake in Haiti has been on and they've just dragged kids out fourteen days later.

During yet another interview suspension, Schembri spoke with a solicitor and it was then that he finally decided to talk—on the proviso that he could see members of his family afterwards.

'There's only part of him [left],' Schembri began. He then told his story, explaining the fight, how Rockefeller was crudely cut up and cremated and was now lying in rubbish bins around town. 'I've got a little piece of him left. The rest of him's gone.'

At around 8.15 pm in the adjacent room, Denny's interview was drawing to a close. Sharyn Bell made one final attempt to extract the truth.

BELL: Is there anything you want to tell me before we go—finish up?

DENNY: The body wasn't left at Heathcote.

BELL: Where was it taken?

DENNY: We went to Heathcote with it but brought it back.

BELL: Is that what's happened? We're of the impression that … We went looking for him …

DENNY: Yeah, I know. I know.

BELL: Yep. Okay. That's done. We're past that now but the thing is …

DENNY: He's not up at Heathcote … All I know, he was taken away and burnt. That's all I know. I didn't want to see. I just couldn't.

BELL: When you came back from Heathcote, where did you go?

DENNY: The next day, the car was taken up to where it was left.

BELL: Yep. But when you came home from Heathcote, was Herman still with you in the car?

DENNY: Yeah he was.

BELL: Where did you put him?

DENNY: In the garage …

BELL: Did you know he was dead then?

DENNY: I don't know. I don't know. Just can't. I can't.

BELL: Okay. What's happened in the garage? Is this the part you're struggling with?

DENNY: He was cut up eventually … He was cut up with a chainsaw.

BELL: Were you there when that happened?

DENNY: I wasn't there … I heard it … I've got no more comment. I can't.

Schembri, too, was coming to the end of his interview. 'I had my whole life ahead of me,' he told Towner and Tim Bell. 'Look what I've done to myself. You know what I've done to myself. I'm fifty-seven and what am I gunna get now? Fifteen years.'

When asked why he killed Rockefeller, Schembri said: 'If I had the answer to that, what would it be? Got out of hand. Went stupid. He tried to defend himself. It made me worse and I just blew up. He was only doing what any normal person would try and do—protect himself. And I don't blame him for that.'

When asked why he unlawfully disposed of the body, he said: 'Trying to get away with the thing, I suppose. Thinking I'm smarter than you guys, probably.'

Investigators managed to locate a small amount of Rockefeller's remains. Pathologists had the impossible task of determining a cause of death from a small amount of bone found inside a bag of ash in the 44-gallon drum in Gottinger's backyard and from bones located in a bag in Schembri's vehicle.

'Due to the destruction of the deceased a post-mortem examination was unable to establish the cause of death,' the police summary states. 'Medical records of the deceased place him in perfect health and many family and friends will attest to his strict fitness regime.'

Jack Gottinger was sickened when informed of what had occurred in his backyard. 'I was just trying to help Mario out. I won't do that again after this,' he told police. 'Mario just told me he'd been burning rubbish.'

Police charged Schembri and Denny with murder. In Melbourne Magistrates' Court on 13 July, prosecutor Beale told Magistrate Sarah Dawes that those murder charges had been withdrawn and a charge each of manslaughter had been filed and served.

'Mr Schembri and Ms Denny have offered to plead to manslaughter … and the Crown accepts that plea offer,' Beale said.

When asked for their plea, Schembri and Denny—separated by a prison guard—stood and uttered the words: 'Guilty, Your Honour.'

During his opening remarks at the killers' plea hearing in the Victorian Supreme Court on 30 August 2010, Beale told Justice Terry Forrest that the couple's accounts fell short of establishing that they 'acted with the state of mind necessary to sustain the charge of murder'.

> Their subsequent destruction of the body is consistent with consciousness of guilt of the commission of the crime of manslaughter. The prosecution case, therefore, based on all the evidence is that on the night of 21 January 2010 the deceased was subjected to an unlawful and dangerous assault by Schembri and Denny which caused his death.

Beale tendered victim impact statements from Vicky Rockefeller, her daughter Sarah, Rockefeller's parents Herman Snr and Edith, and his brother, Robert. None wanted their statement read in open court. The only revelation as to the distress of Vicky Rockefeller was aired via part of a psychologist's report. It read:

> Mrs Vicky Rockefeller is the victim of horrifying traumas. The world as it was known prior to her husband's death is no longer safe or predictable. The traumas that she has experienced and continues to re-live have imposed a life sentence. She is isolated, set apart and defined by her husband's death, horrendous disposal of his body and the discovery of his secret life.

Vicky Rockefeller, face to face with her husband's killers for the first time, sat composed—her facade cracking only once or twice as the most gruesome details were aired. Schembri, a bald squat man, sat seemingly unmoved in the dock as his barrister, Geoffrey Steward, went to work to try to snare him as short a sentence as possible. Steward said it had been eighteen years since Schembri had come to the attention of police or faced a court. In 1992 he received an intensive corrections order for a serious assault in which he punched and kicked a male victim after 'a loss of control'. Steward described Schembri's record of interview regarding the Rockefeller killing as a 'graphic and gruesome' telling of an unplanned crime where 'matters unexpectedly and suddenly got out of hand'.

'He felt that he was being taken for a fool. Taken for a ride,' Steward said.

Justice Forrest had to remind Steward that it 'got out of hand' because Schembri and Denny did not let Rockefeller leave the home.

'[My client] told it as it was or at the very least how he remembered it, warts and all, so to speak,' Steward said.

> Your Honour would have gleaned from the material that he's not a man of sophistication or cunning … It is clear

> that, notwithstanding the passing of a number of days, … there was really, seemingly, no attempt by either Ms Denny or Mr Schembri to get their heads together and come up with a false account.

Steward said his client had saved the Rockefeller family from added heartache by pleading guilty to manslaughter at an early stage, a saintly and noble course of conduct given the evil media interest in the case.

> Had there been a contested committal hearing or had there been a trial, and given the salacious nature of the background and the public's voyeurism—for want of a better word—and the intensity of the media interest from the time of Mr Rockefeller's disappearance—which only escalated once some of the background material was known—one could well have expected coverage of a contested hearing or trial to have reached the level of saturation in the media. It's clear from the poignant and measured and very understandable victim impact statements that Your Honour has received, that one part of the anguish of the Rockefeller family has been how this has been dealt with so intrusively by the media and as a result of the plea … it must be said that obviously a great deal of time and money—and inconvenience—[have] been saved. But far more important than that, as a result of the pleas the distress and anguish of the families has not been exacerbated by various matters being aired in open court and I'd ask Your Honour to take that into account and view it in a circumstance where this came about as a result of Mr Schembri's candour and telling it as it was.

Forrest countered with a blow on behalf of the media:

> I suppose this is unusual in the respect that by the time he was interviewed, the family of Mr Rockefeller had become personalised through the media. [Schembri] knew that they were real, that they were people and that they were distressed and I accept that that seems to have caused him to reflect upon the damage he'd done.

> The distinguishing feature it seemed to me between this and other similar types of unlawful and dangerous act manslaughters, where it's occasioned by battery, is the post offence conduct and it goes without saying that what occurred after [Mr Rockefeller] died not only was designed to conceal detection of the crime, but was also done with a callous indifference to the loved ones of the deceased and it must necessarily add to their trauma substantially—and in fact that's referred to in the victim impact statements and the psychological reports that are attached to them.

Phil Dunn, for Denny, opened his submission with:

> Your Honour, the death of Herman Rockefeller was unplanned, and it was unintended and there was no gain to anybody … It's not Andy Kingston who went out there at all. I mean, he's an educated and (as we know now) married man—a businessman—who was dealing with relative strangers to him who are unsophisticated people. And when this collision of events occurred, what happened was that very quickly Bernadette Denny and obviously her partner found themselves massively out of their depth.

Throughout the plea hearing Denny—a woman of only 150 centimetres—sat sobbing, mascara-black tears running from her eyes. She looked like a mournful little Harlequin. Dunn, quoting from a psychological report, said she suffered a dependent personality disorder.

'She seeks approval and subjugates her wishes to those of her partners and family,' Dunn read from the report.

> She is emotionally needy, under-confident and reluctant to handle life without being in a relationship with someone else who can make decisions for her … Ms Denny is likely to have been dependent on Mr Schembri for approval and her personality structure in my opinion is very relevant to her poor judgement in assisting Mr Schembri to conceal the evidence of Mr Rockefeller's death.

> At the time of the alleged offences, I believe it likely that Ms Denny's dependence on alcohol may have been sexually disinhibiting and associated with poor judgment as well as reducing her ability to think calmly or clearly. In addition, her personality structure is likely to have reduced her capacity to exercise good judgment as she's likely to prioritise her partner's wishes over her own.

According to Dunn:

> Here is a woman in her forties who, in some sense, may have thought that her self-esteem is low and that life has passed her by, and she met a man who she became infatuated with and it's perhaps no coincidence that he's of European background, she's of European background.

Dunn used Denny's first sex session with Rockefeller as an example to prove the point of infatuation with Schembri. 'Having sex with Andy Kingston on the mattress on the living room floor at Hadfield wasn't a romantic situation and she described that to the police as feeling uncomfortable but it was something she thought she had to do to keep the relationship with Mario.'

Dunn said Denny originally lied to police about the disposal of the body due to the realisation of the ultimate horror of it all. 'If she'd just stopped and paused and just had a sip of water and thought for a moment she'd know in the classic words "the game was up",' he told the court.

Prosecutor Beale finished with: 'My learned friend Mr Dunn did endeavour to make something of the lack of sophistication of Ms Denny, and indeed her partner, and he said at one stage that they found themselves massively out of their depth. The only person who was massively out of their depth in any relevant sense in this case was Mr Rockefeller. He had no propensity to violence.'

In sentencing Schembri to a maximum nine years' jail with a seven-year minimum and Denny to a maximum seven years' jail with a five-year minimum, Justice Forrest opened aptly and eloquently:

> Herman Rockefeller made some unorthodox choices in his adult life. So too did you, Mario Schembri, and you, Bernadette Denny. None of those choices was in itself unlawful, nor is it the function of this court to pass judgment on them. The upshot of the choices you made, however, is that the scene was set for the totally unnecessary death of a man. His parents, wife and children are devastated. The harm that you have caused them is profound. They will always carry some legacy of it, and so will you.

Forrest said he formed the view that, perhaps with some justification, Rockefeller was trying to take advantage of the couple.

> I accept that this made both of you, and particularly you, Mr Schembri, very angry and that that anger led ultimately to Mr Rockefeller's death … You cannot be held accountable for Mr Rockefeller's secret life. By your pleas, however, you admit criminal responsibility for his death and defilement of his body. I repeat: the damage you have caused to a decent honourable family is incalculable.
>
> I have found in both cases some remorse and that your prospects for rehabilitation are reasonable. Both of you have a good deal to offer the community, providing you can conquer your demons.

Having experimented with a female prostitute and forayed into the underground world of swinging, Mario Schembri and Bernadette Denny have been left pining for each other from separate jails. Both are no doubt ruing the decision to contact 'Andy Kingston'. As Schembri told detectives: 'With his kind of money he could have bought a bloody whore house or whatever and did what he wanted, but yet he chose to come to us … He betrayed us and then he pushed that button … We just wanted a friend. Someone we could have fun with.'

3

Parting Is Such Sweet Sorrow

A philanderer kills his wife and keeps her close for twenty-three years

'It's hardly sophisticated because anyone who hangs on to his wife's remains in a barrel for twenty-three years can hardly be accused of a sophisticated cover-up.'

FREDERICK BOYLE LOVED HIS wife. Or so he said. Whether she wore a size ten dress or a size fourteen, he didn't care. Or so he said. Despite unfounded suspicions that she harboured feelings for another man, he still loved her—or so he said—even though *he* was having an affair with another woman. His feelings ran so deep for his wife, Edwina, that after murdering her, Frederick William Boyle stuffed her body in a 44-gallon drum and retained possession of it for twenty-three years until her skeleton was discovered inside. Wherever he went to live, so did Edwina, entombed in the industrial-style sarcophagus. Boyle moved house up to five times after the murder; each time, the barrel went with him. He refused to allow it to be carted away to the tip. Edwina, after all, deserved better than that. And the separation anxiety would have killed him … or so he would say.

At family functions and birthday parties, the metal drum remained close by. In photographs taken at such events, there it would be—featured in the background for posterity. Boyle might as well have placed it at the dinner table every night, such was his need to know that Edwina was safe and sound (and not likely to be discovered as a dumped murder victim). Relatives unaware of her grisly demise would say the barrel almost had a persona of its own—an identity. One even joked on occasion that Boyle had probably stuffed his missing wife inside it, even though everyone had been told she'd up and left one night for a mystery truck driver. According to those who knew Edwina Boyle, she lived for her two daughters and would never have deserted them, particularly not the way Fred Boyle had described.

Boyle was born in Wales in March 1949. Edwina was born in the United Kingdom in February 1953. The two met in Wales and married in February 1972. Edwina was a young bride at age nineteen. Less than four months later the newlyweds migrated to Australia, where Edwina gave birth to daughter Careesa. Their second girl, Sharon, came along in April 1975. The family lived in and around the Dandenong district, in the south-eastern region of Melbourne, in the late 1970s and early '80s. The couple were hard workers. Boyle's trade was carpet laying. Edwina worked as a poultry farmhand. Much of their remaining time was spent at the local ice-skating rink where their daughters, Careesa in particular, showed flair and talent. According to younger daughter Sharon, giving evidence during her father's murder trial, ice skating was important to the family. In court she would have the following exchange with Boyle's defence barrister, Jane Dixon, SC.

DIXON: Was your sister a Victorian junior champion ice skater?

SHARON: Yes, she was.

DIXON: And were you also an ice skater?

SHARON: Not as good as her. But yes, I was.

DIXON: Was the lifestyle one of going to the ice-skating rink after school most nights of the week for practice sessions, particularly the focus being on Careesa because of her expertise?

SHARON: That's right.

DIXON: Is it your memory that your mother and father were both very involved in the ice-skating world?

SHARON: That's right. Dad on the committee and mum in the canteen.

While Boyle enjoyed prominence within the skating community, Edwina was content to stay in the tuckshop, close to her girls on the ice. Her friends remember her devotion.

'Quite often at lunchtime she would tell us all about their skating and their competitions and that sort of thing,' work friend Carol Cunningham would tell the court. 'She'd often sit there at lunchtime sewing sequins on one of their costumes for a competition that was coming up and I always just thought "She's such a devoted mum".' Noelene Howarth, a friend from the ice-skating community, added: 'She used to make her roast meals for the girls to take to the rink rather than eat the chips and what have you … and she did their costumes and all that sort of thing.' According to another friend: 'She was a very doting mother. She'd sit up tirelessly till midnight sewing on little sequins and things for her children's costumes.'

Boyle, meanwhile, enjoyed a rapid rise behind the scenes. That's where he did his best work. 'I had a choice to get involved or sit at home and watch the TV, so I got involved,' he would say during his murder trial. 'As a consequence I served as president, competition convenor and test convenor for both the state and the club. At one stage I was doing forty hours for myself [at work] and sixty hours for skating, so it fairly rapidly consumed our lives.'

Apart from his administrative responsibilities, Boyle had something else going on behind the scenes. Her name was Virginia Gissara—a married skating mum on the committee. 'That relationship had been going for something like twelve months prior to the disappearance of Mrs Boyle, and many of the couple's friends suspected that there was a relationship,' Crown prosecutor Gavin Silbert, SC, would say in the Supreme Court.

The affair became obvious to those in the skating community, including Edwina. Careesa remembered, as a child, hearing her mum and dad arguing about his infidelity. 'I would lie awake at night listening to them fight and mum would always say, "You have been with her again," and from that I presumed that dad was seeing somebody else,' Careesa said during her father's trial. 'I don't know that I really knew what an affair was at that time but, yeah, from that I took it that mum meant Virginia Gissara.'

During his trial, Boyle admitted to the affair:

> Over a period of time she was having difficulty at home with her marriage and some sensitive issues. I was a good listener. She found she could talk to me and confided in me and I tried to help her through that. As a consequence we ended up in an intimate relationship.
>
> It's sad to say, I was a man getting his cake and eating it too, so, yes, I was heavily involved with Virginia at the time. But it was never going to be a permanent relationship. I think we both understood that.

Or so he said. In court, Silbert asked Gissara about the affair:

SILBERT: The affair that was going on, was that an affair that was obvious to people at the ice rink?

GISSARA: I would probably say now, yes, it was.

SILBERT: It was fairly well blatant, was it, the way you were behaving towards each other?

GISSARA: I don't know. I hope it wasn't, but obviously it was.

In the months before her murder, Edwina booked in to have some varicose veins removed for cosmetic reasons. She'd lost a lot of weight, and hence looked more attractive and more self-confident than she had before. She confided in friends, like fellow skating mum Wynne Dungan, about her husband's affair. The two had a conversation at the rink one night in October 1983, only days before Edwina vanished. 'Edwina was standing at the edge of the rink against the barrier,' Dungan told the Supreme Court. 'She just looked sad. She had lost a lot of weight and I said to her, "Why are you losing weight?" and she just said to me, "I have to, to keep my husband." My response was, "Don't be stupid, you are very beautiful." She broke down and cried.'

Boyle would tell the jury:

> I can honestly say her weight never bothered me. She was never an overly large woman. She might have got up around size fourteen. Sixteen. That's normal today. And I wasn't Twiggy myself, so I couldn't be demanding that she look like Twiggy. She could have been seeing someone else, I don't know … If she was concerned about losing me to Virginia, then it may well have been.

Boyle claimed that, in the lead-up to his wife's vanishing, their future as husband and wife had looked rosy. 'She had graciously afforded me the opportunity to undo the hurt that I'd done by having the affair,' he would claim. 'I really did stop seeing Virginia. I only saw her spasmodically. We [Edwina and I] owned a block of land in Hastings and we were looking at moving a weatherboard house onto that block.' But Boyle did admit to lingering animosity over the other woman in his life.

DIXON: You've indicated that Edwina was angry about Virginia; were there arguments about Virginia?

BOYLE: Yes, of course there would have been heated words, yes. She had every right to be [upset]. Yes, there would have been terse words and comments from both of us, I guess.

DIXON: What was your attitude towards Edwina? How did you feel about her?

BOYLE: I loved the woman. I still do.

Ice-skating mum Maureen Gibbs remembered the last time she spoke to Edwina; it was the night before her murder.

The two women spoke as they left the rink. Edwina did not seem frightened or hint that she was in any danger. In fact, she was very much looking forward to one of the most important skating meets of the year—the Dawn Hunter Trophy—coming up that weekend.

'We both said, "Goodbye" and "Goodnight" and "We'll see you the following night",' Gibbs would say. 'Edwina said, "Yes, I'll be there."'

Boyle murdered Edwina the following evening—on 6 October 1983. She was thirty years old. According to Justice Jack Forrest: 'As she lay, probably asleep, in the bedroom of your matrimonial home … you used a .22 calibre weapon to shoot her in the head. Your two young daughters were in the next bedroom.'

The next morning, Boyle's brother-in-law, a man named Thomas Turner, dropped in on his way to work as he usually did. Boyle told Turner the fabricated story and showed him a note supposedly left by Edwina. It read:

> I've gone away with someone else named Ray. I don't love you. I haven't for a long while. I'm going interstate for a while until I decide what to do. I'll leave the kids with you because I don't know what I'll be doing for a while and I can't afford to keep them anyway. Try to keep Careesa in skating.

Boyle destroyed the note before anyone else saw it.

Next he had to deal with his daughters. Sharon Boyle was eight when her mum was murdered.

> It was a school morning and I woke up. Usually mum would wake us up to get us ready for school. We woke up on our own and went out to the kitchen where dad was sitting. He had obviously been crying and looked very distressed, and he put one of us on each knee and told us our mum had gone away. I can't remember the exact words he used but it was that she had left or gone away. Obviously at that age I didn't understand what that meant and I just thought,

> 'Why today?' because I had a school dance on and I was more concerned about missing the dance than what I was being told.
>
> Careesa Boyle was eleven.
>
> I remember it distinctly because I had never seen dad cry before. He picked Sharon and I up on each of his knees and hugged us and said that mum was gone. We just sat there and cried. He said that she had left through the night, taken clothes and she had gone away with some truck driver named Ray.

Justice Forrest would express his views on Boyle's subterfuge: 'I regard your decision within hours of the death of your wife to embark upon a plan of deceit about the disappearance of the deceased—your devoted wife and the mother of your two children—as a significant aggravating factor.'

According to Virginia Gissara, she received a call that morning from one of the girls, possibly Careesa.

> She was crying and she said that her mummy had gone, had left them ... I said, 'Well put daddy on the phone', so Fred got on the phone and said Edwina had left him through the night and could he bring the girls down to my place. I didn't know what he was going to do, and I said yes, he could, my children were home.

That night (or the following night, according to Boyle), after leaving his daughters in the care of his sister Mavis Ball, Boyle and Gissara booked in to a motel room. 'When my husband got home from work he was angry that I had had the [Boyle] girls there and we had an argument,' Gissara would say. 'And that's when I left.'

Immediately after the hotel rendezvous, Gissara moved in to Boyle's small flat with her four daughters. 'I had argued with my husband, I just felt I couldn't go back,' Gissara said in court. 'I had hurt him enough, I had hurt my family. I just had nowhere else to go.' Within days, Boyle had organised for his 'missing' wife's clothing to be removed from the home. Gissara would deny she instigated the clear-out. 'Fred had organised for the Brotherhood or somebody to come around.' After moving in, Gissara discovered that Boyle owned a rifle. 'It was in the wardrobe in the main bedroom. It was wrapped in a sheet or a pillowcase.'

Boyle's concocted story about Edwina's sudden departure for another man did not rub with friends. 'She was a totally loving, genuine good mum,' Sandra Pleydell would say in court. 'Edwina was just not the sort of mother to walk away from her children, ever, in my opinion.'

Workmate Carol Cunningham said: 'None of us at work could understand it because our thoughts were that, had she left, she wouldn't have left her two daughters.'

The following month, in November, a detective from Dandenong named Peter Stewart received information about the missing woman from her friends and went to the Boyle home for a welfare check. Boyle stuck to his story, telling Stewart his wife had run off with a truck driver named Ray. Gavin Silbert, in hearing evidence from Stewart, questioned the veracity of Boyle's account.

SILBERT: Did he say where she had gone?

STEWART: Interstate, as far as he knew …

SILBERT: Did he give any indication of her having taken anything with her?

STEWART: Some clothing and about $400 in cash.

SILBERT: Did he express concern for his wife's safety?

STEWART: No, no, he did not.

SILBERT: Did he report her as a missing person?

STEWART: No, he didn't want to.

SILBERT: Did you challenge him about that?

STEWART: I did …

Two months after Edwina's disappearance, as part of his ruse, Boyle sent a letter to her family overseas telling them not to be surprised if they didn't hear from her at Christmas time. That note read in part:

> Edwina took off with another guy. She has been planning this for some time ... I got up for work on Thursday morning to find a letter on the table and $400 cash gone from the bedroom. In the letter she told me that she didn't love me anymore and hasn't for a long time. She also said that she was leaving the kids with me as they were better off with me.
>
> The part that really gets to me the most is the two kids. It's been a month now since they have seen or heard from their mother and for that I'll never forgive her. How do you explain to two kids that not only does their mother not only no longer love their dad, but she doesn't give a stuff for them either.
>
> I have no idea who the guy is and all the people I've spoken to are just as shocked as I was. I don't know where she is either although I've tried to find out. For all I know she could be overseas by now.
>
> I'm stuffed if I know, but for whatever reason she has for going, why has she totally rejected the kids? I can't understand that part at all. If you have already heard from her, please ask her to write to the kids.
>
> Fred, Careesa and Sharon.

Edwina's relatives in England officially reported her missing.

Boyle and Gissara were living together—having moved to a house in Beaconsfield—as the police investigation stepped up a notch. In 1985, detective Geoffrey Beanland received a file about the apparent disappearance of Edwina Ruth Boyle who, unbeknown to everyone other than Fred Boyle, was slowly but surely decomposing in a 44-gallon drum. Beanland picked up the investigation. He confirmed that Edwina had booked in for a cosmetic varicose vein operation and had an IUD contraceptive inserted not long before her disappearance. He was also told she may have been receiving weight loss injections.

On 17 May that year, Beanland questioned Boyle at the Dandenong CIB office. Boyle told him that he fell asleep on the lounge and Edwina went to bed. He said he awoke the next morning to find her note. '[He said] she had taken a few dresses, a few shirts, her driver's licence, $400 in cash, bankcard, keys to the flat and the cheque book,' Beanland would say in court. Boyle also suggested that relatives had seen her overseas and that he had received STD phone calls from someone who would hang up before talking.

However, the usual indicators that a missing person has met with foul play became apparent. For example, Edwina had stopped using her bank accounts. 'Her driver's licence expired and was not renewed,' said Beanland. Another line of enquiry revolved around Edwina's possible forthcoming appearance on an episode of *This Is Your Life* in the UK. A prominent uncle of hers was to be the subject of a show. Beanland would be asked about that during Boyle's trial.

SILBERT: Did you in the course of investigating her have contact with Thames Television?

BEANLAND: I actually had contact with Channel Seven in Melbourne in relation to a program *This is Your Life*.

SILBERT: Did your investigations reveal anything in relation to that program?

BEANLAND: Well, I was making enquiries in relation to a production for George Thomas—Lord Tonypandy I believe is how you say it—and I was advised that that particular program was not Australian and possibly produced in England.

SILBERT: Yes?

BEANLAND: So I obtained contact details of the production people in England as well as America … and I recommended that enquiries be made in London or in England and in America in relation to that production.

As the police investigation beetled along, so too did Boyle's live-in relationship with Virginia Gissara. Having been together for about five years, they split in 1988. During their entire time together, Gissara would say, she never suspected Boyle of having killed Edwina. 'I honestly thought that she had left with whoever Ray was,' she said.

According to Boyle, he ended his relationship with Gissara for the sake of his daughters—who did not get along with her. They had gone to live with their aunt Mavis.

'[Virginia] had basically forced the children to move out,' said Boyle. 'There was no intention on her [part] to be involved with them again, so it was basically abandon my children or move out. So I moved out.' The spectre of his murdered wife also influenced Boyle. 'From my perspective I couldn't honestly hold a relationship with anyone knowing what I have in my possession,' he said.

Boyle and his daughters went to live in a caravan park but their stay was short-lived. By 1990 they had moved to a second Frankston house. Around that time Careesa started dating Michael Hegarty, a good-natured bloke who would later become her husband. Hegarty moved in with the Boyles and began work as a carpet layer. In court, Hegarty would be asked if the topic of Edwina ever came up.

'He [Boyle] would say that she had disappeared with a truck driver named Ray. It was hard not to speak about it because the police came around every couple of years to speak to him about it, so the topic did come up.'

Hegarty said he first saw the sealed green 44-gallon drum sitting in the garage at the Frankston home. He took note as Boyle carted it with him when they all moved in to a house purchased by Boyle and Careesa in 1992 in nearby Carrum Downs. 'It was under the carport,' he said.

When asked if the drum was ever moved from its spot, Hegarty replied 'No.' That year, in March, Homicide Squad detectives Rod Wilson and John Morrish—a veteran investigator known as 'The Pope' due to an ability to gain confessions—formally interviewed Boyle in light of an expected inquest. He stuck to his story like glue. Michael Hegarty, in the meantime, had made his own enquries with Boyle.

SILBERT: Did you ask him [Boyle] what was in it [the drum]?

HEGARTY: Yes.

SILBERT: And what did he say to you?

HEGARTY: It was meant to contain mono spray glue, which is an adhesive for gluing down carpet … I assumed it was still good glue.

SILBERT: Did he tell you whether it was any good?

HEGARTY: Well, at the time, originally yes, he told me that it was good glue that he had saved up from doing jobs … because it was too good to waste.

SILBERT: Did you raise the topic with him more than once?

HEGARTY: Yes.

SILBERT: And what was his response on other occasions?

HEGARTY: That it had become toxic and it couldn't be dumped at the tip.

SILBERT: Did you volunteer to get rid of that drum on occasions?

HEGARTY: Many times.

SILBERT: When you say many times, can you give us an estimate of how many?

HEGARTY: Six or seven at least.

SILBERT: What were the responses when you offered to get rid of it?

HEGARTY: It was toxic and it couldn't be dumped.

Careesa was told the same thing. 'I touched it [the drum] and tried to prod it [at times],' she would say in court. 'Dad said that it had glue in it; glue that had gone off.'

With the drum and its contents starting to haunt Michael Hegarty, he started a running joke that Boyle had Edwina stuffed nicely inside. Michael's brother, Brett, used to laugh—even though he, too, was haunted by its presence.

Michael Hegarty had his twenty-first birthday party in the garage at the Carrum Downs home in February 1993. The 44-gallon drum was among the guests, sitting silently in the background. It even featured in pictures. There it was behind Hegarty's uncle Alan, and again behind aunty Christina and her boyfriend, and also lurking behind cousin Lee and her boyfriend.

By 1993, Homicide Detective Rodney Smith had control of the Edwina Boyle missing-person case. While Geoffrey Beanland had provided a very thorough file, Smith did follow up a couple of avenues of enquiry. One was the *This Is Your Life* angle and the specific program on the life of George Thomas, Lord Tonypandy. 'Basically it was an uncle of Edwina Boyle who was to appear on that show in the United Kingdom, and it was my understanding that it was a possibility that Edwina Boyle was to be a guest on that show,' Smith would tell the Supreme Court.

SILBERT: I think he was a former Speaker of the House of Commons?

SMITH: That's correct sir, yes.

But correspondence from the UK put Smith's line of enquiry to bed. It stated:

> UK representative advises that inquiries at Thames Television, 149 Tottenham Road, London, reveal that whilst research team for the program This Is Your Life were aware of the existence of Mrs Boyle and the family tree, they made no effort to trace her as she is in fact only a distant relative believed to be the daughter of a second cousin of George Thomas.

While cross-examining Smith during Boyle's trial, defence barrister Jane Dixon would throw a well-known criminal into the mix for the jury to mull over. It was Raymond Edmunds, aka 'Mr Stinky'—a killer and serial rapist responsible for the murder of two teenagers near Shepparton, in country Victoria, back in the 1960s. Convicted of several rapes in the 1970s, he is suspected of other rapes and killings.

DIXON: It is the case, isn't it, that around about 1988 [another detective] had commenced inquiries as to whether Raymond Edmunds, who has sometimes been known in the media as 'Mr Stinky', may have had any link to the disappearance of Edwina Boyle?

SMITH: That possibility was explored as well, yes.

DIXON: That was based on the fact that he was living not far away from the [Boyle] premises, knew the area very well having been there in the past, that he had a modus operandi of breaking into women's homes when their husbands were still at work and when there were children in the house—and he had been convicted of multiple rapes and murders?

SMITH: That's correct.

DIXON: Two murders and multiple rapes?

SMITH: That's correct, ma'am.

Detectives interviewed Edmunds in jail about Edwina Boyle and cleared him of any involvement.

DIXON: He denied knowledge of Edwina Boyle?

SMITH: Yes, ma'am.

DIXON: Miss Gissara and Mr Boyle were spoken to and denied knowledge of Raymond Edmunds?

SMITH: Yes, ma'am.

Smith, having exhausted all avenues of enquiry into the disappearance of Edwina Ruth Boyle, compiled a brief of evidence for the coroner.

Meanwhile, Michael Hegarty's joke about Edwina being cocooned in the drum had started to prod and poke at his mind. He was highly suspicious. Could he actually be right, he thought? Could Edwina's body be curled up inside? Boyle's possessive behaviour only fuelled the theory.

DIXON: At some stage you tried to move the drum out into the weather and Fred got grumpy about that?

HEGARTY: I did move it into the weather and it stayed in the weather.

DIXON: He was a bit grumpy about that move?

HEGARTY: Yes.

DIXON: Was there another occasion when you tried to get rid of the drum and Fred really was resisting that as well?

HEGARTY: There was a time when I put it on the back of a trailer and had all the rubbish on the trailer loaded to go to the tip and Fred was supposed to take the trailer to the tip the next day …

DIXON: Yes?

HEGARTY: And the next day the drum was back in the backyard.

DIXON: So it wasn't going to the tip?

HEGARTY: No.

Around July 2006, curiosity got the better of Michael Hegarty. He pierced the drum with a pickaxe four or five times to see what would happen. Carpet glue did not ooze from the holes. He tried to prise open the lid but it was rusted shut. Two months later, Hegarty—still haunted—began a clean-up of the backyard for a forthcoming birthday party. He grabbed an angle grinder and, with the help of brother Brett and a mate named Dean Ellis, cut the barrel in half. The men discovered that concrete had been poured in at both ends. 'There was an assortment of clothes inside and a wool bale,' Hegarty would tell the court. '[And] some women's clothes—socks, and I think a bra.' There was also carpet underlay and a hessian bag. 'It was very dirty and slimy looking and bundled up and closed.'

Brett Hegarty poked at the hessian bag with a stick. He remembered also seeing 'some stockings, knickers and some bras'. But no body. No bones. No Edwina. 'I was joking around with Michael once we had cut the drum open, saying, "Oh well, it doesn't look like there is anything in there. You were wrong [about Edwina] after all these years."'

Michael split the two halves of the drum apart and left the contents—including the hessian bag—on the grass and went inside for lunch. 'Fred sent me in for lunch,' he would tell the court. '[When I returned] some of the contents of the drum had been removed, and I just assumed that it had already been put on the trailer amongst the other rubbish.' He and Boyle later drove the junk-filled trailer to the tip. 'I got out of the car and untied the ropes and packed up the tarp and folded the tarp up while Fred started to unload the trailer,' Hegarty said. He never saw the hessian bag.

After dropping his two sons at school on the morning of 13 October 2006—twenty-three years after Edwina's murder—Hegarty started another backyard cleanup. Inside a wheelie bin, under boxes of power tools and garbage bags, he found the hessian bag.

SILBERT: Did you recognise that hessian bag?

HEGARTY: Yes, instantly.

SILBERT: How come you recognised it instantly?

HEGARTY: Because it was the bag from the drum ... I had a thing about that drum for sixteen years.

Tentatively, Hegarty reached inside, fearing he was about to touch some part of Edwina. He could smell death now. His worst fears were about to be realised. 'I pulled out what appeared to be a pelvis and [a] human leg bone. I just had to confirm to myself that it was human, so I continued to look through the bag and found the skull, which was definitely a human skull.'

Hegarty saw what he thought was some decaying flesh and a section of spinal cord, and he dropped the skull back into the bag. Nauseated, he stripped off his clothes at the back door and had a shower inside. After swallowing down some valium he called his brother.

'He asked me to call the missing persons to see if there was a reward open [for Edwina],' Brett told the court. Hegarty had remembered news of a $50,000 reward for information about Edwina's death and who might have killed her. He would say in court: 'I wanted to make sure there was money to bury her, and the money would have gone to her grandchildren, not to me.'

After calling his brother, Hegarty rang Careesa. '[He was] very upset and hysterical,' she said in court, 'demanding that I come home straight away.' After showing Careesa her mother's remains, Hegarty rang Frankston police station.

Homicide Squad detectives arrived and took control. The human remains were sent for autopsy. Forensic odontologists, through medical records, confirmed the body to be that of

Edwina Boyle. The autopsy to determine a cause of death was a little more involved. According to pathologist Malcolm Dodd:

> It certainly was not a normal autopsy. The majority of the bodies we examine are intact and fresh or lightly decomposed, but several times a year we would be asked to examine grossly decomposed remains or skeletons. In this particular case the first step, after X-ray, was to separate what was obviously human remains from everything else and then clean the bones to reassemble the skeleton, and to determine any areas of trauma.
>
> Once the fleshy components had been separated and the bones had been cleaned and laid out in anatomical or normal body position, we were able to examine all of those bones to determine areas of injury, and the injury was centred predominantly on the right side of the skull.
>
> The injury was readily apparent but the causation wasn't. It required retrieval of those bone fragments which were lost in that area, most of those fragments were found actually inside the skull. Those fragments had to be retrieved and glued back into position by our anthropologist, and that then gave us a clue as to what the injury was caused by.
>
> When the skull was X-rayed we saw several metallic fragments, some of which were lining the inside of the skull and several smaller fragments within what would have been the brain itself … Several small fragments were retrieved from the inside of the skull and sent for metallurgical analysis to the forensic laboratory. I received a verbal report saying that the small metallic fragments consisted of two metals, being lead and antimony.

Only then could Dodd confirm the cause of death as a single gunshot wound to the head. Homicide detectives charged Boyle with murder.

At trial, Boyle ran an unsuccessful defence that he did not kill his wife but did cover up her death by stuffing her body in a 44-gallon drum and sealing it. He claimed he did that because no one would have believed him—a cheating husband—when he said he did not kill his wife. This was his tearful version of events for the jury:

> Well, I'd been to work as normal. I came home, I'd changed and went out because we did have a big [skating] competition coming up on that weekend so there's always things to do—running around organising this, organising that. So I'd gone out. I don't know what time I got home. The kitchen light was on as normal so I sat there and had a coffee. I smoked at the time so I sat there and smoked as well. Then I took myself off to bed.
>
> I got into bed and just laid there and after a while I nudged Edwina and … she didn't respond so I put the light on and she'd been shot through the head and strangled with one of my ties. I didn't know what to do. I went in and checked the girls. They were all right. I went back in and just sat there for a little while. I just didn't know what the hell to do. I went back out in the kitchen and I just sat there for hours. I cried like you wouldn't believe.
>
> I had no idea what I was going to do. And then I thought about, I thought, well, I'm knackered now. No one's going to believe I didn't do her harm. I'm having an affair with another bloody woman and I come home and find me wife shot in the bloody head. Then I decided to make a story and hide it. So I went and got a bag out of the van and went in and I put her body in the bag. I was just chucking things in. As I went I'd find things that maybe looked out of place or something like that and I just put them in the bag. I checked my gun. It was still in its bag wrapped up in the towel. The bullets were still separate. The bolt and magazine was separate. Nothing was out of place.
>
> After I'd put her in the [hessian] bag, of course, you've got the sheets and then there was blood on the mattress so I cut the piece out of the mattress and put that in the bag, and I just didn't know what else to do. I knew that if I rang the police I'd be accused of murdering my wife. I had two

> children that would have no bloody parents, so I had no choice but to do what I did. I've lied about it ever since … There was no sign of forced entry.

Boyle told the jury that he moved the bag into his work van until he came up with his story about Edwina leaving him for another man.

> I wrote a note which took me quite a long time because my handwriting's not very good. I just had to sit there then and wait for Johnny Turner to turn up and for my kids to wake up. He arrived and I was in a hell of a state, but I couldn't tell him what it was about so I gave him the bullshit story that I'd made up and I gave him the note that I'd written. Surprised me more than anything that he believed it.

Dixon questioned Boyle as to what he did next with the foul-smelling bag.

DIXON: Did you do anything with your wife's body? You've said that it was in the van?

BOYLE: Yeah, a day or so later it was obvious I'd have to do something about her body, so I decided on buying a metal drum. I bought a metal drum. I placed the bag in and then I poured some levelling compound across the top and put the lid on and tightened the ring.

DIXON: Did you in any way dismember your wife's body before doing that?'

BOYLE: No, no, she was not harmed in any way other than that she'd been shot. She had not been bashed or bloody dismembered or anything.

DIXON: Where did you put the drum?'

BOYLE: Initially I kept it in the back of my van and it was easy to explain if anyone asked; carrying drums of glue and equipment. After a while I then took it out of the van and put it in the lean-to at the back of the unit and it's remained with me ever since.

DIXON: Can you just elaborate on that comment slightly?

BOYLE: Well, if I didn't want her found it would have been simple to have buried the drum or got rid of it in some way where it would never have been found. My wife died in a terrible way and I was not going to let her remains be thrown down the tip like bloody garbage, so I held on to the drum and it stayed with me all the time.

Boyle described his wife as having suffered 'a single gunshot wound to the head' when he found her dead in bed. Silbert cross-examined with venom, later calling Boyle 'a better pathologist than Dr Dodd'.

SILBERT: You are aware, are you not, that Dr Dodd could not come up with a causation until he reconstructed the skull?

BOYLE: No.

SILBERT: Well, let me just put to you what Dr Dodd told this jury last week.

BOYLE: I heard Dr Dodd's evidence.

SILBERT: I'm going to put it to you again. Because what I ultimately want to put to you is that it was impossible for anyone to tell that there was a single gunshot to the head.

BOYLE: Well … my wife's body was the first dead body I'd seen. There was blood, her head and face were puffed up, I could see blood coming from a wound and I assumed there was a single shot.

SILBERT: Mr Boyle, Dr Dodd told the jury last week, 'The injury was readily apparent but the causation wasn't. It required retrieval of those bone fragments which were lost in the area, most of those bone fragments were found inside the skull. Those fragments had to be retrieved and glued back into position by our anthropologist, and that has then given us a clue as to what the injury was caused by … '

BOYLE: I assumed it was a gunshot.

Silbert also took Boyle to task on his decision not to call the police, saying a ballistic check of his rifle and a forensic check of his hands would have immediately cleared him as a suspect.

SILBERT: If you'd called the police and you'd not been responsible for that gunshot wound, it would have been established within a matter of minutes.

BOYLE: Well, I didn't see it that way. I have a fairly low opinion of the Victorian police—always have had—so, no, I wouldn't have naturally thought to ring the police.

SILBERT: It never occurred to you that ballistics and forensic examination would have cast some light on the situation within minutes of the police attending?

BOYLE: Why? I mean *CSI* wasn't on TV yet. We are all wonderfully aware of what the things are today, but we are talking 1983 in a bedroom in Dandenong and a carpet layer who has just come home and found his wife dead.

Silbert made mention of Boyle's actions with Virginia Gissara immediately after Edwina's death, calling him 'far from a grief-stricken widower'.

SILBERT: You were so traumatised and so grief stricken that you were able to spend the following night with Virginia Gissara alone in a motel room?

BOYLE: That's correct.

SILBERT: And within a day you were able to have Virginia Gissara move into your home?

BOYLE: That is what transpired, yes.

In his closing address to the jury, Silbert described the case as a 'family tragedy of epic proportions':

> All the evidence establishes that Edwina Boyle was a happy, contented, optimistic sort of person; had plans for the future; certainly had no plans for anything of the short term and certainly no enemies; no question of being in any danger and no suggestion that she was likely to meet her demise in the manner and at the time that she did.
>
> It's hardly sophisticated because anyone who hangs on to his wife's remains in a barrel for twenty-three years can hardly be accused of a sophisticated cover-up.

Silbert had said in his opening: 'As long as the remains remained undiscovered, obviously he was safe. The whole thing only blew up once his son-in-law did as he was asked specifically not to do, and that is opened the 44-gallon drum and discovered the remains of Mrs Boyle.'

Dixon told the jury in her opening: 'Frederick Boyle was not the only person with the opportunity to kill Edwina Boyle. Others may have had an opportunity or a motive to do so.' In her closing address she said:

> The curiosity, the greatest curiosity, in this case is the ultimate failure of Frederick Boyle to take the final logical step and destroy the evidence, the very evidence which has caused him to be placed in the dock of this court here. Even through the pressures of questionings and inquests, and so on, even when his son-in-law appeared determined to get in to that barrel, even then he did not destroy his wife's remains. His evidence to you is the reason for that is because he loved her … and that he didn't want her remains just to be thrown down the tip like some garbage.

Boyle left the jury with: 'I'm here to face the consequences of my own stupidity. I did not kill my wife. I loved my wife dearly. I loved her then, I still do now.'

The jury didn't believe Boyle and on 9 February 2008 it returned a guilty verdict. On 18 March, Justice Jack Forrest sentenced Boyle to twenty-one years' jail with a minimum of seventeen. 'I am satisfied that underpinning the motive for the murder of the deceased was your relationship with Virginia Gissara and the effect that it had upon your marriage,' Forrest told the killer. 'It was this relationship that ultimately led you to take the course you adopted … '

> I also regard the manner in which you dealt with your wife's remains as an aggravating factor.
>
> This was a 'bombshell' to your wife's family. Your story, concocted to deflect attention from yourself as the murderer, was devastating to her family, and particularly

> to her mother, who apparently accepted your farrago that Edwina had run off. Your sister-in-law was emotionally and financially committed to discovering whether Edwina had, in fact, run off or whether the explanation for her disappearance was more sinister. She, understandably, is traumatised by the fact that, for twenty-three years, the remains of her sister lay in a metal drum in your possession. According to her, the Welsh side of the family has been destroyed due to your actions and lies.

Careesa Hegarty and Sharon Boyle did not accept the guilty verdict. The court had heard that Careesa and Michael Hegarty had divorced before the trial. Forrest said the daughters' devotion to their father had to be seen in context.

'To some extent, their devotion needs to be considered in light of the fact that, for practical purposes, for much of their respective lives they have not had a mother—she being removed by your actions and her memory erased by your fiction,' the judge told Boyle.

'Despite your evidence that you still love your wife, your actions demonstrate the falsity of this position. You have shown no remorse whatsoever. Rather, you have sought to live a lie with the sole aim of avoiding apprehension for your dastardly actions.'

Boyle sought leave to appeal against his conviction and sentence. In December 2009 the Court of Appeal refused his application.

Edwina Boyle's relatives are not the only ones perpetually haunted by Fred Boyle's cold and callous crime. As Michael Hegarty said at the trial: 'Everything about that drum sticks in my head … It gave me chills.'

4

The Queen of Con

How Australia's greatest con woman broke into bank accounts and stole policemen's hearts

'She has thrown out the challenge in no uncertain terms. It's like a scenario from the Leonardo DiCaprio film Catch Me if You Can.*'*

CONWOMAN JODY HARRIS HAD a thing for cops. Whether tricking her way into police stations as an interstate officer looking for hospitality or charming her way into policemen's beds, the young grifter conned many wary men. During her extraordinary Australian crime spree, she broke the hearts of several coppers and into the bank accounts of many more female victims whose identities she assumed. Police who investigated her—and the ones who slept with her—have grudgingly admitted she is the best female confidence swindler this country has ever seen. Her methods were so proficient that one policeman, during an interview with the *Herald Sun* newspaper, likened her to the famed US con man Frank Abagnale. It surprised police that Harris, now known by the surname Harding, had never heard of Abagnale—the man who inspired the hit film *Catch Me if You Can*—considering their similar stories. As a young man, Abagnale cashed millions of dollars' worth of fraudulent cheques while posing as a pilot, doctor, lawyer and professor. He was the FBI's major nemesis while on the run in the 1960s. He seduced several women along the way.

Harris proved the bane of Australian police during her reign as this country's most brazen con woman late last decade. She posed as an air hostess, doctor, psychiatrist, policewoman and even the niece of slain Melbourne underworld figure Mario Condello to befriend women, before gleaning enough documents and information to impersonate them and fleece their bank accounts. But while Harris's desire to snake her way into the lives of certain policemen helped her perpetrate her crimes, it inevitably proved to be her downfall.

Andrew Lawrence Twining, the son of a former policeman, always wanted to be a copper. He joined 'the job' in Victoria in January 1988 at the age of eighteen. After working the divisional van as a uniform constable, he moved to positions in the then Traffic Operations Group and communications centre D-24. In 1993 he was promoted to the rank of senior constable.

Just as Twining's career was blossoming, so too was that of Queenslander Jody Harris. The daughter of now well-known human rights activist and lawyer Debbie Kilroy, nee Harding, and a violent father, Harris had a dysfunctional and disrupted childhood. 'You were denied in your childhood the safety and stability which family life should provide children,' Judge Felicity Hampel would later explain. After assaults committed on her and her daughter, Debbie Harding left her violent husband and later married Queensland rugby league star 'Smokin'' Joe Kilroy. Both were later jailed for drug trafficking.

From the age of fourteen Harris would begin to commit dishonesty offences and impersonate police. She was a regular in jail. By February 2006, the real starting point for this chapter, she was wanted in several states for financial crimes involving identity and bank account theft. It was around that time that she met Twining on an internet dating site. At that stage of his career he was a motorcycle cop with the rank of acting sergeant.

'Unfortunately … we met on an online dating service called RSVP,' Twining would say at a Melbourne County Court trial while accused of possessing an unregistered handgun. He said the relationship developed 'just the same as any conventional normal relationship'. 'Initially she told me that she was employed as a cabin supervisor with Virgin Blue. And on subsequently meeting her—and going back to her apartment and the like—she had the appropriate uniform items. Skirts. Shirts. Badges. Stubby holders. Things like that. Airline paraphernalia. Flight tickets.'

Twining saw her in the uniform several times. Harris told him she was in the process of relocating to Melbourne after some form of turbulent relationship in Sydney. As their own relationship grew intimate, Harris would regularly stay at Twining's outer suburban unit. He stayed at her inner suburban apartment while on Commonwealth Games duties. In February 2006, Twining had told mate and fellow policeman Glenn Humble that he had a new girlfriend. He said her name was Jody and that she was from Queensland. In the County Court, defence barrister Andrew McKenna would ask Humble about Twining's relationship with Harris.

McKENNA: You were aware that they were seeing quite a deal of each other after February 2006?

HUMBLE: Yes they were.

McKENNA: What did he tell you about what she did for a living?

HUMBLE: He stated that she worked for Virgin Airlines as a hostess.

McKENNA: Did you get any impression from talking to him just how keen he was on her?

HUMBLE: He was very keen on her.

McKENNA: Mad keen?

HUMBLE: I would say that, yes.

According to Twining, Harris would regularly come and go due to her 'job'. When she travelled interstate they regularly talked on the phone. He later said he noticed nothing untoward about her or her movements. 'She would say she was doing a certain jaunt or a trip. She'd say, "Look, by the way, I'm in Sydney now", and some time later she'd say, "I'm leaving for Brisbane and then I'll be back home".'

But Harris was not informing plane passengers about emergency exits or handing out drinks and in-flight snacks. She was, instead, flying the eastern seaboard—usually in business class—perpetrating her fraud crimes. In court, Harris investigator Detective Sergeant Brad Lancaster confirmed that she was a keen jetsetter.

McKENNA: Is it your understanding that the offending of Ms Harris occurred contemporaneously—that is, not at precisely the same time but on and off in Victoria and other states, or at least one other state, during the relevant period of March through to about May 2006?

LANCASTER: She was wanted in Victoria, New South Wales and Queensland.

McKENNA: Was it also part of the evidence, that you understand was being obtained, that she was flying interstate—masquerading as a Virgin Blue Airlines employee—to get her interstate to be able to commit offences?

LANCASTER: I know she was flying interstate.

Harris was using an array of clever covers—sometimes in conjunction with wigs—to befriend her chosen victims and glean personal information. She would then find a way to steal their bank cards and IDs before making a mockery of bank security to withdraw thousands of dollars from accounts. All the while, she was enjoying the trappings. She had a strong attraction to luxury cars, jewellery and designer clothes, a favourite being Louis Vuitton accessories. She also stayed in five-star hotels where, on occasion, she would steal the personal documents—and thus the identities—of staff and guests at the gym facilities. Using her intimate police knowledge learned from past acquaintances, and police apparel and badges she'd picked up along the way, she convincingly posed as a police officer to steal one victim's identity. Alysha Searle, a twenty-one-year-old barista, was driving home from work when Harris—with a police uniform hanging in the back of her car—pulled Searle over.

'The car came up behind me and started flashing its lights,' Searle said in court. 'I kept driving and then the car sped up next to me on my left and the driver signalled at a police uniform that was hanging up in the back seat, so I stopped and pulled over and I waited in the car and a lady came out and said that I'd gone through a red light and that I needed to give my driver's licence.' Harris said she was an undercover rape detective in the South Yarra region and quickly flashed a badge at Searle.

> She said that she had no tolerance for people who went through red lights and that she was going to call the traffic police and get me booked. She was so angry [that] I believed that I did go through the red light, even though I'm sure I didn't.

Harris pretended to make a phone call and, after pocketing Searle's licence, sent the young woman on her way. 'She said, "Get out of here before I change my mind,"' Searle recalled. 'Probably about five minutes later I realised she still had my driver's licence ... She was very convincing.' Using the licence, Harris managed to withdraw $3000 from Searle's bank account and to change the password.

It was not the first time Harris had successfully posed as a copper. McKenna mentioned several incidents while cross-examining witnesses such as internal affairs investigator Detective Sergeant Frank Torcasio during Twining's gun trial.

McKENNA: [Mr Torcasio], did you make some enquiries at all in relation to whether, in 1998, Jody Harris had impersonated police and got access to the Roma Street police complex in Brisbane?

TORCASIO: I personally didn't make any enquiries in relation to that particular event.

McKENNA: You have come across reference to such a—let's call it an allegation—in the material you've been through, have you not?

TORCASIO: Yes, I have.

McKENNA: Have you come across, in the course of your enquiries about her, an allegation that in 2001 she lived with a New South Wales detective in Sydney for about six months?

TORCASIO: Yes, that's correct.

McKENNA: You have made some direct enquiries in your own right or by others in [Ethical Standards Division] in Victoria, have you not, in relation to allegations that she fraternised with police officers in 2000—it might have been 2001—from the Greensborough and Fitzroy police stations?

TORCASIO: September 2001.

McKENNA: And you're satisfied that two police members and almost certainly more than two had direct dealings with her at that time, correct?

TORCASIO: Had socialised with her, yes.

McKENNA: When she was operating under the pretext of being a visiting detective from New South Wales?

TORCASIO: That is correct.

McKENNA: And she was in part doing that by presenting identification of a New South Wales police officer?

TORCASIO: That is correct.

McKENNA: And in fact, it convinced at least one detective at Fitzroy that she was a genuine police officer—at least for a time—didn't it?

TORCASIO: They took it on face value on the flashing of a badge.

Showing hospitality to interstate officers is an unwritten rule in all state and territory police forces. There is nothing untoward about it within the national police 'brotherhood'. As Torcasio explained: 'She [Harris] purported to be a visiting interstate police officer who was out looking to socialise with Victorian police members: a hospitality or courtesy that we would extend to any visiting police officer.'

The fact that Harris actually walked into police stations and successfully duped certain cops showed her brazen and bold abilities. If she could dupe police like that, then banks would prove a cinch.

McKENNA: You have no doubt, do you [Mr Torcasio], that Jody Harris has inveigled herself into the lives and confidences of a number of police officers over the years?

TORCASIO: That is correct.

About twelve years before insinuating herself into Twining's life, Harris had 'befriended' and entered into a relationship with a Victorian policeman by the name of Brett Bardsley. In an interview in the *Sunday Herald Sun* in August 2006, Bardsley told how he struck up a rapport with Harris over the phone on Christmas Day 1993. She was ringing the Russell Street police station to speak to another policeman 'friend' of hers. Unbeknown to Bardsley, she was only fifteen years old. She called herself Jodie Harding and said they should get together for a drink when she was next in Melbourne. A few days later, Bardsley received a mailed photo of Harris wearing heavy make-up and a black lace bra. She travelled to Melbourne and they met up.

'She was impeccably dressed [in a black evening dress] and spoke well,' Bardsley told reporter Carly Crawford. 'She seemed very mature.'

Harris told Bardsley, thirty-two at the time, that she was twenty years old. According to Bardsley, she said she was the daughter of an advertising executive and had attended a prestigious Brisbane girls' school. Bardsley told reporter Crawford that Harris would fly to Melbourne regularly, and that he and his parents even celebrated what he thought was her twenty-first birthday with her. Bardsley reported how, after giving Harris his house keys, she took the opportunity about two months later to borrow his car without his knowledge to go shopping. While driving, she had an accident and Bardsley told his insurance company that he'd been driving. That decision ruined his career. 'I think she just had a fixation with me because I was a copper,' he told Crawford.

In the County Court, McKenna would link Harris with another former policeman—one who had since moved into the world of federal politics.

McKENNA: '[Mr Torcasio] you are aware of some assertions by Bardsley … that he came to know her after she first had a relationship with another Victorian police officer whose last name is Wood? Jason Wood, who was then a policeman at Russell Street.

Jason Wood, the Liberal member for La Trobe and Shadow Parliamentary Secretary for Public Security and Policing, said during an interview with this author that he had known a young Jody Harris. He denied any sexual relationship. 'Jody Harris was under a different name and she used to come around, for example, to East Melbourne and Russell Street police stations,' Wood said.

> I regarded her as a casual acquaintance. I never went out with her. She was like a breath of fresh air walking in [to the police station] when every day you had people walking in having been assaulted or robbed or to make reports. She told me her father was in jail, or something … and hanging out with the police was good for her because it kept her away from hanging out with crooks. She was infatuated with all police members. She would come across as the world's nicest girl … [but] I never had a relationship with her. Definitely not.

In early to mid-2006, the police officer with whom Harris *was* in a sexual relationship was Acting Sergeant Andrew Twining. She was also on an adult sex website, complete with saucy photos, describing herself as a 'bisexual Aquarian who drinks socially and values good looks' in her sex partners. She listed her bedroom interests as participating in swinging sex and spanking, and using handcuffs and blindfolds. Away from cyberspace, Harris was often dining with Twining's folks at their home. Twining even took her to his father's RSL club on Anzac Day. On 17 May, the day Twining was to leave on a European cruise with his parents, Harris drove the family to their point of destination and waved them bon voyage. In court, McKenna would ask Twining: 'Did you have any idea that she was a master con woman who'd been carrying out crimes, it appears, for most of her life?' Twining's reply: 'Most definitely not.'

Jody Harris had hit Victoria Police radar screens in early 2006. The investigation into her Melbourne crimes fell to Senior Detective Paul Bertoncello, of the Embona anti-robbery taskforce. The case was so consuming that Bertoncello became too preoccupied to investigate the pile of 7-Eleven and service station robbery cases piling up on his desk. It was soon decided that it was time to take the con woman story to the media. Bertoncello rang the *Herald Sun* on 19 May. The Jody Harris story ran on the front page of the paper the next day, with the headline 'FIVE STAR STING—Phantom conwoman lives life of luxury'. It was the first story to blow the lid on Harris and her crime wave. The article began:

> An elusive swindler is preying on women in three states, stealing their identities to loot their cash while revelling in a jetset lifestyle. The chameleon-like conwoman—wanted by police in Melbourne, Sydney and Queensland—disguises herself as her victims to bamboozle bank staff. She usually zeroes in on her targets in classy hotels while living it up on the proceeds of earlier five-star stings. Police believe the woman, in her late twenties, has snaffled almost $200,000 in recent months, splurging it on stays in the snazzy hotels and on business-class flights and luxury shopping.

'It's like chasing a phantom,' Bertoncello told this author. 'She's using different names and has proved very hard to track down.'

> We find out about a new name every week or so. She regularly changes her appearance. She walks in so confidently that no one would think she could be an offender ... She's

> travelled business class all down the eastern seaboard and stayed in at least half a dozen five-star hotels. She dresses herself in expensive clothing and buys expensive jewellery—$4000 watches and $2000 necklaces.

And the story went on.

Less than a week later, the Embona taskforce received a crucial telephone call. It was Harris, dangling information about where she'd been living. McFarlane Street in South Yarra, she said—ten minutes from Melbourne's CBD. It was a taunt. Catch me if you can. Police found the correct dwelling: a unit rented out under the name Jodie Kardinis-Harris. The Embona team executed a search warrant. But Harris had moved on. 'We were actually hoping that she would be at the unit when we executed the warrant,' Detective Sergeant Lancaster told the County Court.

At the unit police seized a Queensland police badge, a Victoria Police shirt, and a Virgin Blue hostess outfit along with name tag, pin and crew bag tags. They also found several photographs of Harris, more than likely left there to needle them.

On 1 June, Embona boss Senior Sergeant Glenn Davies contacted the *Herald Sun*. In a second front-page story, Davies threw down the gauntlet in response to Harris's phone call and apparent cat-and-mouse games at South Yarra. 'She has thrown out the challenge in no uncertain terms,' Davies said for the article. 'It's like a scenario from the Leonardo DiCaprio film *Catch Me if You Can*. And, I can assure you, she will be caught … It's only a matter of time before we catch up with her.'

The photographs of Harris left at the apartment were published with the story. Judge Hampel would later say that Harris harboured a hatred for police—Victorian officers in particular—and that she kept abreast of the media reports. She would say to Harris:

> When asked about how you obtained Virgin Blue uniforms and name tags you refused to say how you got the uniforms, apart from saying you paid for them and it was an inside

> job … You were acutely aware of the publicity surrounding your activities, and complained a number of times [in your eventual record of interview] about some details.
>
> Sometimes you blamed the police, asserting they had deliberately overstated their investigative powers; and sometimes you accused the victims of misrepresentation and exaggeration. You expressed great animosity, and even hostility, to[wards] the Victorian police.

The *Herald Sun* articles opened the floodgates for women to ring in with stories of how Harris had conned and fleeced them. Women like Anita Mulligan. She fell and hurt her head in the Melbourne CBD, only to be assisted by Harris who swooped on the situation and drove her to hospital. That night Harris stole Mulligan's licence and credit card and rang her father to glean personal details. 'She told my dad she was a nurse and that her de facto was a police officer,' Mulligan later told the *Herald Sun*. 'She conned my father and got whatever information she needed out of him.' Harris went on to change Mulligan's bank account password and steal $10,500 from her account.

Nova Gordon ran a boutique clothing store. A friend introduced her to Harris, who was posing as the daughter of a wealthy businessman. 'She had all the trappings and pulled up outside my shop in a new four-wheel drive Lexus, dripping in jewellery,' Gordon would tell police. Harris bought some clothes from the shop. She and Gordon then went out for coffee. Harris later fleeced her account of $37,870, using Gordon's licence as identification—despite Gordon freezing her accounts at one stage. 'I found out that Jody had been in the branch and convinced them she was me, and had the block removed,' Gordon would later say. 'Her systems were better than ours.' A Commonwealth Bank spokesman said of that crime: 'Unfortunately a young member of staff was duped. The bank has apologised and we've refunded the customer. We're reviewing our internal procedures to minimise the risk of this [sort of thing] happening.'

Harris met victim Joanne McDonald at the Bridal Show at the Royal Exhibition Building in Melbourne. She told McDonald that she was a clothing company sales representative from Queensland, in Melbourne to attend the funeral of her uncle—slain gangland figure Mario Condello. After a coffee, the two went out for dinner and ended at a Crown Casino nightclub. That's where Harris stole McDonald's licence. She withdrew about $3000 from McDonald's account. 'She phoned, changed the password, then half an hour later walked into the bank and took it out. All she had was my driver's licence.'

Off-duty air hostess Leah Jury sat next to Harris on a domestic Qantas flight in March 2006. Harris told Jury she was a psychologist whose parents had just bought her a house in the affluent Melbourne suburb of Toorak. Jury sensed something about the woman—enough to make her feel 'extremely uncomfortable'—but couldn't quite put her finger on it. 'She had a lot of gold jewellery on, with a massive four-carat solitaire diamond on the right hand,' Jury would tell police.

Despite her first-class appearance, Harris, however, could not fully hide her vulgar traits. 'She said to a hostess, "No glass" [with her drink]—not really what most business-class passengers do,' Jury said in her statement. During the flight, Harris continued to talk up her social status.

> She asked for another Crown Lager and was told by the customer service manager that she didn't think there was any left. [Harris] said, 'What other boutique beers do you have?' and the manager replied, 'I can get you something from economy,' and Harris said, 'I've only been in economy once in my life.'

Jury left her bag under her chair when she went to the toilet during the flight. Harris stole her licence and debit card. After landing, Harris was as cool as a cucumber. 'She commented how she loved my Louis Vuitton shoes and then she got out her travel bag, which was a large Louis Vuitton bag.' Harris later withdrew $5000 from Jury's bank account, before changing the password and withdrawing a further $12,500.

Harris stole Jacqui Young's Visa card, debit card and licence from a gym locker at the Grand Hyatt Hotel. The con woman would later boast of walking past Young, who worked at the very bank branch into which she had strolled to withdraw cash.

'I didn't even know she was sitting at the front desk,' Harris would tell detectives. 'I went past her to the teller and on the way out looked down and I saw Jacqui Young. She works at the bank there, where I took the money from. Her own staff didn't realise. They're a smart bunch in Melbourne, along with their fuckin' police.' Using phone banking, Harris changed Young's passwords and then withdrew $5000 using her licence for identification.

One victim would say of Harris and her methods: 'She lived in the same apartment block as my friend and asked if she could come to the party [we were having]. She was only there for an hour or so and said she was a cabin crew supervisor. I just remember her asking strange questions, trying to find out more about us. She managed to take my licence out of my bag and credit cards from another girl.' Harris withdrew $16,000 from that woman's account.

Another woman would say: 'She was even able to change all my personal details on the cards to hers to the point where, when I tried to change them back to mine, I could hardly prove who I was any more.'

Victim Amanda Urquhart would state: 'You can remove yourself from it if people are using your ID, but if they start pretending to be you, that's when it starts getting creepy.'

Jodie Harris's methods were brazen and basic, and proved the old police adage that sometimes 'you've got to be overt to be covert'.

McKenna would reveal one of her methods in court: 'What she'd sometimes do is she would ring up the customer—or the person from whom she'd stolen the stuff—and pretend to be a bank official and say, "We've got some information that your card's been overused. Would you be good enough to tell us and confirm your pin?"'

Harris told police that on one occasion:

> They had a big alert—'Fraud has been done on this account. Do not give any over-the-counter transactions without contacting Sunshine branch.' The teller read that out to me … and then said to me: 'It's obvious that you're a trustworthy-looking person. Here's the money,' and gave it to me without ringing the Sunshine branch.

While Twining was on his European cruise, Glenn Humble and the Melbourne Embona crew started comparing notes. The news of Harris's antecedents came as a complete shock to Humble—just as they would to Twining.

McKENNA: You got a whole new perspective on Jody Harris from that time, didn't you?

HUMBLE: Yes, I did.

McKENNA: Because what you, in a nutshell, learned at that time was that she was believed to be one of Australia's most wanted fraudsters, or con women?

HUMBLE: That's right.

McKENNA: And was being sought by police in a number of states for repeated and far-ranging credit card and identity frauds.

HUMBLE: Yes, that's right.

McKENNA: You would never have imagined that Andrew Twining would ever be in a relationship with somebody like that?

HUMBLE: That's right.

McKENNA: Because you knew him for quite a while. You knew his family. And that's just not the circle that he would ever mix in socially or in any romantic context?

HUMBLE: Yes, definitely.

After the news about Harris and her exploits broke, Humble delivered Twining the bad news via email. At that stage it was believed that Harris was somewhere in Queensland. Humble's message read in part:

> [Fraud Squad detective] David Lewis has suggested that I change your lock on your house as we both believe she

> may well drive to Melbourne as the net around her is tightening up in Queensland. She will probably not fly as all airlines and banks are aware of her picture.
>
> Jody is very aware of police policy and procedure as she was living with a detective sergeant for a couple of years in Queensland. She has done about eight years' jail for fraud and deceptions. She has assumed the identity and impersonated a police officer in the past and performed mobile intercepts to steal the drivers'—female—licences for her own use and benefit.
>
> When the Embona members did a warrant on her serviced apartment in South Yarra, they found a Queensland 'Freddy' [police badge] that she had made herself. It looked very real and any member of the public would have fallen for it.
>
> David Lewis wanted to know of her exact tattoos on her body so can you, please, let me know and I will pass it on to him.

Humble informed Twining that police had that day arrested a woman at Avalon Airport, having mistaken her for Harris. Jodie Symes, a thirty-five-year-old Melbourne mother, had boarded a flight to Sydney to attend her godson's christening and was waiting for take-off with closed eyes when police stormed the plane. 'I was woken up, and standing in front of me were three uniformed police officers—two male and one female,' Symes would later tell the *Herald Sun*. The officers dismissed her protests and her identification, hauling her off the flight and back into the terminal.

> I burst into tears immediately as I couldn't believe it was happening. It was like a nightmare. I was starting to get very scared because I didn't know what I'd supposedly done, and because I was going to miss the plane and, in turn, the christening. They said I was being held under suspicion of being Jody Harris, who was wanted for stealing people's identities and umpteen amounts of money from innocent people. I told them that I was not her.

To try to prove her identity, Symes showed the cops that she had two tattoos. Unfortunately, Harris had similarly placed body ink. Tattoos were a subject mentioned by Humble in his email to Twining. Investigators wanted his knowledge on the subject.

'Knowing [Harris's] tattoos would make it easier,' Humble wrote. 'Apparently she has the word "karma" tattooed on her lower back—can you please confirm this?' Humble went on:

> David Lewis has asked me to ask you if you are missing any police badges—specifically hat badges or plaques. She will definitely steal same to impersonate a member … She is on the run and will do anything to avoid arrest. She has become desperate and is possible [sic] of [doing] anything—although she has never committed robbery, burgs, assaults et cetera. Only frauds and deceptions.

Humble and Embona officers visited Twining's unit. Humble made his way inside and found—among other things—a black bra hanging on a door.

Still on the cruise ship, Andrew Twining began providing Victorian police with addresses and phone numbers, including that of Harris's grandmother, in an effort to assist investigators in locating the crafty con woman. 'The idea was to continue contact with her with a view to having her arrested,' Twining would say in court. He arrived back in Melbourne after his holiday cruise looking crestfallen and shattered, according to Humble.

McKENNA: You saw Andrew Twining after he came back to Australia, didn't you? He wasn't in a great way, was he? A great state at all?

HUMBLE: No.

McKENNA: Pretty distressed. Upset. Agitated. He felt he'd been cheated.

HUMBLE: Yes.

McKENNA: Conned. She'd exploited his love. He didn't go back to work, or didn't try to go back to work, for some months. Is that right?

HUMBLE: Yes, that's right.

In his own words, Twining said in court: 'Where do you start? I think it's fair to say that I was fairly deeply in love with my perception of what I thought Jody was, in that she worked for Virgin Blue, she was professionally employed on the face of it. Those sorts of people don't have prior convictions. She presents as charming, funny, smart, jovial—all those sorts of things.'

Under cross-examination from prosecutor Aaron Schwartz, Twining would deny that he ever described Harris as a 'woman of little or no worth'.

> What do I say she was? A con woman, a thief, a fraudster, a liar, a deceptionist, a police imposter, a criminal ... As I indicated, I was in love with a person who misrepresented who she was entirely in regards to her employment, her honesty, her criminal background, her criminality, her history impersonating police and associating herself with police. The person that I knew—thought I knew—is not the person that is in prison.

News of Twining and the relationship attracted obvious media attention. 'I had a Channel Nine satellite van sitting outside my address for two days,' Twining said.

As part of a joint interstate police operation, Twining stayed in touch with Harris, pretending their relationship was as strong as ever. He organised to meet her in Sydney on 6 July 2006. She obviously still trusted him, and the sting was set in place. Humble rang and spoke to Twining as he was driving interstate to trip the trap. According to McKenna, 'She was lured to his company while he, behind the scenes, was talking to Glenn Davies from the Melbourne Embona police and with Mr Agostino, who was a New South Wales policeman.'

It was about 4 am and police had saturated a section of Sydney's Chinatown. They were expecting to see Harris walk from a certain hotel room, but she instead stepped from a taxi outside a pub. She hopped straight into Twining's awaiting car. The police contingent swooped, intercepting the car and pulling both Harris and Twining onto the road. The lovers were handcuffed. It wasn't foreplay this time. The elusive 'Catch Me If You Can' con woman's tantalising run was finally at an end.

'The prick has set me up!' she yelled.

After the arrest, Detective Senior Sergeant Despa Fitzgerald, of Rose Bay police, said: 'She didn't know straight away that Twining had tipped off police but, as soon as the lights and sirens went on, she twigged.'

Police found wigs, police property and over 100 items of identification, including a false Australian passport, drivers' licences, bank and credit cards, birth certificates, Medicare cards and even two Californian drivers' licences in Harris's possession.

Fitzgerald would admit that police had missed her 'by a matter of minutes' the previous day. He said they were 'hot on her trail' for three days before nabbing her. 'We had information she was staying at the Avillion Hotel, opposite Central Local Court,' Fitzgerald told the *Sunday Telegraph*. 'We went to reception, asked if anyone had paid cash for a room, and learned that a stolen identity had been used. We looked at the CCTV and, sure enough, it was Jody. She'd left about twenty minutes earlier. It was very frustrating.'

During her record of interview with New South Wales detectives, a belligerent, defeated and drab-looking Harris showed a clear disdain for her captors. 'Fucking Penrite or wherever I am now,' she spat. 'In the middle of nowhere. Fucking Hicksville, full of fucking two-headed cunts—no offence.'

At one point she told police: 'Someone needs to educate you uneducated fuckers. That's not how you spell Vuitton, by the way. Fuckin' triplets. You can't educate someone that shops at Lowes.' When talking of the theft of a victim's identification from a handbag inside a private girls' school, Harris would mutter: 'Must remember never to steal children from private schools ... They probably want to charge me with the fucking Beaumont children [disappearance] ... I walked in the school, I walked in there with the intent not to steal a child but to steal a handbag.'

Harris showed a knack for police vernacular and procedural jargon. When detectives told her they wanted a DNA sample, she jacked up. 'No. Fuck that, no. You get fingerprints and shit for fraud,' she spat. 'I don't know what the fuck you're fitting me up for now. You're not getting my fucking DNA ... Other frauds, they never want any DNA. DNA is for fucking murder and armed robbery and blues and shit like that where you leave blood and fucking spit ... and semen, and that, at fucking scenes of crime. Not for fucking fraud.' In the end she provided a sample.

During taped interviews with the New South Wales police and Victoria's Senior Sergeant Davies, Harris displayed a photographic memory when it came to her crimes. Judge Hampel stated:

> You displayed a precise knowledge of even the most minute details of your fraudulent activities. When given a name, you would generally describe in some detail the circumstances in which you stole that particular victim's identity. You were clearly able to keep track of the individual transactions in respect of each stolen identity, at times volunteering the details of the bank, branch and amounts obtained using a particular identity. You could recount conversations you had with bank officers and sales assistants, particularly when there was a question raised about whether you were the person named on the card you were using at the time. Similarly, you were able to describe the clothes and other goods you bought from particular shops and the identity you were using when doing so.

Harris also showed no respect for the women she conned or the bank staff she duped. 'In your interview,' Hampel would say, 'you were, for the most part, quite extraordinarily frank about your offending.

> Accompanying that frankness was a quite disturbing level of contempt for your victims—not only for those whose

> identity you stole but also for the banking and sales people you deceived.
>
> You boasted about the ease with which you took advantage of people's trust or circumstances, and referred to many of them in the most derogatory of terms.
>
> Your interview makes it clear that you took pride in the audacity of your activity, that you revelled in the publicity and that you used the money and credit to provide yourself with an ostentatiously luxurious lifestyle.

Harris was paraded into Sydney's Central Local Court after being charged following her initial police interview. Magistrate Les Brennan said he had been expecting her.

Betrayed by her copper boyfriend, she was enraged. 'Why isn't he here?' she shouted to the media pack. 'Ask where he is. He's being protected by police.' She held up a wrist to show journalists a tattoo of Twining's name. 'He's got a matching tattoo on his arse, right cheek,' she yelled.

None too surprisingly, the magistrate refused her bail.

In September 2006, Harris—then twenty-eight—pleaded guilty to forty-three charges in New South Wales. The court had heard that she purchased more than $175,000 worth of goods and services using credit and bank cards stolen from thirty-three different victims. Items that she purchased included a $3950 TAG Heuer diamond watch and a $1600 designer 'bichoodle' poodle pup. Her spree had also included the purchase of bags, expensive clothes and shoes, hair extensions, a pearl necklace and hire cars. In sentencing her to four years' jail with a minimum of three and a half, Magistrate Allan Moore said she committed fraud to fund the lifestyle she had grown accustomed to. 'There is little doubt you are a person of intellect; a person of skill. One would have to suggest strongly that this was a matter of greed.'

Harris later unsuccessfully appealed against the length of her sentence, with New South Wales District Court Judge

Peter Berman saying she had 'displayed a continuing attitude of disobedience to the law'. 'Committing these offences must have been something of a full-time occupation,' he said.

Before a move to Victoria in January 2008 under the interstate prisoner transfer act, Harris sent Twining what were described as 'racy letters' from her New South Wales jail cell. In her writings she said that she wanted to be moved to Victoria to serve the majority of her sentence so she could be closer to him. 'I wanted to let you know how I adore you and miss you so much babe,' she wrote in one letter, despite Twining's previous betrayal.

In a true revelation of her reversal of fortune, she asked for money for a pair of prison sandshoes. They don't wear Vuitton behind bars. 'I know you're probably doing it hard down there, but when you can please, please send me some money for my shoes etc.'

In the Melbourne County Court, Harris pleaded guilty to a thirty-six-count presentment. The charges related to fifteen women. Harris had used their money, in part, to purchase plane tickets; fancy dinners; hotel rooms; Louis Vuitton gear; clothing and lingerie from stores such as Portmans, Country Road, Sportscraft, Bras 'N' Things, Jetty Surf and Esprit; CDs and DVDs from HMV and JB Hi Fi; and sunglasses. She even spent forty bucks on condoms on Valentine's Day.

During Harris's County Court plea hearing, defence lawyer Julie Sutherland told Judge Hampel how Harris was abused by an uncle when she was about eleven—while her mother was in prison—and that not that many years later a life of crime began.

'At fourteen she started committing offences,' Sutherland said. 'Even at fourteen she's making out she's a policewoman and committing frauds, and so it goes on—year after sorry year. Her criminal history, in my respectful submission, is a testament to things going wrong with her.' Sutherland said that it was only after her arrest in Sydney that Harris was 'starting to get on top of the demons that afflicted her'.

Sutherland also made mention of the persona that Harris had created:

> The media, and I'm not being critical of the media—they do a tremendous job—but the media has portrayed this young woman as the next 'Catch Me if You Can'. I think it was Frank Abagnale in the *Catch Me if You Can* movie where he was either the hero or the anti-hero. He was the fraudster, had different identities and used to go around to banks and what have you. Ultimately, of course, he pleaded guilty and then became, interestingly enough, a fraud consultant. But the media have painted my client, and one can understand why they have—because of the audacity, because of the boldness and in some respects the sheer bizarre nature of the criminality—as the female equivalent of this anti-hero in the movie. And again, as I say, one can understand that.

Sutherland claimed that some of Harris's methods were so simple 'a child of ten could do it'. It was an extravagant claim, but one that did highlight parlous bank security procedure.

> I mean, she called in to one bank and basically presented a driver's licence. Didn't look anything like the person in the driver's licence. The next minute she was withdrawing money. On another occasion a block, or a ban, had been placed on a certain account. She rang up and basically said, 'Well that's a problem. I want it removed.' And within a couple of minutes it was removed.

At the hearing, Harris's mother, Debbie Kilroy, gave evidence. Kilroy had made an inspirational turnaround. The one-time drug trafficker had become a qualified solicitor with a Brisbane law firm. She was, at one time, the director of a prisoner support group. She had also been awarded an Order of Australia honour. Hampel described her as a 'remarkable and inspirational embodiment of hope and rehabilitation'. In court, Kilroy spoke of the family history. She'd given birth to Jody at age seventeen. 'Her father had always inflicted violence on me and I stayed in that, but the day that he hit her with a broom handle in the chest because she was crying, I actually left the relationship,' Kilroy said. She then told how she went on to marry Joe Kilroy.

SUTHERLAND: And he was a famous player for the Broncos?

KILROY: He was, yes.

SUTHERLAND: And that's a rugby league football team, is it? Up in Queensland?

JUDGE HAMPEL: Even I've heard of them.

SUTHERLAND: As I understand it, Mr Kilroy was a brilliant player?

KILROY: Yes. So the media reported on many occasions ... but, I mean, both of us had grown up in institutions ... So neither of us had good role models in regards to how to be parents.

Kilroy said that, after one of her friends was murdered in jail, she took advantage of a 'window of reform' in the Queensland prison system and utilised new education programs. Her aim was to 'get out and look after my children'. She completed a Bachelor of Social Work and went on to become a lawyer and role model.

The County Court was told that Harris wanted to follow her mother's shining example. Hampel heard that Harris had embarked on a Master of Arts and Writing course and Koori studies in prison. She had also been elevated to the position of Koori peer support person. 'She wants to essentially become—if she can, if anyone can—a person like her mum,' Sutherland said.

On 19 December 2008, Hampel imposed a new sentence of five years and nine months with a minimum of four years and three months in respect to both the New South Wales and Victorian offences. That meant at least an extra nine months in jail for Harris on top of the three-and-a-half-year minimum term she was serving for her New South Wales offences. Her Victorian victims scoffed at the sentence.

Hampel described Harris's offending in Victoria, between January and May 2006, as 'highly organised and systematic'.

> You obtained a total $120,180 cash from various banks, and attempted to obtain a further $8500. There are many victims of your offending. It needs little imagination to understand the sense of violation at having their trust breached, or of being taken advantage of—particularly when some of them were vulnerable due to injury or intoxication, and of having not just their credit cards or licences stolen, but their sense of having their identity stolen as well. In addition, some suffered financial loss or hardship as their accounts were raided. Some had assets frozen, some for considerable time.
>
> It is clear that what you did was professional, calculated and highly organised. Its purpose was to gain material benefit for yourself. Many of the credit card purchases were for high-end consumer goods—some of the cash was spent on luxury cars, travel and high-end-of-the-market accommodation. You displayed an acute awareness of the status symbolism of particular designer labels, luxury cars and prestige addresses. At times you corrected the police on the pronunciation and spelling of some well-known labels, instructed them in the type of jewellery made by particular designers and spoke disparagingly of suggestions that you would buy cheap products.

Hampel made mention of the fact that Harris had sat down with Senior Sergeant Davies to film a video about her crimes. The video, which revealed her method of operation and how she avoided detection, became a training guide for fraud investigators. Just like Frank Abagnale, she shared her criminal expertise with law enforcement agencies. 'I accept this weighs very strongly in your favour,' Hampel said.

> It is evidence of co-operation, which is of benefit to the community generally, and it is also an indicator of your determination to change your ways. Your co-operation does not involve implicating co-offenders or offering to provide evidence against others. Unlike your classic informer case, therefore, you do not suffer the risk of retaliation from co-offenders and do not need as a result to serve your

sentence in harder conditions than those (prisoners) in mainstream—namely in protection.

Jody Harding's immediate fate had been sealed. But what of Andrew Twining?

On 12 July 2006—six days after Harris's arrest—internal affairs investigators found a replica .38 revolver in an office cupboard at his home. On his hard drive they found a Word document entitled 'Deceptions of the Heart'. '[It was] some sort of manuscript by Mr Twining—a pouring out of how he had been deceived by Jody Harris,' barrister McKenna said. 'How it hurt him to the core.'

Twining was charged with possessing an imitation handgun, and suspended from the force. He pleaded not guilty and went to trial in the County Court in February 2009. He said he knew nothing of the gun and that it must have belonged to Harris. The jury deliberated for less than an hour to acquit him of the charge.

'It's the quickest jury deliberation in my personal experience,' McKenna said afterwards.

After his acquittal, Twining told this author that his life had been turned upside down thanks to his Jody Harris experience. 'As I said in court, I was in love with the perception of her. I saw the perception of what she wanted me to see. She's a liar. A thief. A stalker of police.'

5

Seeing Red

A Russian criminal shoots a police informer in the head — and blames a gangland enforcer

'He was blinded by blood and he thought he was dying ... and who can blame him?'

DESPITE BEING A FORMER soldier for the motherland and a Russian policeman, the man who can only be referred to as 'K' had not had much experience when it came to catching bullets. While he knew just about everything there was to know about guns — how to handle them, dismantle them and rebuild them; and, of course, how to fire them — he had never been shot by one in the former Soviet Republic. But one sunny day on the other side of the world, that run of fortune changed in the most dramatic way. A member of a Melbourne-based Russian crime gang, K was now a police informer. His boss, Michael 'Misha' Goldman, had smelled a rat and was now standing over K with a pistol pointed at his head. Minutes earlier, Goldman had shot and wounded K inside his Melbourne flat during a frantic attempt to kill the suspected traitor. 'Who did it, bastard?' Goldman had yelled in Russian dialect. 'Who fucking let me down? Tell me, bastard!' Using a small kitchen table as a makeshift shield, K had somehow managed to ward off Goldman and scramble outside to the roadway. But Goldman had stalked him and now stood poised for the execution. Goldman's angry vision was clouded red. He pulled the trigger. As Goldman's .32 Browning bucked, K's eyes filled with blood.

Michael Goldman, a Russian Jew, was born in Kiev, the Ukraine, in 1948. His father, a qualified engineer, was a captain in the Soviet army. His mother was a qualified architect. According to Victorian Supreme Court judge Robert Redlich, travel restrictions were initially imposed on his family due to their Jewish faith.

'Your family life was one of hardship and I accept that you had a difficult childhood and youth growing up during a period when anti-Semitism was rife in Russia,' Redlich would say.

Due to injuries sustained in a car accident, Goldman was precluded from armed service duties in the USSR. After travel restrictions were lifted, he emigrated to Australia in 1980 aged thirty-two. His wife and child moved later. While working at different times as a salesman, machine operator, pawn shop proprietor and AMP insurance agent, Goldman racked up a history of violence. In 1994 he was jailed for intentionally causing serious injury after ambushing a man outside a reception centre and stabbing him in the stomach. The following year he was charged with the attempted murder of his schizophrenic wife—a charge that was dismissed after a committal hearing in the Melbourne Magistrates' Court. In 1998 he was convicted for again intentionally causing serious injury. The following year he was convicted and jailed for making a threat to kill and threatening to inflict serious injury. That stretch was served concurrently on a jail term previously imposed for breaching a suspended sentence for attempted theft.

'It is not disputed that you are a serious violent offender,' Redlich would tell Goldman.

In the lead-up to the attempted murder of K on 10 July 2002, Goldman had assembled a crime gang comprised of several countrymen. K was one of that gang. It specialised in high-end burglaries. Goldman had also established close ties with gangland enforcer Nik 'The Russian' Radev, a standover merchant and drug dealer destined to be gunned down by one of Carl Williams's triggermen, Andrew Veniamin.

Radev, a Bulgarian immigrant who preferred the 'Russian' moniker, was victim number fifteen during Melbourne's gangland war. Before his murder he built a reputation in underworld and police circles as a violent career criminal and suspected killer. Carl Williams saw him as a threat: a fellow drug trafficker who might attempt to kidnap experts in the art of cooking amphetamines and force them to work for him. A gangland killer who can only be referred to as 'Witness C' reckons Radev owed Williams a lot of money yet still had to be eliminated. A secret police report listed Radev as a high-risk offender.

'He is a dangerous and violent offender well connected within the criminal underworld. He carries firearms and associates with people who carry and use firearms. His conviction history shows a propensity towards violence to extort money. He will assault and resist police.'

Ben Archbold, a former Victoria Police detective who investigated Radev, knows firsthand of The Russian's propensity for violence. Archbold believes Radev killed a fellow Bulgarian migrant by the name of Ivan Tsolakov and assumed his identity until he himself was granted Australian citizenship. Radev wanted to kill Archbold, so put the feelers out for his home address. He even walked into a hotel owned by Archbold's parents armed with a hand grenade one night as part of his vendetta campaign.

'He was a very, very violent man—the most violent to walk Victoria's streets,' Archbold once told this author.

'He was into everything when it came to crime. His favourite method of operation was to stand over people committing fraud or dealing drugs and demand money in return for protection. The victims couldn't report it because they were active criminals themselves.'

As part of a shakedown campaign, Radev once hung an extortion victim from a high-rise hotel balcony by his ankles.

It is criminal folklore that Radev decided against dropping the man for fear of being charged with littering from the seventh floor.

Michael Goldman had a strong affiliation with Radev by the time K fell in with the gang. 'He told me that he was in army … and he went to fight in Afghanistan,' Goldman would say of K during his attempted murder trial in the Supreme Court. 'He was in Special Operations Service … in English it's like paratroopers who jump from the sky and make trouble on earth, and after that he was taken to Soviet police, which was called militia, and in three years' time he was a major. Major is nearly general.'

Of the Melbourne burglary crime gang, prosecutor Boris Kayser would tell the Supreme Court:

> They socialised together, drank together, stole together. The sort of thing they'd do was to cruise around and see if there were any flats under construction or houses under renovation or construction and, when the kitchen equipment went in, they used to burgle those premises and clean out all the whitegoods—the stove, the range hood, the fridge, dishwasher, washing machine, even taps; the sort of thing that they could sell relatively easily and relatively quickly.
>
> They also used to burgle shops where they could break in and quickly grab things like notebook computers. K received a share of the proceeds of the goods that were stolen in the burglaries in which he took part.

According to K, 'We was one crime team.' He estimated that they carried out up to 140 burglaries. In the lead-up to July 2002, however, K said he grew concerned after Goldman began suggesting the gang carry out more violent crimes with firearms.

Detectives from St Kilda were investigating the gang, and arrested K, Goldman and others in early July 2002 and questioned them. In an interview room away from unwelcome ears, K told investigators he wanted out. He said he was prepared to turn informer in exchange for indemnity. He told the police he had fired shots during one burglary and would later tell them he had a pistol 'in an underground position' in his front yard, in case he ever needed it. He also mentioned that Nikolai Radev was a Goldman associate.

'I never said I am white and soft,' K would say in court. He went on:

> Of course I said, 'I am really bad guy and I want to stop my criminal connection and I am ready to help you in your investigation of my crimes ... I did it [became a police informer] freely. My family give me deadline to stop my criminal activities or they leave me alone. Another point: I didn't want to be involved with really high dangerous crimes any more.

Goldman's barrister, Peter Chadwick, would express a different view, telling the jury that K was controlling the situation to suit himself. 'He baited a hook,' Chadwick said in court. 'And the method was to drop a name—Nik Radev. And what a name to drop. What a name to drop to the Victoria Police. It would be like dropping Osama bin Laden's name to George Bush; you can bet on a reaction. And he got one.'

K's decision to turn police informer was a dangerous one. Any criminal who turns 'dog' knows they are stepping into a world of peril—even if they are a Russian ex-combat soldier. K had served in the war in Afghanistan from 1985 to 1989.

KAYSER: How long were you in Afghanistan?

K: Three years, six months, fourteen days.

KAYSER: And during that time you saw weapons?

K: Yes, of course.

KAYSER: And you saw what weapons could do?

K: Yes, absolutely correct.

KAYSER: Did that have any effect on you?

K: Yes, of course. It made quite a big impression on me.

The Supreme Court heard that K had quite a distinguished military and law enforcement career before he came to

Australia in 1996—where he surprisingly turned to crime. Chadwick questioned K's credentials.

CHADWICK: You are saying that you were a major in the Soviet police?

K: Yes, it is correct.

CHADWICK: A little over three years was your service in that time?

K: A little bit more than three years.

CHADWICK: And do you also claim that you went into the Soviet police force as a *praporshchik*, as a junior officer, and left as a major?

K: Yes, that's correct.

CHADWICK: You see, I suggest to you, sir, that is simply you lying about your background; do you agree or disagree?

K: I disagree.

CHADWICK: Have you also claimed not only to having been in the Soviet army, to having been in the Soviet police, but to also being a qualified lawyer in the Soviet Union? Have you said that?

K: Yes, after leaving police career.

K knew exactly what fate awaited him if word got out that he had become a registered police informer. 'If Michael Goldman or Nik Radev receive any information about my connection with police, they kill me, no choice,' he said in court.

The day after their arrest and questioning by the St Kilda detectives, the Russian gang met at an Elwood restaurant to debrief about their capture and release. 'We talk about all the aspects of our arrest and we talk about future crimes and we talk about maybe some one of us is police informant,' K would recall.

KAYSER: How do you know that Michael Goldman thought that one of you might be a police informer?

K: We talk with each other and Michael Goldman tell me his opinion about it.

KAYSER: What did he say?

K: I not remember word by word. He means it is not possible for police to receive information about our activities without help of informer and he thinking one of us is a police informer.

Detective John O'Connor, of the Special Response Squad, was K's handler. While being briefed by O'Connor at the TRS office in the St Kilda Road police complex on 10 June, K received a phone call from Goldman ordering him to his flat in Hampton, a bayside suburb about twenty kilometres south-east of Melbourne. K was strapped with a tape recorder and sent off to gather evidence. What he would record would be 'Misha' Goldman's attempt to murder him.

'He was wearing that tape recorder when he entered Goldman's flat,' Kayser would tell the court.

> He was wearing that tape recorder when Goldman shot him once; he was wearing that tape recorder when he was shouting at Goldman; he was wearing that tape recorder when Goldman spoke to him and told him why he was shooting him; and he was wearing that tape recorder when he managed to escape from that flat and go across the road before he fell to the ground and was shot in the head by Goldman.

Several weeks before the shooting, K and another member of the crime gang had burgled some 485 T-shirts, 515 pairs of jeans and about 260 designer jackets from a warehouse owned by a friend of Radev's. According to K, the burglary was committed on Goldman's order. Goldman denied any knowledge. Radev was angry about the heist and called for a meeting at a cafe in Acland Street, St Kilda, to discuss the matter.

'I was a bit tentative and had good reason to be,' K said.

Kayser agreed. 'You are not dealing with Snow White. It was Nikolai Radev.'

Radev demanded that the stolen goods be returned but he was told they had already been sold and the money spent. But the clothes were, in fact, sitting hidden in a self-storage warehouse, and police found them during a raid. According to

Goldman, Radev complained that K had lied about the stolen property, and that was when Goldman ordered the 10 July meeting at his Hampton flat. According to Chadwick, Goldman was an 'honest broker bringing these people together' by arranging the meeting. Goldman claimed that Radev arrived wearing a long raincoat and a stylish beret, and that he snorted a few lines of cocaine before pulling a .32 handgun from the waistband of his pants. He claimed he thought that Radev was going to 'force K to repay what he took in a peaceful, nice way', despite saying in evidence: 'I know that he has served time in jail and that he was very feared by his enemies. He was like a very good friend and very bad enemy.'

According to Goldman's disputed version of events, Radev opened the raincoat and showed him an automatic rifle on a sling—and then 'shoved it in my face'. 'He started whispering loudly, salivating in my face,' Goldman would claim. 'He said, "All you have to do, just grab this, squeeze and pull. Give him one in the head and I get rid of the body. Come on! Do it!"'

With surveillance police following at a distance, K—all wired for sound—arrived at Goldman's flat at about 1.30 pm. Goldman opened the door. 'He have two doors—one normal one and another security door,' K recalled in court.

> He opened security door and say, 'Please come in. How are you?' or something like that. Then I coming inside his flat. I make maybe couple of steps. Inside he ask me where I have been in the morning. I said, 'To a doctor.' He asked me which … and what car I am using for coming to his flat. I said, 'It's my wife's car.' Then he shot me in my body. He shoot me in my left side of my body.

K's legs crumbled and he collapsed to the kitchen floor. 'I fell to the floor because I lost feeling in my leg and I could feel pain.'

Goldman had the .32 Browning semiautomatic pistol wrapped in a tea towel. The cloth over the self-loading weapon was the only thing that saved K's life, as he frantically grabbed at something—anything—to shield himself. He up-ended a small table as he lay on the linoleum and used it like a shield in battle. 'I took this table, rolled over and try to cover my body,' he said in evidence.

Goldman went to fire off another round, but the tea towel jammed the Browning's ejection port and slide action. According to K: 'I just hear click but not shoot.'

Goldman pulled on the trigger again. It was all very frantic and panicked. K's tape recorder captured the drama, all yelled and protested in Russian. Goldman wanted a confession from K about informing to the police.

K: Misha, this is not my fault!

GOLDMAN: Whose fault is it then?

K: I didn't do it. Misha, what are you doing? I didn't do it, I swear.

GOLDMAN: Tell me everything.

K: Misha, I didn't do it.

GOLDMAN: Tell me, bastard, who did it?

K: Don't shoot! I didn't do it.

GOLDMAN: Tell me! Who then? I am going to shoot.

K: Misha, I'll tell you. I didn't do it!

GOLDMAN: Tell me, bastard. Tell me … bloody bastard!

K: Misha, I didn't do it! I swear … Please stop!

GOLDMAN: Who did it, bastard?

K: Misha, wait …

GOLDMAN: Who fucking let me down?

K: Misha, I swear I didn't do it. I swear by my mother.

The questions and denials went on.

GOLDMAN: Wait a minute, you've been saying things against me all the time?

K: Are you stupid? Why would I say something against you?

GOLDMAN: I am not stupid.

K: Misha, I haven't said anything against you.

GOLDMAN: I *was* stupid …

K: Misha, I swear to you … I haven't said a word about you. This is not my fault.

GOLDMAN: Tell me, bastard.

K: I didn't do it.

GOLDMAN: Tell me, bastard! I am going to fucking shoot you dead.

K: I swear by my mother. I didn't do it.

K spied a nearby window and considered trying to leap through the glass. Goldman's Browning, after all, was not going to click away harmlessly forever. K inched his way towards the window but didn't have the strength to jump. 'I'm looking for way to save my life, to protect myself, but I don't feel my leg,' he told the jury. '[It was] impossible to jump through window because one of my legs doesn't work.'

According to Kayser, '[K] was in great pain. He was losing blood. [Goldman] was standing there doing his best to fire this gun at him a number of times but not succeeding.'

As the gun continued to misfire, K staggered out of the flat. As he passed through the doorway, Goldman managed to fire off a second round. It missed. According to Goldman, Radev was hiding in the flat during the bullet-riddled argument and appeared and pushed the barrel of his automatic rifle into his stomach and ordered: 'Go cunt, quickly, and finish him. I fuck you, I fuck your family … '

In court it was suggested that, if in fact Radev was present and threatening, then Goldman could have tried to defend himself. Chadwick would retort: 'It is only people like Steven Seagal and Harrison Ford and so forth who can deal with such situations. The rest of us, we just do as we are told and hope to survive the experience. To have a shootout with Radev would have been simply suicidal and that was the very threat that was being made to him, wasn't it? "Do this or you will die."'

As K staggered outside into the bright sunshine, he had two things on his mind—an armed Goldman on his tail and a quick police ride home.

'I believe Goldman [would] not follow me to the public place because it was middle of day, a lot of sunshine and people around,' K said. 'I am trying [to] escape from him that way.' But Goldman was like a jackal. Holding his wound, K limped along a pathway to the side of Highett Road. Goldman closed in, his gun still wrapped in the tea towel.

Janet Bedlington and her daughter Gemma were driving along Highett Road when they saw K stagger and collapse on the opposite nature strip. Goldman was close behind. 'The second man was walking in a kind of determined way … and the first man was stumbling, trying to get out of the way,' Gemma Bedlington would tell the jury. K recalled: 'Power leave my body and I crawl.'

As K looked up, Goldman was standing over him. The informer raised his hand for mercy. He did not receive it. In plain sight, Goldman pulled back the slide of his Browning to clear the weapon and took out the magazine. Pulling fresh rounds from his pocket, he pushed a couple into the magazine and slid it back into the gun. Goldman pulled back the slide, loading the pistol, and stepped to within arm's reach of K for a roadside execution. K recalled: 'He hold the gun by two hands. He was aiming at me. I was begging him not to shoot … not to kill me. [The gun was pointed] in my face.' Goldman pulled the trigger.

K would have died, had it not been for a reflex action. '[K], at the right moment, miraculously turned his head,' said Kayser. K said: 'When I saw him move his finger on the trigger, I just move my head and I feel the bullet punch me in my face. I believe I died because the bullet punch me [in the] middle of my eyes and blood cover my eyes.'

Goldman had a different version. He claimed he shot to deliberately miss K's brain, despite Radev having taken up a position with an automatic rifle through the open lounge room window—with *him* in his sights.

GOLDMAN: I shot deliberately to miss … If I put gun between K's eyes [and wanted to kill him], I think half of his skull would go.

KAYSER: Well, half his nose did.

GOLDMAN: I must be magician to do like this, if I aim straight in the head from such distance and do such a [small] wound.

KAYSER: He moved, I suggest.

GOLDMAN: Moved?

KAYSER: He moved his head as you pulled the trigger … And I suggest to you the reason you didn't kill him was because [K] moved his head, number one, and secondly, that he was fortunate that you had a Browning .32 and not a .38.

Kayser put this to Goldman: 'I will make this clear to you. I suggest to you that the story of Nik Radev is just a fairytale; it didn't happen.' Goldman's reply: 'It did happen, sir … I kept the gun pointing on [K] because I was under gun myself.'

After shooting K, Goldman walked back to his flat and made a call to 000. He admitted to the shooting. When asked by the operator who he'd shot, Goldman replied: 'You will see. You come. You will see. I don't resist. I wait outside.'

Kayser had a theory about the 000 call.

KAYSER: You feared being shot by police because you believed you had shot a police informer.

GOLDMAN: No, I didn't know.

KAYSER: And you feared that the police would come with guns blazing, didn't you?

GOLDMAN: It is Australia. Why police come with gun and shoot me? This is not somewhere in Africa, you know.

Out on Highett Road, Janet Bedlington had stopped her vehicle. According to K, 'Through blood I saw two women in a red four-wheel drive. They stop and come out of car and come at me and I said, "Michael Goldman shoot me" because I believe I will die. I try to leave more evidence about my killer.'

When asked by Kayser why he thought he was going to die, K replied: 'Because chance of stay alive after injury in the head between eyes—it's very, very small.'

Janet Bedlington immediately noticed two holes in his head, 'one between his eyes and the other on the right side of his nose, the bridge of his nose … He asked me to call the police.'

Plumber Phillip Smith had heard the shots and ran to

the injured K. 'Half his nose was a bit blown away, it wasn't looking too good. I could see a bit of bone hanging out there and it didn't look too nice.'

Police units began to arrive.

'I don't know where they all came from in such a hurry, but they must have been hanging around,' Smith would say. 'It happened that quick, I mean by the time I was still onto the operator, the whole area was just cordoned off in a matter of minutes.'

K, in the meantime, was desperately trying to contact Detective O'Connor on his mobile phone. In a show of contempt, Goldman walked from his unit and slapped the phone from his hand.

Janet Bedlington shouted, 'That's him! That's the one who shot him!' Goldman appeared almost proud. 'Yeah, I shot him,' the gang boss said, as more police officers arrived.

Constable Glenn Saddington tried to calm the bleeding K. 'I attempted to talk to the male and he was able to respond, but I couldn't make out what he was saying. It was broken English and he seemed to be in a lot of pain.' According to Kayser, 'He was blinded by blood and he thought he was dying … and who can blame him?'

As K mumbled to the cops, 'I have tape recorder on my back', Senior Constable Dean Isles was speaking to Goldman.

ISLES: What happened, mate?

GOLDMAN: I shot the guy.

ISLES: Where is the gun?

GOLDMAN: It's inside.

Police went in and established a secondary crime scene. They found the fired weapon, spent bullet casings, fired projectiles and upturned furniture. Paramedics rushed K to the Alfred Hospital trauma unit. He was in a critical condition when he arrived, with head and abdominal injuries. According to Dr Marek Garbowski: 'The injuries were obviously life-threatening and the patient required urgent operation.'

Goldman was charged with attempted murder. During the Supreme Court trial, Kayser told the jury that Goldman's motive and intention were obvious:

> Members of the jury, the Crown case is that the accused man decided that [K] was an informer, talking to the police about him and his criminal activities. He decided that this man had to be eliminated.
>
> The prosecution says and submits to you that the accused man is guilty of attempted murder. He shot [K] twice—shot him once in the abdomen and shot him the second time between the eyes and tried to shoot him at least, the prosecution submits to you, five other times. He did his best to kill [K] and he did so with the intent to kill because there can only be one intent in the head of a person who points a gun at another human being and pulls the trigger not once but a number of times, follows him outside and then, when he is on the ground, points the gun between his eyes and pulls the trigger. There can only be, in my submission, one intent—an intent to kill.
>
> You have seen [K]. Tough! Boy, he has got to be tough, that fellow! The accused man, Mr Goldman, was a man never lost for something to say. And a man, you might think from the way he bore himself, used to having his authority accepted.
>
> He told you about this Nikolai Radev, the man on the grassy knoll. I don't know how many of you remember the day when you turned on the radio in the morning to listen to the news—it was a Saturday morning—and you heard that President Kennedy was shot. Well, we all know Lee Harvey Oswald up in the Texas book depository shot President Kennedy, but there was the man on the grassy knoll. How many people said that they saw the man on the grassy knoll and that he did it? That is Nik Radev—the man on the grassy knoll!
>
> If Radev was there, then why didn't *he* shoot [K]? In my submission, if he was there, he would have without any doubt at all—if you accept what Goldman says about

Radev's state. It is just inconceivable, in my submission, that Radev was there. This whole story of Radev is a fairytale … The accused man did his best to kill [K]. That he did not succeed is almost miraculous.

In his closing address, Chadwick attacked K's credibility.

Are we dealing with a Russian man of high intellect with capacities both practical and esoteric: a trained lawyer in his early 20s, a combat officer, a police officer? This man was set up for a glittering career with that sort of background, but what was he when he came to Australia, the land of opportunity? A thief and a burglar with his own criminal history. You see, I'd suggest to you we are actually dealing with a lying, self-serving crook.

On the flip side, Chadwick painted Goldman as an unassuming, law-abiding man with a menagerie of associates.

There is no lavish lifestyle [for Goldman]. What we have is an immaculately kept flat, nicely furnished, but not lavishly furnished. This is meant to be the home of a criminal gang leader. Or is it the modest home of an older man with the trappings you would expect to find in Australia, here in Melbourne: a couple of televisions, a washing machine, a fridge? We also hear that he socialises in what is sometimes called a cafe society; a very European way of living, I would suggest, socialising particularly with his countrymen and -women … and acquaintances, as he told you, from many and varied walks of life. Some of us like to keep a close-knit group of friends very similar to ourselves. Others of us like to have a broad cross-section from the community and even take pleasure from a few colourful characters. What is the expression in Sydney? 'Colourful Sydney racing identities'. Damon Runyon characters. People who add to the colour of life. Of course in that group that Michael Goldman associated with, his acquaintances included [K] and it included Nik Radev.

Radev is a man who has little or no regard for human

> life. But what better way to punish [K] than by having [K's] friend, the man who brought them together, pull the trigger. It is an act of sadism, isn't it, but it has a horrible but compelling attraction, I suggest.
>
> Unlike [K], Michael Goldman doesn't believe that he can control people; in fact, quite the opposite. I suggest to you that he had no control. He was trying to do his best to bring about peace and he failed—and we all fail at times, no matter how noble our intentions—but on 10 July 2002 Michael Goldman's good intentions ran into Radev's evil intentions, and in this struggle of good over evil, evil won out and he was completely overwhelmed by Radev.

After a lengthy trial and two days of deliberation, the jury found Goldman guilty of attempted murder. Justice Redlich sentenced him on 27 May 2004, dismissing the claim that Radev forced him to open fire on K.

'I am satisfied that on each occasion [on which] you discharged or attempted to discharge the pistol you were not acting under any coersion from Mr Radev,' Redlich said.

> [K] was lured to your flat by you with the intention that you would kill him. You believed that [K] had informed on you in relation to your criminal activity. Your anger and desire to kill [K] [are] evident upon listening to the recording.
>
> You viewed [K] as disloyal—as one who had broken the code of silence. The sentence which I must pronounce must reflect both the seriousness of an attempt to take the life of another human being and also the motive for doing so. I agree with the learned prosecutor's submission that I must view your decision to kill a potential witness against you as a serious case of attempted murder.

Redlich handed Goldman a maximum fourteen-year jail term with an eleven-year minimum. Goldman unsuccessfully applied for leave to appeal his conviction and sentence in the Court of Appeal, and then the High Court. He showed true red defiance to the end.

6

An Eye for an Eye

A grieving suburban grandmother hires a 'hit man' for some torture and murder

'I'd like her to be tortured.
Put in a hole. Cemented alive.'

FOR A LOVING GRANDMOTHER who takes her coffee with four sugars, Petra Traycevska is not a sweet elderly woman when it comes to matters of revenge. She is instead, arguably, the oldest person in Victoria—if not Australia—to incite another person to commit murder on her behalf. During chilling conversations with a man she believed to be a hired killer, Traycevska ordered two deaths as calmly as she spoke about recipes for home cooking: talk of drilling out eyeballs and kneecaps interspersed with recipes for paprikas, tomatoes and fetta cheese. Her prime target was a woman by the name of Natalia Oscianko—her adult son's lover who'd been acquitted of his murder. A male friend of Oscianko, a truck driver named Christoffer Dowsett, did the killing. According to her barrister, it may have been done in an attempt to 'covet her and her baby'.

'I'd like her to be tortured,' Traycevska would tell the 'hit man'. 'Put in a hole. Cemented alive.'

Her second target was to be Oscianko's father. Traycevska feared he would seek revenge over his daughter's death—so wanted him gunned down. 'I want him knocked off,' the granny would say. 'I don't want him around.'

A religious woman with her soul destroyed, Petra Traycevska held firm the virtues of the Old Testament: a breach for a breach, an eye for an eye and a tooth for a tooth.

The day was as cold and grey as shark skin when undercover cop Mick Farnworth—not his real name—pulled up at the rendezvous point for his first meeting with Traycevska. Farnworth was working an operation codenamed Coffer being run by Altona North detectives. According to his briefing, the granny was looking for a hit man to kill a mark by the name of Natalia Oscianko—a twenty-eight-year-old woman who only three and a half months earlier had been found not guilty of murdering her partner, a bloke called Michael Traycevski.

'The time is now 9.28 am on Wednesday the 22nd of July, 2009,' Farnworth narrated into his secret recording device as he pulled in to the kerb for the meeting. 'I'm a member of the Victoria Police force attached to the undercover unit. In relation to Operation Coffer I'm using the assumed name of Mick.'

Farnworth and Traycevska met and headed off for a drive. 'We'll get a coffee and go and have a talk,' Farnworth said reassuringly.

They headed for a nearby coffee shop down by Port Phillip Bay on the western side of town.

'My nerves have been shattered for the last two years, you know,' Traycevska began, before bringing up the topic of her dead son.

> His name was Michael. They used to call him Mick. The Micka. He was well liked and he was one of a kind. Not because he's my son ... but he was one of a kind, you know. He had a good heart. He wouldn't get into any bullshit like, you know, stealing cars. You know, like these young ones. Young louts. You know, they bash these Indian guys.

Farnworth nodded his head. 'Yeah,' he said.

GANGLAND KILLED

Greed drove him

A LIFE ON THE EDGE

October 14, 1970
Carl born

1995
Convicted of attempting to traffic amphetamines

1997
Brother died of a drug overdose

October 13, 1999
Shot and wounded by rival brothers Mark and Jason Moran in Gladstone Park in a dispute over a pill press

November 1999
Arrested on drugs charges after police found him fully clothed in bed with a pill press whirring in room next door

June 15, 2000
Police believe he shot dead Mark Moran as Moran parked his car outside his Aberfeldie home

Early 2001
Married Roberta Hughes

March 21
Daughter Dhakota born on that year

May 2001
Arrested with Roberta for drug trafficking

July 2002
Bailed after corruption claims made against drug squad officers

December 2002
Williams gave a criminal associate freed from prison the job of watching Jason Moran as part of plan to have him killed on anniversary of his brother Mark's death

June 21, 2003
His henchmen carry out the plan a week late, shooting dead Moran and his bodyguard Pasquale Barbaro at a kid's footy clinic

Mark Mallia, who was tortured, strangled and dumped in a West Sunshine drain

October 23, 2003
Had two offsiders murder hot dog vendor Michael Marshall, who was shot dead outside his South Yarra home

March 23, 2004
Close friend and ...

boyfriend of lawyer Zarah Garde-Wilson, shot dead by the men Williams paid to kill Lewis Moran

June 2004
Arranged for two hitmen to murder Mario Condello outside his Brighton home, but police foil the plot thanks to listening devices planted in ...

Carl's birthday

Roberta Williams and her daughter Dhakota at Barbara Williams' funeral.

Carl Williams (far right) as a boy with his family: brother Shane, father George and mum Barbara.

to become a killer

Carl at his mother's funeral.

October 2005
Found guilty of Marshall murder and sentenced to 27 years with a 21-year minimum, but verdict kept secret until 2007 for legal reasons

Early 2007
Splits from wife Roberta

March 2007
Pleads guilty to murders of Mallia, Jason and Lewis Moran and conspiring to murder Mario Condello. Sentenced to life with a 35-year-minimum

November 22, 2008
Mother Barbara Williams found dead after prescription pill overdose

January 2009
police take Williams and his father George out of prison for a week for questioning over police corruption

June 20, 2009
George Williams walks free from jail after serving 20 months for drug trafficking.

Yesterday
Williams killed at Port Phillip Prison

Carl and Roberta Williams.

Carl with his mum, Barbara.

MULTIMEDIA TIMELINE: We track Carl's life in crimes

heraldsun.com.au

Newspaper coverage of the life and crimes of gangland killer Carl Williams, the day after his jailhouse death

Murdered multimillionaire Herman Rockefeller led a dark — and eventual deadly — secret life

The backyard where Rockefeller's body parts were burned

Sick reminder: partygoers enjoy the 21st unaware the barrel in the corner contains a body.

Happy snaps hold grim secret

Kate Uebergang

PARTY guests celebrating a 21st birthday were oblivious to the horrific contents of the barrel in the background of these happy snaps.

As party-goers ate and drank, they could never have imagined that the body of their host's missing wife was hidden just metres from them.

The guests were marking the birthday of Michael Hegarty, whose former father-n-law, Frederick Boyle, was ound guilty last week of murdering wife Edwina Boyle and hiding her remains in the drum for 23 years.

Mrs Boyle went missing in October 1983.

Her husband told family and friends she had left him to start a new life interstate with a truck driver named Ray.

Almost a decade later, on February 19, 1993, Mrs Boyle's loved ones were among guests gathered at the Boyle family home in Carrum Downs to celebrate Mr Hegarty's big day.

Mr Hegarty's family and friends mingled in the backyard and under the carport — where the 200-litre drum had sat since his partner Careesa, her sister Sharon and Boyle moved into the home.

Mr Hegarty became emotional as he recalled his 21st birthday while giving evidence before a Supreme Court jury.

The three snapshots tendered to the jury show guests partying underneath the carport, which is festooned with balloons and streamers.

Mr Hegarty identified his cousin and her boyfriend posing in one image and a friend and his uncle in another.

In one photo his aunty sits on the lap of her boyfriend as they both smile at the camera.

The green drum features in each shot — just metres from the celebration.

Mr Hegarty's former wife, Careesa Hegarty, told the jury of her frustration with the mysterious green drum that remained with her family.

"I was always infuriated at the fact that there was so much rubbish around the yard," she said.

"It was heavy. I have touched it and tried to prod it . . . (my father) said that it had glue in it, glue that had gone off."

Mr and Ms Hegarty separated in 2006 — an event that precipitated the discovery of Edwina Boyle's remains.

During a clean-up of the family property Mr Hegarty finally cut open the drum.

Last week a jury found Boyle responsible for shooting his wife and for the macabre cover-up.

Boyle, 58, is in custody awaiting sentence by Justice Jack Forrest.

Oblivious: guests chat in the carport where the barrel was kept for years.

ABOVE: The metal drum containing Edwina Boyle's body was even invited to parties

LEFT: Val Bordley is still haunted by her sister's grisly demise

Australia's greatest con woman Jody Harris in a picture she left for the cops

Harris's cache of stolen and fake IDs

WITHDRAWAL

Westpac Banking Corporation ABN 33 007 457 141

Westpac

Withdrawal Request

Date 23/7/09

Branch where account is held

Account name Petra Traycevska

Amount in words Four ~~thousand~~

Signature
Sign in front of Customer Service Representative

Initials & Bank Stamp

23 JUL 2009

Account number

Tranco

SB number 733067 520957

$ 4000

+074+

ABOVE: The withdrawal slip for a contract kill

RIGHT: Petra Traycevska's handwritten description of target Natalia Oscianko

NATALIE OSCIANKO
age 28.
~~Deer~~ park shopping
3 BuckLand Ave
NewTown.
Fair Clomp. 5.8-
Sold build
Spiky Hair
big butch Looking
big boosts.
Andrew ↑ 5D.

Gangland player Nik 'The Russian' Radev

Petra Traycevska, finally granted bail

Crime author Douglas Robinson and accomplice David Campbell, up to no good

Manhunt for 'out-of-control' fugitive

ANGEL OF DEATH

THIS is the violent Hells Angel bikie who is on the run from police after the cold-blooded shooting that left a heroic father of three dead.

Fugitive Christopher Wayne Hudson was branded "dangerous" and "out of control" by police as the national manhunt continued after the fatal shooting of solicitor Brendan Keilar and the wounding of two others on a busy city street on Monday.

Hudson, 29, was yesterday cut loose by his motorcycle gang as his parents begged him to surrender peacefully, and details emerged about the second man gunned down in Monday's shooting.

He was identified as 25-year-old Dutch backpacker Paul De Waard, who had been in Australia just four days as part of a round-the-world trip.

Mr De Waard was shot three times when he and Mr Keilar went to the aid of Kara Douglas, 24, who was being attacked. He was in a serious condition in the Royal Melbourne Hospital last night.

And the *Herald Sun* has obtained this exclusive photo of Hudson, taken

Tribute: a city worker leaves flowers at the scene of the fatal shooting.

ABOVE: Newspaper coverage following Christopher Wayne Hudson's CBD gun rampage

RIGHT: Bikies turn up to court to support Hudson and his parents

ABOVE: Attempted killer Cameron Cook's car retrieved from Port Phillip Bay

RIGHT: Career bandit Alexander MacDonald back in custody after killing an innocent man

ABOVE: Blood-stained concrete remains after Tyler Cassidy's body is taken from the scene of his fatal confrontation with police. An autopsy would reveal he was shot five times.

BELOW: The aftermath of the Hoddle Street massacre still haunts those involved to this day

652 1111 CLASSIFIED 662 2222 MELBOURNE MONDAY AUGUST 10, 1987 WEATHER: FINE. PAGE 14. 40 CENT

GOLD TVGUIDE

The Herald

FINAL EXTR

Slaughter on Hoddle St

A driver, propped up by his seatbelt, sits dead behind the wheel.

A motorcyclist lies under his bike where he was felled by the gunman.

A mother, dead, slumped across the front seat of the family car.

Two bodies, partly covered by police jackets, lie in the gutter.

PICTURES: LEIGH HENNINGHAM, MARK MORRISSY AND ROB BAI

'They get a hard time [those Indians], don't they.'

At the coffee shop, Farnworth bought the grandmother a strong cappuccino with four sugars while she bought herself a packet of Winfield Blue cigarettes.

'I'm not an intelligent person but … I'm not an idiot,' Traycevska offered, obliviously unaware of who she was talking to. 'I can see things with people. I don't like a person that speaks shit. I can tell straight away if people speak shit.'

FARNWORTH: So what exactly do you want done, mate?

TRAYCEVSKA: I'd like her to be tortured.

FARNWORTH: Tortured?

TRAYCEVSKA: Tortured … I'd like one of them … what do you call them … drills in her eye.

FARNWORTH: Yep.

TRAYCEVSKA: I'd like her to be tortured. Put in a hole. Cemented alive.

FARNWORTH: Okay. That's what you want done?

TRAYCEVSKA: That's what I want done.

Traycevska said she wanted Oscianko's father, Andrew Oscianko, 'knocked off' too. Riddled with bullets, she insisted. Shot. Gunned down, she would later confirm.

Farnworth agreed to 'do one at a time'.

'These things take time … and very, very methodical planning on my behalf,' he said.

The grieving grandmother said she wanted the woman done first. 'I don't want her walking around free, you know.'

FARNWORTH: Yep. Yeah. Yeah. And how would you like her done? I'll put her in the ground, but how would you like it done prior to that?

TRAYCEVSKA: As I said. I'd like to drill through her bloody eye. I'd like her tortured … You know all about that.

FARNWORTH: Yep.

TRAYCEVSKA: And put her in the ground under cement.

Pausing for a second, Traycevska quizzed Farnworth on any last words he should whisper on her behalf.

TRAYCEVSKA: What would you say to her if she says, 'Why are you doing this?'

FARNWORTH: What do you want me to say? You tell me.

TRAYCEVSKA: You could mention Michael. What would be the best thing to say? A payback?

FARNWORTH: You can say what you want. Who's she gonna tell?

TRAYCEVSKA: Well, what would you say if you lost your son?

After a bit of small talk Traycevska decided: 'Just say it's a payback.'

Traycevska began to write out a note for Farnworth with an address and other particulars. Unfortunately, she didn't have a photograph of Oscianko. They'd all been ripped up. Farnworth asked for a description. Blonde-brown spiked hair, broad shoulders and 'big boobs', Traycevska said, and scribbled it all down.

'Just write "big boobs",' Farnworth told her. 'That'll do. Big boobs.'

After handing Traycevska a contact phone number, Farnworth asked the suburban granny about the price she was prepared to pay. Due to the economic financial crisis, death contracts were apparently negotiable.

TRAYCEVSKA: Well, the problem is, I'm on the disability pension … I'm waiting for some money from Victims of Crime [Assistance Tribunal] at the moment, to come up … I did have plans with the money.

FARNWORTH: Yep.

TRAYCEVSKA: But as far as I'm concerned, stuff the car. Stuff money for other things. I'd rather have her annihilated. The father annihilated.

Saying he had a 'little bit of a heart', Farnworth would eventually agree to do the job for a total of $16,000. That included Oscianko and her father in the deal.

TRAYCEVSKA: That's peanuts compared to what people do pay out.

FARNWORTH: I get paid a lot for some ... But I know the situation you're in.

Then came the subject of a down payment. It was $3000 for Oscianko's scalp and $1000 for her father's. Traycevska—whose disability pension was worth about two hundred dollars a week—said she'd have to juggle that payment with day-to-day living expenses. 'At the moment I've got credit cards to pay. I've got bills to pay.'

Traycevska reckoned she could scrape together the required deposit within a couple of days. 'And I'm waiting on this money from Victims of Crime, which could be probably fifteen to twenty grand,' she said. 'If I didn't have me bloody husband around I'd sell my home. I'd sell my house and I'd pay fifty, a hundred grand.'

During the drive to try to locate the victims' homes, the granny and the 'gunman' covered a range of topics. The subject of Melbourne's gangland war involving Carl Williams and the Moran clan was a hot topic for Traycevska, as was crime matriarch Kath Pettingill.

TRAYCEVSKA: Did you know Jason Moran, and all those? Did you know all them?

FARNWORTH: Um, yeah ...

TRAYCEVSKA: Do you know the Pettingills?

FARNWORTH: Pettingills? Nah.

TRAYCEVSKA: I knew Kathy a long time ago.

FARNWORTH: What was she like?

TRAYCEVSKA: She's settled down, you know? Going good.

Traycevska talked about her granddaughter—the little girl she was planning on turning into an orphan. 'In August she turns three.' She mentioned her own seven children. Farnworth asked about her favourite music.

TRAYCEVSKA: I like Stevie Nicks.

FARNWORTH: Do ya?

TRAYCEVSKA: Fleetwood Mac ... I still like Midnight Oil.

FARNWORTH: Yeah? Do you like Prince?

TRAYCEVSKA: Yes I do.
FARNWORTH: I love Prince.

Traycevska told Farnworth she was born in Germany to a German father and a Danish mother, who both died in a car crash. She was brought up by her grandparents. 'I haven't had an easy life, you know. I don't dwell on it. Some people have good luck with their lives, you know. They have good lives, some people … Some of us have to battle for it.' There was talk of religion and chats about home cooking.

FARNWORTH: What kind of food do you cook at home?
TRAYCEVSKA: All sorts. I cook a lot of Macedonian food.
FARNWORTH: What's Macedonian food?
TRAYCEVSKA: Those green paprikas.
FARNWORTH: Is that like capsicum or something?
TRAYCEVSKA: They're long and green.
FARNWORTH: Like a chilli?
TRAYCEVSKA: Like that but they're not hot. You can get the sweet ones and you can get the hot ones. Cut 'em up. Fry 'em up with tomatoes and with fetta cheese.
FARNWORTH: Oh, nice.

From fetta and fried tomatoes the conversation wove its way back to triggers and torture. Andrew Oscianko was mentioned again and Natalia Oscianko's demise was confirmed.

TRAYCEVSKA: Drill her knees.
FARNWORTH: Yep.
TRAYCEVSKA: You know what torture is.
FARNWORTH: I do.
TRAYCEVSKA: Yeah. And then bury her.
FARNWORTH: Yeah.
TRAYCEVSKA: Under cement.
FARNWORTH: Yep. Do you want her to be dead first?
TRAYCEVSKA: No.
FARNWORTH: No. Okay. Still alive when I put her …
TRAYCEVSKA: … down. And she'll suffer.
FARNWORTH: Yep. No worries.

TRAYCEVSKA: Michael had to go through that.

FARNWORTH: Yes.

TRAYCEVSKA: Strangulation.

FARNWORTH: Yeah.

TRAYCEVSKA: No breath … But you're sure you can find her?

FARNWORTH: Hundred per cent.

TRAYCEVSKA: You've looked for people before?

FARNWORTH: That's what I do. All the time.

Nearly three hours after having met, Farnworth and Traycevska parted ways. They agreed to meet two days later. Despite the grave nature of the conversation that had just taken place, Traycevska appeared unfazed—not the least bit rattled or concerned. The meeting to organise two murders had been just one of several tasks on her list of things to do that day.

FARNWORTH: What are you gonna do the rest of the day?

TRAYCEVSKA: Probably just fold up the washing that I took off the line yesterday … Um, go and buy some steak for tonight.

FARNWORTH: Oh nice. What are you cooking?

TRAYCEVSKA: I'll cook Scotch fillet … Make some wedges in the deep fry.

FARNWORTH: Yeah.

TRAYCEVSKA: [Use some] sour cream and make a salad.

FARNWORTH: Beautiful.

To confirm the kill plot and guarantee the deposit, Traycevska told Farnworth she would take out a bank loan if all else failed in her efforts to scrape together the money. In the grandmother's mind, the fate of Natalia Oscianko—and her father—was signed, sealed and soon to be delivered.

Natalia Oscianko and Michael Traycevski had moved in together in 2002. A couple of years later, while selling perfume at a stall at the Laverton market, Oscianko met a truck driver named Christoffer Dowsett. He and his de facto wife had a son but were unable to have more children. At that stage Oscianko was four months' pregnant with Michael's child. Not long after the baby was born in 2006, Oscianko visited Dowsett's home and said she wasn't coping. She said the baby wasn't eating or sleeping and that she and Michael were often fighting. Dowsett became involved, and physically fought Michael a couple of times. According to Justice Jack Forrest: 'On at least two occasions you [Dowsett] became involved in physical altercations with [Michael], including striking him with a baseball bat which resulted in him being hospitalised.'

While giving evidence against Oscianko in the Supreme Court, Dowsett would unsuccessfully claim that she told him that Michael 'had to die'. Prosecutor Maitland Lincoln would ask Dowsett if there was any discussion about how Michael should 'meet his death'. Dowsett replied: 'Yes, there was.'

LINCOLN: Who raised that?

DOWSETT: Ms Oscianko did.

Dowsett would claim during Oscianko's murder trial that an early idea to throw Michael off a bridge was hatched but dismissed.

LINCOLN: At some stage did you ever go out and spray-paint a bridge?

DOWSETT: Yes, I did.

LINCOLN: What bridge was it?

DOWSETT: The EJ Whitten Bridge.

LINCOLN: Why was that done?

DOWSETT: Because I was annoyed with Ms Oscianko ringing and complaining all the time. She was that insistent on getting rid of him that I … just to shut her up, went out and sprayed the EJ Whitten Bridge with some markers.

LINCOLN: Can you recall when that was?

DOWSETT: It would have been about, say, three months prior to his death.

And later:

LINCOLN: What part of the bridge was it?

DOWSETT: It probably roughly would have been the highest point of the bridge.

Lincoln asked Dowsett why he marked the bridge.

DOWSETT: Once again, it was in order to keep Ms Oscianko off my back about where we were going to put him.

LINCOLN: And what was the point of marking the bridge? What were you going to use the bridge for?

DOWSETT: To throw him over the edge.

LINCOLN: What did you finally decide?

DOWSETT: I had no intentions of throwing him over there whatsoever at any point. It was merely just to shut her up.

Dowsett would say: 'The whole incident was morally wrong … It would have made a mess at the bottom of the EJ Whitten Bridge.'

In evidence, Dowsett claimed that three final methods of killing Michael were considered.

DOWSETT: One was to shoot him. One was strangulation. One was a drug overdose.

LINCOLN: Were you able to get a gun?

DOWSETT: No.

LINCOLN: What about drugs?

DOWSETT: No.

LINCOLN: What about strangulation?

DOWSETT: Strangulation seemed to be … the lesser way of doing it without much blood or DNA.

LINCOLN: Did you have a discussion? Who raised strangulation?

DOWSETT: Ms Oscianko.

LINCOLN: Did you agree with her?

DOWSETT: Stupidly, yes.

According to Dowsett's unbelieved testimony, it was decided that Michael would be strangled on the night of 14 September 2007 as he slept in his bedroom with a few drinks under his belt. Dowsett told the jury that signage on the side of his panel van was covered with grey duct tape and his number plates altered, and he went to Oscianko and Michael's house.

Dowsett said he jumped on the bed and tried to wrap a cord around Michael's neck.

'That failed. It startled him. He then got up, thrashing his arms and legs around. I then quickly grabbed him—had my forearm around the throat and had him in sort of like a headlock.'

Dowsett claimed that Oscianko sat on top of Michael 'so he couldn't throw any punches'.

LINCOLN: Did Michael Traycevski say anything or shout out anything?

DOWSETT: 'Can't we talk about this?' [and] Ms Oscianko replied: 'It's done. It's over. You've got to go.'

LINCOLN: What did you do next?

DOWSETT: I then proceeded to strangle him.

LINCOLN: Where was Ms Oscianko when you were doing that?

DOWSETT: She left the room.

Dowsett said it took three minutes for Michael to die. He claimed that he and Oscianko dressed Michael's body and carried it to the kitchen before cleaning the bedroom and mopping the dead man's urine from the carpet. 'He released all of his bodily fluids,' Dowsett told the court.

Dowsett also claimed that he was told to write a note saying 'Told you not to fuck with Kellie', as an attempt to frame someone else for the killing. The note was then shoved into a pocket of Michael's tracksuit pants. According to Dowsett's refuted version, he and Oscianko placed the body in his panel van and drove to the EJ Whitten Bridge for a look, before Michael's body was dumped in shrubs next to Hume Road the following night. Two days later, a factory worker on his lunch break came across the body 'lying face down in rocks and prickles'.

In a statement to police, Oscianko said that her car broke down on the night of 14 September and Dowsett drove her to a supermarket where she bought Michael three cans of Jim Beam and cola. She said she and Michael later argued and he stormed out. 'He walked out the front door, which he slammed behind him,' Oscianko said in her police statement. 'This is the last time I saw him or spoke to him.'

She and Dowsett were both charged with murder.

Dowsett pleaded guilty and agreed to give his evidence against Oscianko. Before her murder trial began, Justice Forrest sentenced Dowsett to a maximum fourteen years' jail. That sentence would have been somewhat greater ('well in excess of twenty years' imprisonment') had Dowsett not pleaded guilty and agreed to testify.

'Your actions in the brutal killing of the deceased were premeditated and merciless,' Forrest told Dowsett. 'However, you have agreed to give evidence against your co-accused, Natalia Oscianko, and that fact alone necessitates a reduction of what would have been a very long period of imprisonment.'

Oscianko pleaded not guilty to murder. During her trial, defence barrister Stratton Langslow said the case against her was substantially dependent on Dowsett: a 'tainted witness' who'd done a deal for a reduced sentence in the face of a fail-proof case against him.

LANGSLOW: You were told that the case against you was overwhelming, isn't that right?

DOWSETT: That's right.

LANGSLOW: And one of the things that was absolutely damning against you was this wasn't it—that fingernail scrapings had been taken from the deceased and examined for DNA and your DNA was under the fingernails of the deceased. Isn't that right?

DOWSETT: That's right.

Langslow told the jury:

> There is a great incentive to tell lies to cast blame away and to cut a deal, as it were, and get a benefit. What I want to say to you [the jury] is that you, right from the outset, need to look at the evidence of this man with exceptional care.
>
> It appears that both he and [his de facto partner] coveted [Oscianko's] baby and maybe there is a good deal

> to consider in relation to that … They wouldn't be the first, in effect, to find a way or have a fantasy about how they might be able to obtain another child.

Langslow said the only evidence as to when, where and how the murder took place came from Dowsett:

> He says it took place inside a house. It may have done. It may have taken place outside a house, too. It may be that Dowsett saw an opportunity and caught up with Michael Traycevski and the killing took place and he did it on his own. But there was interest—there is no doubt, it was obvious—there was an interest in Oscianko.
>
> It may be that this fellow who claims for very little reason to have involved himself in the murder really had some fantasy about either taking over Oscianko or taking over Oscianko and the baby that he coveted, and he decided that if they were fighting and carrying on—struggling a bit—that the best way to [stop Michael coming back to Oscianko] so far as Dowsett was concerned was to get rid of this man altogether.

On 3 April 2009, the jury found Natalia Oscianko not guilty of murdering Michael Traycevski. The dead man's family erupted, yelling abuse at Oscianko and the justice system.

On the morning of Friday 24 July 2009, 'hit man' Farnworth again spoke into his secret recording device. It was time to net Petra Traycevska for two counts of incitement to murder. 'I'm about to call the target of this operation,' Farnworth narrated, 'and organise to meet her later today and collect a deposit for the murders of Natalie and Andrew Oscianko. I'll now place that phone call.'

Farnworth organised to meet Traycevska in his vehicle near her home. 'I can see the target standing on the corner,' he recorded. 'The target's got a black handbag.'

The granny hopped in the car and they sat and talked. Farnworth confirmed that she was still committed. The murder of Oscianko, and preferably that of her father as well, was to occur that weekend.

FARNWORTH: Are you a hundred per cent?

TRAYCEVSKA: Hundred per cent I want to go through [with] this thing … I want her extremely just taken off the face of the earth, you know. Disappear. Disappear. You know what I mean.

FARNWORTH: And I will do that.

TRAYCEVSKA: And I want her to suffer … like my son gasped for the last few minutes to breathe.

The plan to shoot Andrew Oscianko was also confirmed.

'Full of bullets. All right. Cool,' Farnworth nodded.

Traycevska handed over a white Westpac Bank envelope containing forty $100 notes. The down payment was complete.

FARNWORTH: Three for Natalia and one for the old fella.

TRAYCEVSKA: Yeah.

FARNWORTH: Yep.

TRAYCEVSKA: I just wanted to show you a picture of my son.

FARNWORTH: Yeah, show us. Gee, he's a good-lookin' young bloke.

TRAYCEVSKA: He was. To be with that thing.

With the plan set in stone—just as Traycevska wanted Natalia Oscianko's body to literally end up—Farnworth put the finishing touches to Operation Coffer. He and Traycevska needed a code to signify that the murders had occurred. It was to be confirmed via a phone call.

'If she's done, I'm gonna go, "Is Nikola home?"' Farnworth decided. 'If they're both done I'll say, um … "Coming around for some cheesecake".'

Traycevska said she would stay home that night, or take a walk up to the shops where people would see and recognise her.

TRAYCEVSKA: Everyone knows me … I've got me granny … I call it the bloody granny trolley.

FARNWORTH: As long as someone sees ya tonight.

The next morning, at about 7.15 am, Traycevska received a knock on her door rather than a telephone call from Farnworth. A group of detectives had arrived. And they weren't there for cheesecake. They were armed with a search warrant and arrested her. They seized a handwritten note with Andrew Oscianko's address on it and two *Herald Sun* articles about Oscianko's murder trial. Traycevska was taken to the Altona North CIU office and participated in a 'No comment' interview. Investigators charged her with two counts of inciting another person to commit murder. She later pleaded guilty.

In a written submission during her Supreme Court plea hearing, Traycevska tried to explain the effect of her son's death on her. Here is the heartbroken mother's submission, in part:

> Homicide detectives came to my home to break the devastating news. That was when the whole world came down on me … I just can't take the picture out of my mind of my son gasping for his last breath. I break down and feel so empty that life and everything in it feels so worthless. When Michael's life was taken, that was the moment my life, my world, my existence was taken. I had to hear that he was initially to be thrown from the EJ Whitten Bridge.
>
> Entering the morgue I screamed [upon] seeing Michael cold and lifeless. I collapsed and I couldn't believe or want to believe in my son being dead. I visited the Altona Cemetery to find a plot for Michael but there was nothing good enough for my boy.

The crux of her plea, in March 2010, was that she was remorseful. She said she felt the justice system had let her down so had tried to 'get justice my way'.

Defence barrister Julie Sutherland said that while she did not condone the rationale, it was Traycevska's 'background' to the offending. According to Sutherland: 'They say that there's no stronger love than a mother's love for a child and I think that's right.'

Justice Paul Coghlan said: 'But to say that the solution is

to take this course when we know so much about so many other people who have been through processes just as bad as this with results they regret in the same way, suffering from the same level of depression and sometimes worse … they do not see that the solution could possibly be that you go out and murder another person.'

Traycevska admitted her actions were 'demonstrably wrong'. 'Even though she still remains disappointed, she has no feelings of wanting to seek revenge in any shape or form against this woman, her family or anyone, for that matter,' Sutherland told Coghlan.

Prosecutor Doug Trapnell, SC, said the proposed torture of Natalia Oscianko was a 'significant aggravating' factor. 'That was not just a throwaway line. It was intended that her death be a painful and lengthy death because of the prisoner's perception of how her own son had died.'

Trapnell described the proposed murder of Andrew Oscianko as 'entirely gratuitous':

> Really, the only reasons she could give for that are to prevent the proposed victim seeking revenge against her because he'd work out who it was that had killed his daughter. There is [also] certainly a reference to the granddaughter and the fact that if the grandfather [Andrew Oscianko] is killed as well as the mother then the prisoner would be able to get custody of the granddaughter, and that clearly is an extremely serious way of perceiving the world.

Coghlan said: 'While understanding all the matters personal, the courts have got to probably say something about you simply can't take the law into your own hands.'

Coghlan said Traycevska's estranged husband had been trying to deal with their son's death in polar opposite fashion to her. 'Due to his Macedonian background, he appears to prefer solitary methods of dealing with his grief over the loss of Michael and takes refuge in alcohol.'

Traycevska's general practioner wrote of her outlook in a report: 'Petra is a very vulnerable person with significant depressive illness complicated by recurrent bereavements and post-traumatic stress syndrome. The stress of prison would be a very great psychological burden for her.'

Justice Coghlan sentenced the granny to a maximum seven years' jail with a minimum four-year term, with the following summing up:

> Your wish to see Ms Oscianko tortured is a matter of aggravation, as is your calculated view that her father should be murdered to prevent revenge, and it may well have been motivated by issues relating to the custody of your granddaughter.
>
> I am satisfied that on the whole of the evidence, you were suffering from a combination of major depression and post-traumatic stress disorder at the time of offending. Those conditions do reduce your moral culpability to a degree. Many people in the community would empathise to some degree with your position, but it cannot be condoned. The aggravating features are important and although your moral culpability is reduced, there is still a need for punishment and denunciation. You simply cannot take the law into your own hands.

7

Who Killed Michael Grech?

A published true-crime author becomes the lead character in a real murder mystery

'He said to me that a person will only go missing over revenge, hate and money, and that's when I told him, "There is money involved".'

CONVICTED ARMED ROBBER TURNED true-crime author Douglas Robinson knows a good murder yarn when he hears one. A former jail mate of 'society murderer' Matthew Wales, Robinson wrote the double killer's biography and sold it over the internet. Entitled *Warts and All*, the book told Wales's account of how and why he drugged and bludgeoned to death his millionaire mother, Margaret Wales-King, and his ailing stepfather, Paul King, before burying them in a shallow rural grave. It was a crime that intrigued the nation. Robinson has written half-a-dozen crime books, but it was the Matthew Wales biography that really put him on the map as a true-crime author.

It was therefore an ironic scene in the Supreme Court in February 2010, when Robinson found himself smack-bang in the middle of a gripping court-room drama involving a blood-soaked murder in Melbourne's western suburbs. Through circumstances sparked by an apparent desire for quick cash, he was charged with murder and thus became a lead character in a seedy story about a dead loan shark, turncoat criminal associates and a litany of lies.

The murder victim in this story is sixty-one-year-old Michael Grech, who worked with his carpenter nephew and ran a money-lending business 'on the side'. 'He would lend amounts of cash, with interest, to friends and associates,' prosecutor Peter Rose, SC, would say in the Supreme Court.

Grech was bashed to death—presumably with a hammer—at a house being rented for the growing of cannabis. His body ended up in a shallow semirural grave.

'In this case there were, on a conservative estimate, eight to ten or more fractures, or blows,' Rose would say. 'It is accepted he was murdered. The issue is who did it.'

The main character is Robinson, a sixty-three-year-old former bandit who, in his own words, turned from the life of a worker to that of a criminal because he 'found he couldn't settle within himself'. While in jail in 2002 he began to write his crime books. 'He's put a lot of work into writing books,' his barrister, Mark Rochford, would say in court. 'He's been interviewed in magazines, [on] television, talkback radio, et cetera, and believed that, coming up to 2005, he was, in his words, "rehabilitated and able to go back into mainstream life as a successful author".' Robinson was charged with Grech's murder.

One of the two other characters is an unemployed crook called David 'Tonto' Campbell. At age forty-nine he carried a conviction for murder. According to consultant psychologist Bernard Healey: 'In view of his just average intellect, limited personality functioning and many years of institutional experience, it was evident that he lacked discretion and interaction with prison associates, to whom he felt a sense of loyalty—never anticipating, however, that he could be involved in such serious matters.'

The last character is an unemployed drug criminal by the name of Corrado 'Corey' Motta, who admitted to a string of prior convictions—most committed because he was on heroin. '[If] that's what you want to call a career criminal, well I'll be embarrassed then, yeah,' the forty-one-year-old would say in court. Asked if he was a dishonest person, Motta said, 'Yeah, I suppose I am.'

Campbell and Motta, despite their histories, were the two key prosecution witnesses in the murder case against Robinson. But, as Rochford would tell the jury, 'The accuracy, the reliability, the credibility, the truthfulness of Motta and Campbell are in issue in this case. Very, very, very much so. I can't stress it enough. You have to accept them to find the Crown case proven.'

Robinson had pleaded not guilty to the charges of murdering Grech by caving his head in with a hammer and stealing two gold chains from his body, but had pleaded guilty to cultivating cannabis. His trial began on 17 February 2010.

'In the twelve months preceding Mr Grech's death, Mr Grech was regularly socialising with both Mr Robinson and Mr Motta,' prosecutor Rose said in his opening at the beginning of the trial.

> The prosecution will say that Mr Robinson was gambling heavily during 2007. He was utilising a self-made gambling system. It's the prosecution case that this gambling habit of his led to the loss of large amounts of money and financial hardship for Mr Robinson, and that between 9 March 2006 and 31 March 2008 Mr Robinson withdrew some $68,210 from his father's pensioner security account with the Commonwealth Bank and gambled away this money.

According to Robinson's older sister, Bette Block, their father had been in nursing-home care for about three years. 'Dad is physically immobile,' she said in a police statement.

> Mentally dad is not always lucid and is not able to speak above a whisper. In April 2002 dad signed over power of

> attorney for both incapacity and financial affairs to both my sister Jean and I.
>
> I have since received documentation from Commonwealth Bank Australia which indicated that dad gave Doug third-party authority to operate his CBA pensioner security account on the 13th of September 2005. I estimate that dad would have had approximately $50,000 in the account at this time. As of September 2005 Doug had been visiting dad in the nursing home on a regular basis. Approximately early March [in 2008] my sister received a letter requesting her to sign a new contract for dad's residency and care as a guarantor. I went to the CBA and picked up bank statements for dad's pensioner security account for the previous two years. Dad's latest statement showed a balance of $7.38. I then checked through all the statements and saw numerous large withdrawals. I found forty-four withdrawals from dad's account by Doug totalling $68,210.

Peter Rose told the jury that, in August 2007, Robinson and Motta went to Grech's home where Robinson signed a contract to borrow $15,000 in cash—with $3750 interest.

Motta witnessed Robinson sign the statutory declaration binding him to the terms of the loan. Motta then signed the document as a witness. 'I believe he picked up the money the next day or a couple of days later,' Motta would say in court. 'He came to my place and basically said, "I got fifteen grand. Are you coming to the casino with me?" He lost nine thousand of it within three days.'

Rose told the jury that Robinson had agreed to sign over to Grech the total percentage of his inheritance upon his father's death should he fail to meet Grech's repayment deadline. According to Motta, Robinson had come looking for a separate loan from him around August 2007. '[He said] basically he wanted a loan—a $30,000 loan—because he's got a system on at the casino that cannot lose. Yeah, foolproof.' When asked if he knew of any losses Robinson had allegedly incurred using the system, Motta said: 'He lost $40,000 one night, with a friend of his.'

ROSE: Did he indicate to you that he was still trying to go back and have a successful system?

MOTTA: Wasn't actually chasing the money but couldn't lose, basically … yeah.

ROSE: Later on, what did he tell you about the money he'd got?

MOTTA: That the money was coming from his dad's account.

ROSE: Did you ever go gambling with him on occasion at the casino?

MOTTA: I did a couple of days, yes.

ROSE: Was he a winner or a loser?

MOTTA: Loser.

A good mate of both Grech and Robinson, a builder by the name of Neil Scott, would tell the Supreme Court that he was also aware of Robinson's gambling habits.

> Doug had a system which was playing pretty much the odds and evens—fifty/fifty type stuff—and his idea was that if he was to make a single bet and was to lose it, he could then double up with two people and eventually retrieve and make money … Every time I saw Doug, he lost.

It was in September 2007 that Robinson and Campbell agreed to go into business with Motta to grow a hydroponic cannabis crop at a rental property. Using fake employment and bogus landlord references, Campbell rented a farmhouse on Coburns Road in the western suburb of Melton on the outskirts of Melbourne.

'He just asked me if I'd be interested in growing or helping him grow a marijuana crop and we could both make a bit of money out of it,' Campbell told the jury.

> Initially I told him that I didn't have the sort of money that would be necessary for that sort of an enterprise and he said that I didn't have to worry about money—that everything would be paid for and he'd finance it and I was just basically going to be a house-sitter.

In crucial evidence that would effectively sink the Crown's murder case against Robinson, Campbell told the jury that 'it was either right at the end of October or it was maybe 1 November' when the real estate agency informed him that he'd been granted the Coburns Road lease. According to Campbell's testimony, equipment was brought in to grow marijuana plants but the operation initially stalled due to a disagreement over the size of the crop.

> The argument was mainly about the amount of dope we were going to grow. Doug wanted to fill the whole house up, because we had rather a sizeable house—I think it was about four bedrooms or something—and Doug wanted to put a power box at each end of the house and just basically fill the whole joint up. But me and Corey only wanted to do a dozen to maybe sixteen plants tops.
>
> We had set up a test of four plants. We didn't have any chemicals or anything to put in it. We just put water in it.

ROSE: Did Mr Robinson express any reason to you as to why he wanted to go so big?

CAMPBELL: He needed money pretty quick.

ROSE: Did he say why he needed the money?

CAMPBELL: He owed a fellow a sizeable amount of money.

ROSE: Do you know who that person was?

CAMPBELL: The name Michael Grech was mentioned … He said that he had a deadline coming up. I think it was the following month. He'd borrowed an amount off him, I think it was around about fifteen thousand and he had to pay back three $10,000 instalments to Grech.

ROSE: At some later stage did you have any discussion with Mr Robinson about the debt and how he might get the money to pay back the debt?'

CAMPBELL: He made mention once when we were out at the farm … about owing money and was saying that he had several options that he could think of as to how to get the debt either paid or whatever. He came up with several options about how he could commit an armed robbery or he could do over a jewellery place or he could actually get rid of the debt altogether by getting rid of Mr Grech … Me and Corey, we weren't interested in stuff like that. We just wanted to grow dope.

Motta said in evidence that he believed Grech was killed 'under a month' after they started renting the Melton house.

> There was a lot of Sundays we used to go down [to the property] and Doug used to basically call them 'meetings'. They were basically a waste of time, really. But one Sunday, yeah, not long before Michael's death … yeah, there was a discussion.
>
> [It was] basically about the house and then he brought up, 'I owe Michael money', and I sort of bit me tongue because I'd given him a bit over $14,000 to pay the debt off. I suppose I realised that he'd gone back and blown that at the casino as well.
>
> It must have been at this stage where there was armed robberies—an armed robbery talked about—a diamond place up near his way … Dave basically came out with, 'Why don't you just put a bullet in his head?' Didn't take it too serious, but.

Under cross-examination, Campbell said he meant nothing by the comment. 'It is just a conversation-ending line that I use,' he told the jury.

Before Grech met his death, according to Campbell, Robinson drove him to bushland in a suburb called Toolern Vale, near Melton. 'He showed me an area at the bottom of a gully and asked me if this would be a good spot to hide something that wouldn't be found easily,' Campbell claimed.

ROSE: Did he indicate to you what he had in mind to hide?
CAMPBELL: No.

At about 8.30 pm on the night of Monday 19 November 2007, Grech and Robinson spoke on the phone and arranged to meet. Grech's nephew, Jeffrey Zammit, dropped Grech off at his home and was to pick him up for work the following morning. 'I was to pick him up between seven and quarter-past seven like normal and go back to the job site,' Zammit would say in court.

Robinson, meanwhile, had travelled to Motta's home. According to prosecutor Rose: 'They'd made an arrangement to attend at Coburns Road in company with Mr Grech that night, and it was ostensibly for the purpose of discussing whether or not Mr Grech was interested in funding the hydroponic crop.'

Campbell claimed that he was of the belief that Robinson was bringing more hydro equipment to the house. 'I was waiting for Doug to bring some gear out—tubs, lights, chemicals and things like that. I was supposed to be out at the property and I was supposed to wait for Doug and give him a hand to get the stuff out of the car.'

According to Motta, he and Robinson picked Grech up. 'Doug was driving, Michael was in the front seat and I sat in the back. I remember that while Doug was driving he sent a text.'

Campbell told the court that he was in bed when he received the text message at about 11 pm saying, 'We're on, open up', to which he replied, 'Gate's open', before going back to sleep. The court heard that Robinson, Motta and Grech arrived at the Melton property where Grech then met his demise.

'It's the prosecution case that Mr Robinson struck Grech to the head with a hammer, causing him to fall to the ground,' Rose told the trial. 'He then continued to strike Mr Grech to the head with multiple blows—and it's these blows it is said that killed Mr Grech.'

Motta alleged that he heard a 'real weird noise' and, after running around the house, saw 'Doug going to town on Mick, basically'.

Campbell told the jury:

> There was a heap of banging on the back sliding door and a voice saying, 'Dave. Dave where are you?' That woke me

up … I got up and I went around to the laundry door and opened up the laundry door and there was Doug to my right covered in, well, had blood all over him holding a hammer and a fellow lying at his feet on the ground.

ROSE: Was Mr Robinson doing anything with the hammer at that stage?

CAMPBELL: No, he was just standing there with it.

ROSE: Can you tell us as best you can where the blood was and on whom or what?

CAMPBELL: Blood was all over the bloody place. There was a big pool of blood on the ground near, under and around Mr Grech's body and there was blood all over the front of my car and there was blood over the walls, the sliding door area and the windows. It was just sort of all over the place.

ROSE: What happens then? Was anything said between the three of you?

CAMPBELL: I've walked out and I've seen this and I've gone … excuse the language but, 'What the fuck have you done? What's going on?' That sort of thing.

ROSE: Has Mr Robinson responded?

CAMPBELL: He just said sort of like, 'Just help me clean this mess up. Don't concern yourself too much.'

Campbell claimed that Robinson dropped the hammer and entered the house through the laundry—before walking back out to take off his blood-stained shoes. 'He was carrying on about microscopic bits of DNA and stuff like that,' Campbell alleged.

It was alleged that Robinson went back inside and returned with plastic, before asking Campbell to move his car. 'He asked me and Corey to give him a hand to move the body onto the plastic,' Campbell claimed. 'I just said, "No. My back's buggered. I can't lift anything … I won't be doing that." He said, "Well, if you're not going to help, fuck off and stay out of the way."'

Motta claimed he helped Robinson roll the plastic up around Grech. 'I basically give him a hand,' Motta told the jury. 'He [Robinson] sticky-taped the top part of the plastic and the bottom part of the plastic to the bulk of the body.'

Campbell said that when he walked back in to the carport after going inside the house, the body was almost wrapped. 'Doug got some black nylon cord and proceeded to tie it around the plastic top and bottom and middle,' Campbell told the jury.

> [Doug] and Corey picked it up and put it in the boot of the car … A bit of a search went on under the carport, having a look around and this and that and the next thing, picking things up that may have fallen and we actually, we went back inside for a short time. Doug had a heap of cash that he'd picked up … he'd either taken it off Mr Grech or it had fallen on the ground or something. But he had a heap of cash. He counted it out. It was about two thousand dollars, and he put it in his pocket. [He] had a black phone … and took that out into the carport and smashed it under his foot, picked the pieces up and put it in his car and just said that everything has to go, nothing can be left behind and had a look around, picked a hammer up and then picked another hammer up that I hadn't seen earlier. A wooden-handled hammer. The head and the handle were separate. It had broken, and [he] put them in a garbage bag and chucked them in his car and said to me to stay and clean the place up as best I could and that he'd be back shortly.
>
> He and Corey jumped in the car and left … I grabbed the hose and a broom and I proceeded to wash down the walls, the pavers and wash the blood away and scrub it with a brush.

In cross-examination, Rochford asked Campbell why he did not ring the police or jump in his car and 'hightail it out of there' if the murder had happened as described.

'I didn't know what to do,' Campbell claimed.

Later, when asked why he failed to alert police after Grech's disappearance was announced on the news, Campbell said: 'I had no proof. I had no evidence of any sort.'

Motta told the jury that he travelled with Robinson to

dispose of the body. 'I wasn't very comfortable but basically I was a robot,' he claimed in court. According to Motta, a hole had already been dug at the secluded burial site and covered with corrugated tin.

> I was supposed to be helping carry [Grech]. I suppose I couldn't have done a good job because the plastic ended up in my hands before we got there. The plastic's just hanging on. He [Robinson] has dropped Michael in and put dirt over it. We put dirt over the top. I could not take my eyes off Doug. For some reason I thought I was next.
>
> On the way home I was basically asking him why he went that far.

JUSTICE COGHLAN: Did he reply to that?
MOTTA: He didn't have a choice.
ROSE: Did he say why he didn't have a choice?
MOTTA: I assumed he was talking about the money.

Coghlan homed in on what would prove a crucial element in the case.

COGHLAN: Mr Motta, how long before this night—that's 19 November or perhaps by now the early hours of 20 November—was it that you'd been out to that [Toolern Vale] site with Mr Robinson?

MOTTA: How often?

COGHLAN: No, how long before that night was it you'd been out to that site? You told us that the three of you went out there at some stage and you talked about that being the spot where the equipment and so on would be left. How long was that prior to the night of 19 November?

MOTTA: We actually went there within the first week of getting the house.

COGHLAN: Yes, but how long was that prior to the murder?

MOTTA: Two, three weeks, I believe.

Coghlan was told Robinson had a shower back at the Melton property after the burial and changed into one of

Campbell's clean T-shirts. Campbell said discarded clothing went into a 44-gallon drum at the property and was later set alight.

The morning after the murder, Jeffrey Zammit pulled up outside his uncle's home and sounded his car horn a couple of times. When Grech failed to appear, Zammit rang him on his mobile. He knocked on the door, thinking Grech must have slept in and not heard the call. There was, of course, no one home. Later that day Zammit returned and broke in through a laundry window. He found his uncle's wallet. The next day he became concerned and rang Robinson.

Zammit explained in evidence:

> I said to him, 'Have you seen my uncle in the last couple of days?' He goes, 'No.' And I go, 'Well, Monday you were supposed to meet him, you know,' and he goes, 'Oh, I was supposed to but you come home late blah, blah, blah.' And I go, 'Well, the last time I spoke to my uncle it was at ten o'clock and he said that you were still coming over.'

Zammit went to the Keilor Downs police station and reported his uncle missing. That night, he said, he met with Robinson at the Kentucky Fried Chicken store near Melbourne's Westgate Bridge.

> I was a bit worried because he was the last person to see my uncle. He walked in first and then he looked up and he seen the [security] camera up ahead so he turned around and sat [with his] back to the camera and I go, 'Why did you do that?' and he goes, 'We've got a smart one here, have we?' Then he just put his hand in his shirt and I didn't know what he was going to do. He pulled out a wad of money and threw it on the table and said, 'I don't need money.'

According to Zammit, the money was a wad of $100 notes with a Crown Casino wrapper around them.

> I said to Doug, 'Why should I think you haven't got nothing to do with my uncle being missing?' He goes, 'Oh no, youse worked too late. I didn't come and see him,' or something like that. He said to me that a person will only go missing over revenge, hate and money, and that's when I told him, 'There is money involved.' He said, 'I paid your uncle all the money that I owed him.'
>
> He said to me that he lent money off my uncle … he had some sort of system in the roulette at the casino. He said he had a bad run or something and that's about it.

Under cross-examination, Zammit would admit that Robinson told him to ring the police about the apparent disappearance.

ROCHFORD: He went on to say that in relation to your uncle, that he loved the bloke. [He said] 'We were a tight group.' Do you agree with that?

ZAMMIT: Yes, he did.

Neil Scott told the court he met with Robinson at his house on 22 November—three days after Grech was killed.

> When Robinson turned up I was actually quite concerned at that particular point. I didn't want him in the house and arranged to go down the pub to have a discussion with him. The nature of the discussion was what had happened to Michael and the first words that Doug said to me when we went into the pub was, 'I know what you're thinking. I didn't knock off Mick.'

In Campbell's final version of events that he settled on in court, he said he returned to the Toolern Vale site in December on Robinson's request to look for 'clones' that may have been 'dropped off out there'. 'Clones are cuttings of a main marijuana plant,' Campbell explained. 'It had been raining pretty heavily and when I got out there the place just looked like a lake.'

Campbell claimed that he returned about a week or so later and came across part of an exposed knee jutting up through the earth. He told the jury that he 'didn't know where the body was' up until that point in time.

'I shit myself, basically. I was sort of having a look around to see who was watching and what was going on. The only thing I could think of doing at the time was to go to my car, get a shovel and cover it up.'

Rochford would ask Campbell why he did that.

'I panicked,' Campbell said. 'I needed time to think.'

Campbell would even admit to returning to the area to look for clone plants on another occasion. Rochford did not entertain that claim.

ROCHFORD: After you've told him [Robinson] that the knee was exposed, are you seriously suggesting that he's saying to you he's arranged to have some clones put there for you to pick up? Of all the places in the world, that spot there? Is that right?

CAMPBELL: Well, the knee had been covered up. It hadn't rained since. There was no reason to think that that had happened again.

During the trial Campbell claimed that, in the week following Grech's death, a Stanley knife was purchased from Bunnings and used to cut up carpet inside the Melton home. He said brick pavers in the carport were also of concern.

'I'd cleaned them as best I could and a few days later Doug had arranged to meet out there so that we could go over the pavers, the walls, the windows again,' Campbell said in court. 'He had bleach and stuff with him and we did it all again, and then at the end of that he decided they [the pavers] had to go anyway.'

James Pastou, a smoking and coffee-drinking buddy of Motta, provided a tip truck and helped Motta pull up the brick pavers, for which Robinson paid him. 'Campbell was too fat and too tired to pull up anything,' Pastou would tell the court. 'All he did was made coffees for us.' To replace the pavers, Campbell bought crushed rock from a nearby garden supplies outlet.

After he and Robinson sold two of Grech's gold chains to a jewellery shop for $1300, Campbell contacted the police through an acquaintance in the Fisheries Department. Detectives located Grech's decomposing body in the shallow grave on 12 April 2008. Pathologist Professor Stephen Cordner found that the cause of Grech's death was 'consistent with multiple skull fractures caused by numerous blows to the skull vault and face with a blunt implement'. Campbell and Motta were arrested and charged with assisting offender by being accessories after the fact to murder. They were also charged with cultivating a narcotic plant. Robinson was arrested and charged with murder and other offences.

As a chef would a raw onion, Rochford peeled away Campbell and Motta's credibility during Robinson's trial. While cross-examining Campbell first, he established him to the jury as a man who originally lied to police.

ROCHFORD: Your attitude was, wasn't it, 'I'm going to tell them [the police] everything that happened', correct?

CAMPBELL: More or less.

ROCHFORD: Well, is that correct or not, Mr Campbell?

CAMPBELL: Well, yes.

ROCHFORD: But you didn't, did you?

CAMPBELL: No.

ROCHFORD: You left things out, didn't you.

CAMPBELL: Yep.

ROCHFORD: You lied to them, didn't you.

CAMPBELL: Yep.

ROCHFORD: Made things up, didn't you.

CAMPBELL: Yep ... I was trying to minimise my own part in what was going on. I wasn't doing a very good job of it.

Rochford also established that, according to a real estate agent's pre-tenancy report and a signed contract, Campbell did not take control of the Coburns Road rental property in Melton until 17 November—only two days before the murder. That meant events that were said to have happened in the weeks leading up to the killing—the arrival of drug equipment, the Sunday meetings at the property and visits to the Toolern Vale bush site—could not have happened as described. Rochford showed Campbell the signed pre-tenancy condition report during the trial.

ROCHFORD: It says the inspection date was 15 November 2007, the agent's name being C Cartwright. Do you agree with that?

CAMPBELL: That's what it says but the date's wrong.

ROCHFORD: It says that you commenced tenancy on 17 November 2007, doesn't it?

CAMPBELL: It says that but it's wrong.

ROCHFORD: You've signed that document and you agree with that, don't you?

CAMPBELL: Yes.

Rochford even showed Campbell photographs—dated 15 November 2007—taken during the pre-tenant condition check. 'The camera's wrong,' was all Campbell could offer. 'The settings on the dates and times are wrong on the camera. There's no way known these dates are right. Not possible.'

Property rental manager Catherine Cartwright testified that the pre-tenancy inspection was definitely carried out on 15 November. 'We do not release keys until a tenant has actually signed their lease and paid over bond monies,' she said. 'He had an appointment for 3.30 on the 16th of November, the lease starting on the 17th of November.'

Rochford revealed to the jury that, on the night Grech was killed, Campbell was on parole for 'an execution-style killing where a person had been taken out into the bush and shot in the head'. (In 1984, Campbell had been charged with murder and in August 1987 he was sentenced to life imprisonment with a minimum eighteen-year term. He was released from jail on parole in April 2004.)

Rochford also took Motta to task about the timing of the lease. Rochford suggested that the trio would not have had hydro equipment and test cannabis plants growing in the house if an estate agent was coming to check the property and take photos. 'No, I've got that wrong, haven't I,' Motta would say.

It was Rochford's submission that Motta was the man who killed Grech. He submitted that all three of the men played a part in either the transportation or burial of the body.

Motta strenuously denied the allegation that he killed Grech.

Rochford also established that Motta's initial versions of events to police were lies. 'I lied about a few things … because I was scared,' Motta said.

ROCHFORD: So you didn't see him hit Mick two or three times in the head area with the thing he had in his hands? Is that right?

MOTTA: No, I didn't. No …

ROCHFORD: So, you will just tell them [the police] anything that pops into your head, will you?

MOTTA: First couple of interviews—well, I basically said the truth but danced around a little bit.

ROCHFORD: Talking about dancing, did you ever say you saw Mr Campbell doing an Indian rain dance?

MOTTA: Yes, I did.

ROCHFORD: On the grave?

MOTTA: Because I remember he did it on another day. It just stuck in my head, but it wasn't on the grave site. No.

ROCHFORD: You just made that up, did you?

MOTTA: Yes, I did.

ROCHFORD: Complete rubbish?

MOTTA: Yes.

Despite admitting he lied to police, Motta told the jury he was telling *them* the truth. 'The reason I've done what I'm doing today [by giving evidence] is, well, the truth's got to come out and I'm not going to get blamed for something I didn't do,' he told the jury.

But Rochford did blame him, alleging he killed Grech by hitting him in the head with the hammer 'until it broke'.

'I never hit anyone in the head with a hammer,' Motta said. 'Why the hell would I kill Mr Grech?'

Rochford suggested: 'Because you were upset with him about the drug dealing that you had been doing with him.'

Motta replied: 'No … so how many dealers would I have killed in the past, then?'

In a direction to the jury, Coghlan said Campbell and Motta were witnesses who may have had something to gain by testifying in the manner they did. 'Their evidence in particular needs to be subjected to very close scrutiny indeed,' Coghlan said.

> You ought consider … the great difficulties that arise in their evidence, particularly out of the fact of the occupation of the house no earlier than the 15th at the absolute earliest and probably the 16th—with it being absolutely certain that the murder occurred on the 19th—and how what are said to be quite important features of the case fit in with that, particularly any trips in advance that might have been made out to the grave site.

Prior to Robinson's trial, Campbell and Motta had pleaded guilty to being accessories after the fact to murder and were jailed for their cover-up. At the duo's sentencing Coghlan had said:

> In your case, Campbell, you are to be sentenced on the basis of assistance you gave on the night of the murder, the burning of the clothes, as well as your cleaning up of the premises, your subsequent actions in assisting with removing any evidence of the deceased's death from the Coburns Road house by washing and removing the pavers, your visits to the makeshift grave and your effort to secrete the body of the deceased.
>
> In your case, Motta, you are to be sentenced on the basis of assisting in wrapping up the deceased's body and placing it in the boot of Robinson's car, then going to the burial site with Robinson and assisting in the burial of the deceased's body. You also have admitted to removing the bloodstained pavers from the Coburns Road house.

In his closing address during Robinson's trial, Peter Rose said it was not in dispute that Grech was bludgeoned to death at the Melton property on 19 November 2007, in the presence of

Robinson, Campbell and Motta—before his body was buried in the shallow grave.

'The only evidence that you have before you as to who carried out the killing is that of Mr Motta and Mr Campbell,' Rose told the jury.

> Both have at times, in their early dealings with police to protect themselves or others, given false accounts of what happened. They've admitted that. It's a matter for you, ladies and gentlemen of the jury, as to whether or not you accept when they gave evidence before you that they were doing their best to tell the truth—particularly on the essential issue as to who killed Mr Grech. There is no evidence that Mr Motta or Mr Campbell was the perpetrator involved in the killing of Mr Grech.

Rochford's message was simple:

> The Crown case is a mess … I'm going to show my age here, ladies and gentlemen, because when I was younger there used to be shows on TV like *Perry Mason* and now it's all *Law & Order* and *Special Victims Unit* and *CSI* and it's all about the prosecution and the investigation, et cetera. But Perry Mason, he used to get people in the witness box and break them down and they'd confess in the witness box. But this isn't TV land. This is the real world. Do you really think that Mr Motta and Mr Campbell, if they had killed Mr Grech, were going to confess to it here because they were just asked about it by me? 'Oh yeah, I'll come clean. You've got me. Yeah, I did it.' Is that really going to happen? They are unreliable witnesses.

The jury acquitted Robinson of murdering Michael Grech, but found him guilty on the lesser charge of assisting offender in that he was an accessory after the fact to murder. Before Robinson was sentenced, Coghlan and Rochford agreed that he should probably stick to writing about crime rather than committing any more of it.

COGHLAN: He looks a persistent more than a successful armed robber, I must say, in terms of his prior convictions.

ROCHFORD: He keeps on getting caught.

COGHLAN: He kept getting caught, yes … and I don't expect him to tell us about any he didn't get caught for, but there are plenty that he did get caught for and got decent sentences for.

ROCHFORD: He's mixing with the same old people, the same old groups and it's one of the …

COGHLAN: One of the conundrums.

ROCHFORD: Yes, one of the difficulties with the system. Once you get out [of prison], if you're an old lag, who do you hang around with? Mr Grech was the same. He's associating with people that he knew from jail. It's the way society often works.

Coghlan sentenced Robinson on 8 April 2010, saying he had a 'long but seemingly unsuccessful criminal history' from 1967 to 1996. He served his first jail term in 1968. Robinson's priors included dishonesty offences and six armed robbery convictions, for which he received lengthy sentences. He also had form for assault and firearm offences.

'You have, however, achieved some success since your last release from prison in December 2004 by becoming a published author of true-crime books,' Coghlan said. 'The financial rewards, however, have been modest. After your latest release you also seemed intent upon making money out of a system which you devised for the playing of roulette. Like all such systems it was ultimately unsuccessful.'

Of Grech's death Coghlan said: 'Almost immediately on arrival [at Coburns Road] Michael Grech was murdered by being beaten to death with a hammer. It is not possible to say how or at whose hand he met his death. In [Campbell and Motta's] case you were the offender. In your case, either or both of them are the offender. Nobody has been convicted of a murder which must have been committed by one or more of you.

'Just what happened at Coburn's Road is not known, and perhaps it never will be known.'

8 Hell Boy

The anatomy of a bikie's city gun rampage, six days after a wild night with an AFL star

'Although anabolic steroid abuse and the lifestyle led by Mr Hudson suggest narcissistic and antisocial features, it is more likely that he was seduced by the lifestyle offered by joining motorcycle gangs.'

COLLINGWOOD FOOTBALL CLUB STAR Alan Didak didn't know it at the time, but he was playing with fire the night he took a drink from a stranger inside Melbourne's upmarket Spearmint Rhino strip club in the city. A recognisable AFL gun, Didak was out on the town a little later than his club would have preferred. It was after 1 am on Tuesday 12 June 2007—more than eight hours after Didak had played a blinder against the Melbourne Demons in the Queen's Birthday weekend AFL clash at the Melbourne Cricket Ground. Having started drinking at 9 pm, Didak was now on a blinder of a different kind as nubile women worked the shiny poles around him. Didak and mate Colin Sylvia—a Demons footballer—had started at the Bar 20 strip club in King Street before moving down to the Spearmint Rhino club to continue drinking amongst the flesh.

'At some stage one of the waitresses came up to Colin and I and told us that a guy wanted to buy us a drink,' Didak would recall to police. 'I was drinking vodka, lime and soda most of the night mixed up with bourbon and coke and a few shots in between. The drink that the waitress poured me on this occasion was a bourbon and coke.'

The Collingwood footballer asked who'd ordered it. He was directed to a man sitting on a nearby couch. The man was apparently a fan.

'I would describe this guy as a big lad,' Didak told police. 'I went over and thanked him for the drink. The guy introduced himself as Huddo. I remember speaking to Huddo for a bit about the game that day and football in general.'

Sylvia had to be helped from the club by bouncers but Didak stayed with his new-found friend and the two continued to drink. When Didak said it was time for him to go, Huddo offered him a lift home. The two walked to a black Mercedes-Benz coupé parked in a side street nearby.

'The car was pretty shmick,' Didak would later comment.

Unbeknown to Didak, Huddo was, in fact, twenty-nine-year-old Christopher Wayne Hudson—a fully patched member of the Hell's Angels outlaw motorcycle gang.

'I'm not sure if Huddo told me he was a Hell's Angel or I just assumed he was from a tattoo I saw on his forearm,' Didak said in his police statement. 'I'm pretty sure the tattoo just said Hell's Angel. By this stage I started to become a bit concerned because I didn't really know what was going to happen.'

While driving across the Bolte Bridge with music blaring, Hudson pulled a black handgun from near his right leg. 'He held the gun in his right hand and showed it to me,' Didak told police. 'I didn't know what to do. I didn't want to upset Huddo in any way, so I sort of gave him a half smile to acknowledge the fact that he had the handgun.'

Didak's predicament worsened when Hudson pointed the gun out his open window and let a few rounds go.

'Even though the music was blaring I could hear Huddo firing shots from the handgun,' the Collingwood star said in his statement. 'I don't remember how many shots Huddo fired but by this stage I was shitting myself. We then continued along the freeway. I had no idea where we were going or what suburbs we were going through, but we were travelling away from the city.'

Instead of pointing towards home, Hudson and Didak were headed for the Hell's Angels East County clubhouse in the outer western suburb of Campbellfield. Like most outlaw bikie clubhouses, it was nestled in an industrial estate. Another club member opened the door to let them in. The three sat at the clubhouse bar and drank more bourbon.

'I can't remember if I had another drink or another three—but about half an hour later I told Huddo I had to go,' Didak would tell police.

Didak piled into the Mercedes with the two bikies. He was in the back seat. Huddo was driving, with the other bikie riding shotgun next to him. 'I remember travelling on the freeway and Huddo driving like a lunatic,' Didak said. 'He was constantly changing lanes and speeding, and at one stage I sat forward and asked Huddo to slow down. Huddo just laughed it off and ignored me.'

At 4.45 am police constables Christina Wallis and Steve De Giorgio, in a divisional van with call sign Broadmeadows 311, saw the Mercedes speed through a red light. Wallis took off in pursuit but couldn't catch the vehicle. To try to lose the cops, Hudson parked hidden for a couple of minutes before hitting the road again. When Wallis and De Giorgio saw him fishtail back onto the road they commenced another pursuit. 'The vehicle was again travelling at a fast rate and in an erratic manner,' Wallis later said. 'There were two vehicles ahead of the [Mercedes] this time and it was weaving around the vehicles.'

A driver of one of those cars, Robert Hemmings, would tell police he saw three people in the Mercedes. 'The person in the back was sitting upright in the middle between the two bucket seats.' The driver of the other vehicle, Mathew Chase, would say: 'I remember thinking the person in the back seat would be in trouble if they crashed the car, driving the way they were.'

Hemmings said the Mercedes swerved 'aggressively' and overtook him before cutting straight in front of him at 160 kilometres an hour. Constable Wallis, still in pursuit, said it was around that time that the driver of the Mercedes fired three gunshots out his window.

'I was quite shocked at what I was observing,' the policewoman said in her statement. 'I could see the flash in the air.' She said the Mercedes continued to travel 'very fast and erratically'.

> The vehicle has then stopped approximately twenty metres ahead of us in the middle of the road … on a slight angle. The person [driving] has then put his arm out the window. I saw the person fire three shots in quick succession. I could see the muzzle flash from the firearm. He didn't appear to be shooting at us. However, I felt it was a direct warning for us not to come any closer.

De Giorgio said: 'It appeared as if he was warning us off.'

Hudson then sped towards the CBD, outrunning the police van on his way. At about 5 am he pulled up close to the Victoria Police Centre in Flinders Street. Emergency Services Communications Officer Mark McDonald was outside the police building having a cigarette. Loud music coming from inside the Mercedes drew his attention to the car. 'It was extremely loud,' McDonald later remembered. 'I couldn't tell what sort of music it was but it sounded like "thump thump, boom boom".' McDonald said three men got out of the sleek vehicle and appeared to talk for about two minutes, before Didak was sent on his way.

> It seemed as though he was being motioned away because they'd had enough of him … He didn't appear distressed or worried in any way. He didn't act as though something bad had happened and that he needed police assistance. The Melbourne West police station was right in front of him and he could have gone there if he wanted to.

McDonald said Didak had a conversation with a cab driver at a set of lights. 'He waved an amount of money at the driver. The driver appeared to ignore him and drove off.'

Police constables Peter Maynard and Joe Anderson were driving past the station in their divisional van and recognised Didak. The footballer waved at them to stop. The cops pulled over. It was 5.20 am. According to the officers, they had the following conversation with the footballer:

MAYNARD: Alan, what are you doing out so late?

DIDAK: I've been out drinking with some mates.

MAYNARD: And what are you doing standing out here?

DIDAK: I've been standing out here in the cold for an hour trying to catch a taxi but none will stop. Can you guys give me a lift home?

MAYNARD: Where do you live?

Didak told them his suburb.

MAYNARD: I would, mate, if you didn't live so far away. I'd need to get permission from the boss to go that far out of my patch and I don't think he'd say yes.

ANDERSON: Crown [Casino] is just around the corner. Why don't you walk there? You've got a better chance of getting a taxi there than you have here.

DIDAK: How far away is that? I'm freezing my arse off.

ANDERSON: It's a five-minute walk, mate …

DIDAK: Fair enough. You guys can't give me a lift, though?

ANDERSON: Sorry, mate. You'll need to walk over and catch a cab.

DIDAK: Well, thanks anyway, guys.

Maynard would later say of Didak:

> His manner was good. He appeared to have been drinking but was not intoxicated. His speech was not slurred, although you could smell intoxicating liquor on his breath. I did not feel it was appropriate to give Didak a lift home or have him lodged for drunk for his safety. Didak did not

state who the people were that he had been drinking with or what establishments he had been at.

When later interviewed by detectives, Didak would only mention the Bolte Bridge shooting incident. He said nothing of the police pursuit and shots being fired in Campbellfield. 'I don't remember any further incidents involving Huddo and the handgun apart from the [Bolte Bridge] incident that I have already described,' he would say. 'I was fairly well intoxicated. Over the next few days I discussed what had occurred with a few close mates from the [football] club. I had considered going to the club and telling them about the incident but I was scared and just didn't have the guts to go through with it.'

Six days after showing off in front of Didak and warning off police with a volley of gunshots, Chris Hudson—burning on amphetamines and armed with the same .40 calibre pistol—would unleash all hell in the Melbourne CBD. It would be a morning that would shock the city to its core.

Hudson, born in Tweed Heads in northern New South Wales on 24 May 1978, first found himself in trouble for truancy. A bloke who'd struggled with literary skills at school, he started a plastering apprenticeship with his father's business and worked as a Gold Coast nightclub bouncer. He would tell forensic psychologist Jeffrey Cummins that it was while bouncing that he started using designer drugs. 'Through his association with the nightclub industry, he was introduced to ecstasy, cocaine and amphetamines at around age nineteen/twenty,' Cummins stated in a report. 'Shortly later he was introduced to crystal amphetamine.'

Hudson joined the Finks outlaw motorcycle club in about 1998. The Finks are renowned for their stronghold on the Surfers Paradise nightclub scene and its lucrative drug profits. Around late 2004 Hudson defected, or 'patched over', to become a member of the much mightier Hell's Angels gang. During his time as a bikie he had several aliases, including Paul Richard Lewis and Milan Radmanovic. The offences he committed included assault occasioning bodily harm and weapons offences in Queensland; and grievous bodily harm, assault and destroying property in New South Wales, for which he was jailed for a minimum of eight months. Other offences included drug possession and fraud. It was his defection from the Finks to the Angels—or fury over a stolen sapphire—that sparked a wild brawl at a kickboxing tournament at the Royal Pines Resort near the Gold Coast in March 2006. The all-in—involving fists, feet, bottles, chairs and other weapons—was nicknamed the 'ballroom blitz'. A Finks member shot Hudson in the jaw and the back. Other bikies were shot and stabbed. According to Cummins's report: 'He said [that] following the shooting incident of 2006 he became a very heavy and often daily user of amphetamines and crystal amphetamine. He said he would then sometimes also use Xanax as a "downer".'

Hudson also started carrying a gun. Cummins: 'He admitted at interview [that] he was intermittently in the habit of carrying a firearm as a result of having been shot in the jaw at the affray at a kickboxing event.'

Consultant psychiatrist Dr Danny Sullivan would make the following report on behalf of Hudson:

> After being assaulted in 2006 he had increasingly used speed and ice—snorting and smoking but not injecting. He related to me that he would use up to two grams per day and would take this for up to a week at a time before he needed to sleep for a couple of days. He told me he would use up to half an ounce of amphetamines over this period. He reported that he enjoyed feeling 'up', happy, drinking and socialising. However, he noted a propensity to paranoia, often thinking that someone was coming to get him.
>
> He reported that his stimulant use had increased significantly following the [Royal Pines Resort] shooting: prior to this he had tended to use cocaine and ecstasy more than amphetamines. He reported using up to two grams of cocaine when working as a bouncer.

> He denied having used hallucinogens such as LSD or magic mushrooms although acknowledged having tried ketamine and gamma hydroxylbutyrate [known as GHB or grievous bodily harm], which he had not particularly enjoyed.
>
> Mr Hudson told me that he had used anabolic steroids first in 1999 and had had five to six cycles for two to three months each.
>
> Mr Hudson stated that his concerns about his safety dated back to being shot in 2006, after which he had carried a weapon.

Melbourne-born model Kaera Douglas had met Hudson through her boyfriend in Sydney while working at a menswear store in Darling Harbour. At twenty-three years of age, the attractive Melburnian was enjoying Sydney and its vibrant nightlife. Like most young women her age, Douglas enjoyed nightclubbing. In 2007 she started a new job as a part-time travel consultant. Hudson was sweet on her and made a move after she split with her boyfriend.

'I would say hi to him if I saw him,' Douglas would say of Hudson.

> Then in Sydney I wasn't paying the bills with [the wages I earned at] Flight Centre as I was only new and I went back to [nightclub] dancing every now and then—maybe once a week. On a weekend [in late April 2007] I came down to Melbourne and I was out at a day club … and just about partying 'cos I'd got out of a relationship, and Chris apparently found out that I was there and came down. We spent maybe three days together then I went back up to Sydney for two weeks.

According to Douglas, their casual relationship continued via text messages—as Hudson was living in Melbourne. 'I think I came down to Melbourne once to see him for two days.'

He travelled up to Sydney to see her. During a police interview, Detective Sergeant Paul Tremain of the Victoria

Police Homicide Squad would ask Douglas if she knew of Hudson's outlaw bikie background.

DOUGLAS: I did, yeah.

TREMAIN: Right, so Chris was involved with the Hell's Angels.

DOUGLAS: Yeah, yeah, he was. I'd prefer not to talk about them, to be honest.

Tremain would ask Douglas about the relationship as it blossomed.

DOUGLAS: I think it borderlined on friends, and sometimes sexual.

TREMAIN: And from that time whilst you were in his company … was there drugs being taken or used at the time?

DOUGLAS: I'd done them with him a couple of times, yeah. A lot of drinking, to be honest … He's just a terrible, terrible drunk.

TREMAIN: Right, and what sort of alcohol does he drink?

DOUGLAS: Um, anything.

TREMAIN: Okay. And what sort of drugs were being used?

DOUGLAS: Um, not a lot, to be honest, but I had tried, um, like amphetamines and stuff with him.

TREMAIN: When you say amphetamines, what type of amphetamines?'

DOUGLAS: Um, like speed … I know that he did them a lot … snorting a lot of speed.

Hudson took Douglas on a trip to Adelaide, where they stayed in an exclusive hotel. It was there that the bikie revealed his inner beast by bashing her. 'He got very violent with me there,' Douglas would say. 'It terrified me to the bone. I just remember crying for my mummy and daddy.'

Douglas said she returned to Sydney (with black eyes) for a couple of weeks 'to get away' from Hudson, before coming home to Melbourne at the start of June. She had organised a transfer with Flight Centre and was looking to start afresh. 'My coming home was to get away from bad people and any negative influence in my life and … just to stop drinking and just to lead a good life,' Douglas would say. But Hudson pursued her regardless. 'I was driving home from Sydney and he started smooth-talking me,' she said in her police interview. 'He just kept the pressure on. Kept ringing and ringing and ringing nonstop.' Douglas ended up spending a night with Hudson at an apartment in which he was living in the inner-Melbourne suburb of Richmond.

Kaera Douglas was a known face at the Spearmint Rhino strip club. She was on friendly terms with some of the exotic dancers there, including a relatively new girl by the name of Autumn Daly-Holt (stage name Savannah). Hudson was a semi-regular at the venue, having ingratiated himself with the staff and strippers.

One of the dancers, Marie (stage name Jazz), would tell police: 'Huddo had informed me that he was part of the Hell's Angels motorcycle group. I don't know why he told me he was with them; however, he was very proud of belonging to them. He referred to them as "The Brotherhood".' Spearmint Rhino waitress Cassie said: 'I know that Huddo is in the Hell's Angels. He always used to say that we were going to get married.'

Hudson was afforded VIP status. Spearmint Rhino general manager Steve Kyriacou said in his police statement that he knew Hudson only as Huddo. 'Huddo is what I would describe as a cool dude. A very sharp kind of guy in that when he comes in he exchanges small talk, is very smooth with the girls and is normally well dressed.'

Hudson told forensic psychologist Cummins that he classed himself as a 'good acquaintance, if not a friend, of the manager of Spearmint Rhino'. 'He said he had been introduced to the manager of Spearmint Rhino through his previous relationship with a woman named Shantelle,' Cummins stated in his report.

> He explained [that] because of his relationship with the manager at Spearmint Rhino it was unusual for him to have

> to pay for alcohol when at Spearmint Rhino or when at Bar Code [next door], which was a bar also managed by Spearmint Rhino. He also explained [that] as a result of his relationship with the manager of Spearmint Rhino he was invariably given VIP status when he attended, which meant he was able to interact with the exotic dancers in a more private area of the venue.

According to Douglas, she and Hudson had an argument at the club on the night of Saturday 9 June 2007.

TREMAIN: What was the argument about?

DOUGLAS: Um, he wanted attention off the girls … I don't even know, to be honest. I just know that he was really rude to me.

Douglas told detectives she didn't speak to Hudson during the following week, but did see him as she was 'coming and going' from a room she rented out at the Punthill apartments in Flinders Lane in the city. 'We sort of saw each other,' she said.

Exotic dancer Jazz, a backpacker, would later remember there being a good vibe in the Spearmint Rhino VIP room on the night of Sunday 17 June. It was 'disco' theme night. Burn, baby, burn. 'Everybody seemed to be happy and in party mode,' she would recall.

New girl Daly-Holt, who had finished her 'official' stripping shift, and manager Kyriacou, who was off duty, were enjoying the club's grog. 'I was drinking heavily,' Kyriacou would later tell police. Daly-Holt would admit to police: 'I would estimate that I consumed far more alcohol than I usually would have.'

Jazz said Daly-Holt appeared to be having a 'good time' while 'drinking a lot of shots with Steve'. Hudson arrived at around 3 am. He too was in party mode and began drinking beer and spirits. 'When I finished my dance I went over to Huddo and said hello,' Jazz said. 'Huddo was in a good mood. He offered me a drink and I accepted it.' A group of staff and strippers—and Hudson—drank there until about 5 am. Hudson then suggested to Jazz that they continue the party at Bar Code. Jazz said she and another dancer, Carly (stage name Brianna), would meet him there. Kyriacou and Daly-Holt headed to Bar Code and were joined by waitress Cassie and Danish stripping sisters Nadia and Nina.

'If I was to score each of them out of ten—ten being the highest level of intoxication—I would say that Steve was an eight out of ten, and Nina and Nadia would have been about a seven or eight also,' Jazz said in her police statement. 'Autumn and the waitress would have been well over ten. I would say that both of them were the drunkest I have ever seen anybody in Australia.'

By that stage there were about ten other people in Bar Code. 'There were two girls that were affected by pills, as one of them approached me and asked me if I had any drugs for sale. I told her that I didn't do drugs and basically brushed her off,' said Jazz.

Jazz and Brianna couldn't immediately find Hudson. They went on a search and found him in the disabled toilet. Both girls suspected he was snorting speed. 'Huddo appeared a little agitated and distant,' Brianna would recall. 'I asked him if he was taking any drugs and told him that if he was I wanted some. Huddo told me that he was not using anything. I then observed half of a long drinking straw floating in the bottom of the pan.'

According to Brianna, Hudson soon returned to the toilets with another man for about twenty minutes. 'When they came out both of them looked happy. I said to them, "Excuse me, where is the love?" meaning, where is my share of the drugs. Huddo replied to me that it wasn't his to share.'

Daly-Holt seemed to be in a frisky and flirtatious mood and was having trouble keeping her clothes on and her hands off colleagues. Jazz: 'Autumn and the waitress [Cassie] began to kiss each other and put on a bit of a show for Steve.'

Cassie told police she was pretty intoxicated thanks to shots of peach schnapps, vodka and cranberry juice—drinks referred to as 'Fresh Pussies'. 'Steve introduced me to Savannah, which is Autumn's stage name,' Cassie stated.

'Savannah then grabbed me and started kissing me and because I was drunk I just thought "Okay". I kissed Savannah once or twice.'

Jazz believed Daly-Holt's affections appeared 'desperate'. 'Huddo agreed ... and stated that he was not happy with how she was carrying on,' Jazz told detectives. Brianna described the girl-on-girl performance as a sixteen-year-old show. According to her: 'Huddo and Steve were watching Autumn kiss the girl and were smiling and whispering to each other.'

At one point Hudson called someone on his mobile phone, quite possibly Douglas. 'Huddo did not seem to be making sense to whoever he was talking with,' Brianna said. 'When he got off the phone he stated something and then he crunched his phone in his hand and broke it to pieces before throwing it across the floor.'

It was 6 am when Douglas—tucked safely in bed in her rented room at Punthill apartments—was woken by a text message from Hudson. From whichever mobile phone he was using, the Hell's Angel was demanding her presence at Bar Code. And somehow he knew she would have no option but to meet him.

'Saturday night I went out with a girlfriend to a nightclub and I came back and slept all day Sunday and all Sunday night,' Douglas said. 'I woke up at six o'clock [on the Monday] morning to him texting me, going, "Come down to Bar Code. Everyone's at Bar Code." I was just like, "No way."' Douglas got up and went into the bathroom. That's when she noticed her keys and all her money missing. She knew Hudson had them.

'My plan was to go down there and get my keys to my car, catch a cab back and get my things and leave. I knew that he'd been drinking and everything like that, and even on a friendship basis we weren't really getting along, to be honest. [I was] seriously scared after what had happened in Adelaide.'

Inside Bar Code, the Daly-Holt show was continuing. After her passionate kissing session with waitress Cassie, she'd started performing a lap dance for her boss. It was about 7.20 am and she was stripping seductively. 'I noticed Autumn begin to remove her top and dance for Steve. I pointed this out to Nina and Nadia and they shook their heads in disbelief,' Jazz said.

It was around this time that punter Ben Smith and a mate walked in to Bar Code looking for a last pit stop after a night out. The young blokes couldn't believe their luck. 'When I arrived I saw a young female with dark hair and brown skin with her top off stripping for a large guy with a receding bald but shaved head who was sitting at a two-seated couch near the main dance floor,' Smith would recall. 'The female was quite an attractive girl. Slim build. Stripper type. She was topless but wearing her jeans. I got myself a drink and sat with my friend and watched what was happening and enjoyed the show. The female stripped down to her G-string and was doing a lap dance.'

Hudson saw the impromptu lap dance, and a caustic mix of alcohol and methylamphetamines exploded in his head. With fire in his eyes he stormed over to Daly-Holt and stood on a ramp behind her. 'He reached down and grabbed Savannah by the hair and lifted her up slightly,' Kyriacou recalled in his statement. 'She began to cry and he stopped doing it. I told her to put her clothes on because she was creating a scene.'

Hudson walked back towards Jazz who, by that stage, had picked up a male admirer by the bar. In chivalrous tones about two minutes too late, the new guy told Hudson there was no need to go pulling a girl's hair.

'Huddo pulled up his sleeves and pointed to his tattoos and said, "Do you know who I am? I'm a Hell's Angel",' Jazz would recall. Ben Smith thought Hudson 'appeared high on something, possibly ice'.

It was around this time that the bikie left the bar. Outside he bumped into a passer-by named Chris Cocossis. 'It was an uncomfortable, unnerving situation because I could see this guy was off his face,' Cocossis told police. 'This guy was racing. By this I mean off his face to the point where his movements and speech were extra fast. He was on edge.' Hudson showed Cocossis a tattoo across his abdomen and boasted about his membership with the Hell's Angels. Cocossis immediately noticed a gun shoved down the front of Hudson's pants. Hudson tried to force Cocossis's hand towards the weapon, before babbling about trouble inside Bar Code.

By the time Kaera Douglas arrived at Bar Code, according to Jazz, the drunk Daly-Holt was sitting on a pool table wearing little if any clothing. 'Kaera looked sober and did not look happy at all,' Jazz said. 'She appeared to be fresh looking. She did not look like she had been out partying all night.' Jazz said at that stage a topless Daly-Holt grabbed her from behind and tried to hug her. Jazz told her to get dressed. The party was finally over. 'Autumn was struggling to put her top back on,' Jazz recalled.

It was daylight outside Bar Code and city workers were making their way to their city offices for the beginning of another working week. Autumn Daly-Holt sat on the steps of Bar Code, drunk and dishevelled. She sat with her bag containing her stripper's kit and make-up. Hudson was circling. Daly-Holt knew of him through Douglas.

'On the previous Friday after work, Kaera [had] told me that she was going back to a city motel room to visit a guy who she had been sleeping with,' Daly-Holt would tell police. 'I kind of said, "Who is this guy? Is it a boyfriend?" She replied, "Oh, he's just a guy I've been fucking." She dismissed him as someone not very important to her.'

Hudson was about to seriously injure Daly-Holt at 7.55 am on the King Street footpath in front of scores of witnesses.

'I can recall brushing Chris away with an open palm manner because he was invading my space,' Daly-Holt recalled. 'The next thing I knew I was being beaten.'

In what Supreme Court Justice Paul Coghlan would describe as a brutal attack, Hudson kicked the petite woman in the face with his left foot, grabbed her by the hair, punched her in the face and then threw her off the steps onto the footpath. He threw her bag at her. As a stunned Daly-Holt struggled to her knees, Hudson took a 'three step build-up' and kicked her in the face with his right foot. According to Coghlan: 'That kick was delivered with as much force as you could muster.'

Witness Shannon Molloy said: 'This guy's casual manner of the way he walked towards her and kicked her made me feel sick. He just clearly looked as though he didn't give a shit about what he was doing or who was around.'

Daly-Holt later said of the attack: 'I felt sharp pain in my face. I remember clutching my nose and my face and thinking, "Fuck, that hurt." From then on I remember being struck again with force and then drifting in and out of consciousness.'

Molloy called 000 and Douglas and others were soon around the bleeding Daly-Holt. 'Her face appeared to be caved in, with blood coming out of her nose and her mouth,' Bar Code patron Ben Smith said. 'She sounded like she was choking on her own blood and was making a gurgling sound. She was limp on the ground and not in a very good condition.'

Despite her state, Daly-Holt heard Douglas's distressed voice. 'As I was drifting in and out I remember Kaera's voice saying, "Oh my God. I can't believe he did this to you. I'm going to get an ambulance".'

According to Douglas: 'She was on the ground topless. She was absolutely beaten. I was just, like, shaking. I'd just woken up to this disgusting zoo of people. [It was] just repulsive. I knew that he [Hudson] had done it. I didn't see it but I knew that he'd done it.'

At that moment, Hudson appeared on the corner of Flinders Lane and King Street. He was motioning Douglas to come to him. She approached with caution, wanting her missing keys and money. Hudson lifted his top and revealed his semiautomatic pistol. 'That's when he grabbed me and goes, "Walk with me,"' Douglas recalled. 'And that's when it started. It was horrid. It was psychotic.'

TREMAIN: What was in your mind in relation to your welfare?

DOUGLAS: 'How do I get out of this? How do I get away from this? He's bigger. Faster. Stronger than me.' I could absolutely not believe that it was happening … He was just completely out-of-his-mind insane. Just completely gone … He had me by the arm, going, 'Walk, cunt.'

Douglas said she was so petrified that she could barely put one foot in front of the other. 'I was just shaking. Absolutely beside myself.'

Hudson forced a struggling Douglas down a building stairwell and, with gun in hand, pushed her hard against a wall with a forearm against her throat. He was almost salivating. 'I was just going, "Please, you don't have to do this. Why are you doing this?"' Douglas said.

Cleaner Emmanuel Borg was putting rubbish in a skip bin when he heard Douglas's pleas. 'It was a combination of like crying and screaming,' Borg would tell police.

> He looked like he was using his body weight to keep her from going anywhere. As he was holding her up against the wall he was holding a black handgun in his right hand. As soon as the male saw me he raised his right hand and pointed the gun straight towards my face.

Borg ducked for cover and bolted up onto the street. He ran to an adjacent building to report the gunman to security. Douglas, meanwhile, had used the distraction as a chance to break free. She made a desperate run for it, darting up the stairs to the corner of William Street and Flinders Lane. She tried in vain to leap into a passing cab, but all its doors were locked.

'The girl was very pretty and tall,' city worker Edith Aquino remembered. 'She was dressed very stylish and well presented … She was screaming hysterically. The man wore a tracksuit top of a dark colour with white stripes on the sleeves. The girl was struggling to get away.'

Hudson was behind Douglas and had a handful of her long black hair. According to Douglas: 'That's when Brendan stepped in and sort of said, "Hey what's going on here?"'

Brendan Keilar, a property solicitor and partner of law firm Norton Gledhill, was walking to his office when he witnessed the street assault. A forty-three-year-old father of three young children, married to his university sweetheart, Keilar had been admitted to the bar as a practising solicitor in 1988. He became a partner at his firm twelve years later, in 2000. Born and bred in country Warrnambool, he was a dedicated husband, father, colleague and friend to many. He excelled in both his professional and sporting pursuits, namely football and cricket. According to his brother-in-law, Paul Firth: 'Brendan's life can only be described as a success. He was a bright, effervescent and strong person. He held his immediate and extended family close to his heart. Brendan was well read and held strong convictions about social issues.'

Danish backpacker Paul De Waard had slept at Southern Cross railway station that Sunday night to save on accommodation. The twenty-five-year-old was on his way to a free newspaper and coffee refills at McDonald's when he, too, stepped in to help Douglas.

'Hudson looked pretty strong and he looked like he'd had too much to drink,' De Waard said in his police statement.

> I couldn't smell any alcohol but he was being unreasonable. The thing that stood out about him most was that he had a mad look in his eyes. I remember the look in the girl's eyes and she was totally frightened and so scared. Her voice sounded scared. She was saying, 'Help! Help!' I thought about the recent commercials in Australia about violence against women. I felt that I had to stop him.

Keilar and De Waard intervened together.

> That made me feel stronger because Brendan looked stronger than me and I thought that together we could stop the man. As we walked towards them I said something like, 'What are you doing, mate? Let her go.' I can't remember if Brendan said anything. It all happened so quickly.
>
> I was just trying to settle [Hudson] down by talking to him. When he pulled the gun out, he didn't say anything. I can't remember him saying anything at all.

Witness Russell Baker watched Keilar and De Waard's heroic attempt. 'I was absolutely shocked when I saw the gun.

The gunman appeared to be quite calm and deliberate when he started shooting.'

In front of hundreds of shocked witnesses, Hudson unleashed an angry snarl of gunfire from his pistol. At point blank range he shot Douglas in the stomach before gunning down Keilar and De Waard. 'People were just dropping,' witness Donna McGowan recalled.

Rian Chapman was walking to work when the shooting played out like a scene from a movie.

> The gunman held the gun towards the stomach of the girl and shot her. He was point blank and had the gun against her clothes. She fell to the ground on her side. The guy with the gun, I think he turned to his left towards [one of] the other guys, pointed the gun at him aiming low and shot him in the stomach. He was very close to the guy he shot. The guy went down to the ground.
>
> [The gunman] has then pointed the weapon towards the other person. Again it was aimed at the lower torso. [Hudson] was only a few steps from that person. That person also hit the deck.

The horrified witnesses watched Hudson stand over the wounded men and fire more rounds into them.

'I remember shots and pain in my chest,' De Waard recalled. 'I don't know who was shot first but I remember being shot twice. I also remember Brendan being shot. I think I heard three shots in all. There might have been more but I was in too much pain.'

Outside Bar Code, one block away, paramedics were loading Autumn Daly-Holt into an ambulance. They all heard the crack of gunfire—even Daly-Holt, despite her injuries. 'I recall a conversation where [it was said that] people had been shot,' she said. 'I became concerned about whether my friend Kaera had been hurt or whether she had been involved.'

Back at the intersection of William Street and Flinders Lane, Hudson was surveying his handiwork. His pistol was dry and his victims bleeding out.

'The girl was screaming out that she had been shot,' witness Aquino stated. 'She was hysterical. The guy who was on the road [Keilar] was not saying anything or moving. He was very pale and gasping for air.'

Hudson walked away along Flinders Lane.

'I thought that he heard me scream and would come after me,' said witness Natalie Gullace. 'He turned and faced me and waved the gun left and right in my direction twice. I hid behind the wall of the building where I was working. I thought that he was going to shoot me because I was a witness. I thought he was going to kill me.'

In the aftermath, screams and distant sirens were all that echoed in a brief and unnerving calm. Everyone was trying to come to terms with what had just occurred. Keilar lay on the street in an expanding pool of blood. He was shot through his chest, abdomen and left thigh. De Waard was shot twice. The rounds had pierced his stomach and buttock. Douglas was shot once, through the torso. The bullet had torn apart her kidney. 'I just don't remember any of it—the shooting,' she would later say. 'All I remember is lying on the ground and having people around me … I knew I'd been shot in the stomach.'

Donna McGowan was one of the first to reach the injured. She went to the aid of De Waard. 'I remember Donna as I was lying on the street,' the Dutchman would later say. 'Donna was telling me to stay with her and she wouldn't let me close my eyes.'

According to McGowan:

> I held his hand and told him to look at me because I didn't want him to pass out. I tried to keep him conscious. I asked him what his name was. He said his name was Paul and I told him my name was Donna. I didn't know how many times he'd been shot and he didn't want me to leave him. I think it was a fireman that came over to cut his backpack off, but Paul didn't want me to go. I kept holding his hand and telling him how brave he was. The fire brigade or ambulance cut his shirt off while I was holding his hand and

> I saw the gunshot wounds in his front and his back. There was a big hole in his chest.
>
> I saw the other guy (Keilar) gasping for breath. He couldn't breathe. It didn't look good.

Russell Baker and a trained nurse, Coralann Walker, had reached Keilar. 'I lifted up his shirt and saw that there were two holes in the left side of his abdomen,' Baker said of Keilar's fatal wounds. 'I applied pressure to the bullet holes. About this time a nurse arrived and helped.'

Nurse Walker later said:

> His pulse was very weak. I tried to reassure him that he was going to be okay and stroked his hair. I told him to keep breathing. He stopped breathing and I felt no pulse. Someone came, a man with a resuscitation bag and mask. This man started to give the victim oxygen via this mask whilst I commenced cardiac compressions.

Metropolitan Fire Brigade crews were the first of the emergency services on the scene, followed by ambulance paramedics. Despite their fears about the gunman, they went to work on the shooting victims.

'As I pulled up I noticed three people lying on the ground,' West Melbourne Senior Station Officer Rick Gili would tell the *Herald Sun*.

> I cut the clothing off the backpacker and found a bullet hole just above his heart and another coming out of his chest on the right-hand side. I told him to relax but I thought he was on his way out. People go a different colour when they pass away, and he was that colour. We had other people working on the girl, applying bandages to her bullet wounds. We had a number of people rotating continuously [performing CPR] on the solicitor.
>
> I had concerns for my men, myself and everyone else. For all I knew, the shooter was still in the area, on top of a building somewhere. But we did what we had to do.

Metropolitan Ambulance Service Manager Lindsay Bent adds: 'I remember the chaos. I remember the uncertainty, not knowing where the gunman was and the potential for more shots to be fired.'

Police—including members of the specialist Force Response Unit—blocked off city streets and began a sweep for the gunman. Buildings were secured. The heart of the city was in lockdown. By that stage, Hudson had picked up his pace a little. Passengers on a tram say they saw him point his gun under his chin near Flinders Lane and Market Street, despite knowing full well there were no rounds left in the weapon.

Justice Coghlan would say to Hudson during his eventual sentencing: 'I do not accept that the action of putting the gun under your chin was suicidal or shows any signs of regret.'

Hudson moved south down Queen Street and was heading east along Flinders Street when he removed his Adidas tracksuit top, wrapped it around the gun and threw the bundle into a construction site. He then managed to backtrack to the Punthill apartments. That was the last reported sighting of him in the Melbourne CBD. One person who had been with Hudson before his meltdown—Spearmint Rhino waitress Cassie—had no idea of the terror he had just inflicted as she stumbled from Bar Code. 'I remember when I came outside it was daylight and there were police everywhere,' she said in her statement. 'Someone told me that there had been a shooting but I was so drunk I didn't think anything of it.'

At the shooting scene, paramedics had stabilised Douglas and De Waard and were loading them for transportation to the Royal Melbourne Hospital, where they underwent emergency surgery. Paramedics were unable to resuscitate Keilar, who died on the road at the city intersection.

'I watched him die,' Donna McGowan later said. 'I've never seen anything like that before. There was so much blood.'

The shooting had rocked the city. And the gunman was still on the run. Police quickly nominated Christopher Wayne Hudson, a Hell's Angels bikie, as the trigger man. His face was duly plastered across media reports.

'This is the violent Hell's Angels bikie who is on the run from police after the cold-blooded shooting that left a heroic father of three dead,' the *Herald Sun* reported, alongside a prison photo of Hudson proudly showing his tattoos.

Alan Didak read all about it. 'I remember seeing the newspaper the morning after the shooting incident,' he said. 'On the front page was a picture of a person police were looking for. I remember talking to a friend of mine and saying that the photo of the guy looked similar to the guy that I'd been with on the Queen's Birthday long weekend.'

The Hell's Angels motorcycle club became a major focus for police—and the media—as the hunt for Hudson intensified. It was unwanted heat for the outlaw club and its members. Hudson's father, Terry, made a public plea for his son to surrender. Speaking on Channel Seven from his Gold Coast home, he said: 'Please, Chris, if you're watching this, surrender peacefully to the nearest police station to avoid any further conflict or injury to any party, including yourself ... Mate, we love you. Please give in. Give up.'

Chief Commissioner Christine Nixon confirmed that Hudson had been wanted for questioning over the shooting incident in Campbellfield a week earlier. 'This is a big city—3.5 million people,' she said. 'We had resources focused on him, but we didn't find him.' She sent a message to the Angels. 'I would hope they would hand him over. I think this person's clearly out of control.'

Kaera Douglas, twenty-four, awoke from a medically induced coma on 20 June minus one of her kidneys. Knowing their daughter was out of mortal danger, her parents issued a statement:

> Our thoughts turned early to the courageous Brendan Keilar and the devastating effects on his family. His actions were selfless and truly heroic. We are eternally grateful and deeply saddened at the same time. To Paul De Waard, he too risked his life to save Kaera and for that we are eternally grateful.

Late that afternoon, Hudson—with Hell's Angels president Gregory Edwards as a chaperone—walked in to Wallan police station in semirural Victoria. On duty were Acting Sergeant Ivan Ravanello and Senior Constable Scott Patton.

'How are you going?' Edwards said as he walked in with Hudson, whose left wrist was bandaged with a sock. 'This is Chris Hudson. He's here to hand himself in. I'm the president of the Hell's Angels down here.'

Detective Inspector Kim West, of the investigative Taskforce 500 unit, and solicitor Patrick O'Dwyer, for Hudson, had orchestrated the peaceful surrender. Hudson had been concerned about 'what may ensue' if police came across him. West had assured him safe passage. 'What I was concerned about was preventing the chance meeting of Mr Hudson with police in the street,' West would say.

Edwards asked the cops if it was all right for Hudson to ring his father and report safe passage. 'Yeah, no worries,' Senior Constable Patton replied.

In his statement, Patton recalled: 'Edwards explained how the Hell's Angels had received some bad publicity and that Hudson was facing up to what he had done, or words to that effect. During my involvement with Hudson I found him to be softly spoken, polite and compliant to all requests.'

Due to the remote location of the police station and Hudson's status, Ravanello locked down the small building and asked Hudson about his wrist wound.

HUDSON: I did it with a knife.

RAVANELLO: When?

HUDSON: About twelve o'clock today.

RAVANELLO: Why?

HUDSON: I thought of doing myself in.

Homicide detectives arrived and took Hudson into their custody. Back at the St Kilda Road police complex, the killer bikie gave a 'No comment' record of interview. He was charged with offences including murder, attempted murder and intentionally causing serious injury.

The following day, De Waard awoke in hospital surrounded by his proud and very relieved family—dad Hans de Waard, mum Marjan Heyden and older brothers Bartjan and Erik. They'd just arrived on a plane from the Netherlands. Bartjan and Erik were straight in their little brother's ear, joking and saying: 'Let's go and get a Grolsch beer.' Doctors said De Waard was a miracle man to have survived. More than ten litres of blood—apparently twice the amount carried by an average adult male—bled from him in the hours after the shooting. Cardiac and vascular trauma teams had worked in tandem to keep him alive. A bullet was still lodged in his pelvis. 'Paul was as close to death as you get without going there,' Royal Melbourne Hospital trauma surgeon Russell Gruen said.

Hudson, meanwhile, had undergone surgery in a secure hospital wing for his self-inflicted wrist injury.

It was Thursday 28 June when Alan Didak first went public after telling the Collingwood Football Club and making a statement to police about his time with Chris 'Huddo' Hudson a week before the CBD rampage. He made a brief media statement about 9 pm at Collingwood's home base, the Lexus Centre. In a carefully worded statement, club CEO Gary Pert told how Hudson and Didak had met by chance at the Spearmint Rhino strip club. 'Prior to this ordeal Alan had been drinking very heavily and as the night's events unfolded he became increasingly concerned for his own safety,' Pert said.

A sheepish Didak said: 'The club and I felt it important to face the media tonight. I am only now fully aware of the situation I found myself in. I deeply regret the embarrassment caused to myself, my family and the football club.'

Detective Sergeant Michael Engel, of the Armed Crime Taskforce, described Didak as nothing more than a witness to the previous shooting incident in Campbellfield. 'Alan has provided officers with a statement in relation to knowledge of a particular incident. Alan has made a fault in relation to judgement and that's really as far as I'd like to take it.'

Brendan Keilar's mother, Moya Keilar, was upset with Didak for not immediately reporting his 'ordeal' to his club and the police. 'I would have expected any decent person in that situation would have reported it to the police,' she told the *Herald Sun*.

The football club announced that Didak would refrain from drinking alcohol during the season, was to seek alcohol counselling, would observe a 1 am curfew and avoid nightclubs. 'I think some of the decisions that I've made under the influence of alcohol haven't been the best,' Didak told the media.

As the dust settled around the Collingwood Football Club, focus returned to the heroes of the saga. A gaunt and pale Paul De Waard made his first public appearance. Flanked by his family, he said he would 'do it again' if the same situation arose. 'I was not supposed to die at that moment—it was not my time,' he said from his wheelchair. 'The worst was lying there on the road and everybody—my family—was on the other side of the world. I was lucky there was a lady—Donna—looking after me. I felt so lonely at that moment.'

Christopher Wayne Hudson pleaded guilty to murder, two counts of attempted murder and intentionally causing serious injury. Defence barrister Phillip Priest, QC, told the Supreme Court that his client was in a psychotic drug-fuelled rage the morning he unleashed hell on the city. Hudson admitted to having used excessive amounts of methylamphetamine and drinking an excessive amount of alcohol. He was also a regular steroid abuser. Dr Danny Sullivan wrote in his report for the defence:

> Mr Hudson reported that at the time of the index offence he had been taking anabolic steroids for around a month, having been concerned that people had stated that he was looking 'skinny' (weighing by his account 82 kilograms) and felt that he had possibly taken more than he would usually do. In addition he reported that for the few weeks prior to the index offence he had been taking large amounts of stimulants, drinking copiously and that he was, as a

> consequence, much more paranoid than usual. He informed me that his paranoia was that he would be shot by people from other motorcycle gangs, or that he would be arrested by police and found to have a firearm.
>
> There is no overt personality disorder present. Although anabolic steroid abuse and the lifestyle led by Mr Hudson suggest narcissistic and antisocial features, it is more likely that he was seduced by the lifestyle offered by joining motorcycle gangs—and that his peer group and lifestyle encouraged self-centred and aggressive attitudes.

Prosecutor Ray Elston, SC, called for a life sentence. 'Only the medical practitioners prevented Hudson from facing three counts of murder,' Elston told Justice Coghlan.

On 22 September 2008, Coghlan sentenced Hudson to life imprisonment with a thirty-five-year minimum term. A group of bikies were in court, offering Hudson smiles and hand-on-heart salutes. Before speaking of the CBD shootings, Coghlan mentioned the gunplay Hudson had embarked upon in Campbellfield six days before the CBD murders. 'You appear to have been intent on impressing Didak,' Coghlan said.

> Your behaviour on that occasion has never been explained. It is not of great significance when compared to the other matters which bring you here, except that it shows your general attitude. It involved the use of the same firearm you used on 18 June 2007.
>
> The events [in the CBD] occurred at a place where ordinary people are entitled to feel safe. Two of your victims were not known to you and were shot for doing no more than trying to help the young woman you were assaulting. She was shot too. None of your victims represented any threat to you, imagined or otherwise. Your conduct is all the more chilling because it remains unexplained. It was calm and deliberate.
>
> Many adjectives may be used to describe it but it speaks for itself. It is appalling ... There were a large number of witnesses to the events, probably hundreds to different

> aspects of it. They will carry the images of those events with them for a very long time.

The Keilar family remain haunted over the cold-blooded murder of an ordinary man who showed extraordinary courage. Father Peter Hosking said at Keilar's funeral: 'Brendan did not want to die, yet he died standing up for what he thought was right—helping another and trying to stop violence. Love and sacrifice make the world a better place. He died making the world a better place.'

Close mate Gerard Dalbosco praised Keilar, saying he had many fine qualities.

> Central to them was a moral compass that gave him a strong sense of what was right and what was wrong … Whatever sport he played, there was one common theme and that was courage. Invariably he was the smallest player on the ground, but he was fearless and never took a backward step and regularly put his body on the line. This resulted in many knocks, several concussions and broken bones. But he always bounced back bigger and bolder than ever. There wasn't much that could keep him down.

Keilar was posthumously awarded an Australian Bravery Medal.

Kaera Douglas continues to live with the mental and physical scars. She describes De Waard as her 'rock' and says there is nothing she could ever say to express her thanks to Keilar. She told the *Herald Sun* in late 2008 that she was attending church and Alcoholics Anonymous, had applied for university, volunteered for a children's charity and wanted to work as a guidance counsellor for adolescents. She said she wanted to warn young women about the dangers of drug and alcohol abuse.

'I know people will be saying, "Who's she to be preaching to us? She's that stripper who got shot,"' she told reporter David Hastie. 'I want to say to all the young girls out there who ever think of taking a drug, who ever think of dancing, dating a bikie—don't do what I did. It's not pretty. There's nothing glamorous, nothing cool about it.'

Paul De Waard was adopted by Victorians as a de facto Melburnian for his bravery. He received several awards.

'I'm a very positive person and will always tell people I'm fine and doing well. However, my life has changed forever and I'm still struggling with my health every day,' he said. As Justice Coghlan remarked: 'His conduct is marked by the same elements of decency and selflessness as that of Mr Keilar.'

In the Melbourne CBD, at the intersection where Keilar lost his life and De Waard almost did, a little plaque is etched with an inscription: 'May their selfless courage in going to the aid of a stranger inspire in us all a greater sense of community and concern for others.'

9

I Will Survive

A chained and beaten wife cheats death by escaping a sinking car in the bay

'I'm not a religious person but my step-grandfather had died the previous day and we believe he had not fully crossed over and was looking over me.'

WITH FOREARMS TETHERED TOGETHER and mouth covered with gaffer tape, the woman who can only be referred to as 'Jessica' lay chained in the back seat of her family car looking into the face of death through blackened eyes. Her husband Cameron Neil Cook, the man sitting behind the wheel, had chained her tight. Cook, a former policeman, sat staring at the black abyss beyond the end of Mordialloc pier. It stared straight back into him. Jessica's eyes were swollen and so bloated and black that she could hardly see. Her nose, right eye socket and cheekbone were fractured. The copper taste of blood coated her throat. She tried to scream, time after time, but the gaffer tape smothered her voice. Cook revved the engine. It was night and fishermen's lights lit up the pier like a runway. Cook turned to his whimpering wife. He was in control, not her. This was his moment. He was the man, the boss.

'I'm sorry,' he said in a ruthless tone. 'But I am taking you with me.'

Jessica's eyes widened as Cook began to speed towards the pier.

'Don't do this! Don't do this!' she screamed through the tape, as a bell on a nearby fishing boat rang out a 3 am death knell.

The woman at the centre of this miraculous tale of courage and survival cannot be named due to a suppression order made by a Victorian Supreme Court judge. Neither can her son. For the purposes of this story she asked to be called Jessica.

Cameron Cook and Jessica had been married for ten years. They had first met, ironically, at the scene of a car accident Cook attended as a policeman. They stayed in touch and started going out together not too long after. Two years later they were engaged and then married. They had one son.

'During the course of our marriage, there had never been any form of physical violence between Cameron and myself but there was a lot of verbal and emotional violence issues,' Jessica would tell police. She would say that the animosity intensified after the birth of their son. 'There were just more arguments and difficulties in trying to juggle shift work with Cameron being in the police force, and my job issues.'

According to Jessica, Cook seemed to suffer from depression. 'A number of times Cameron would go into the bathroom and sit in a warm bath most of the day and just read books and not come out,' she said. 'This lasted for about a five-week period and then he seemed to have recovered and commenced normal family duties.'

To alleviate the stresses at home, it was arranged that their son would be placed in full-time child care. Cook went part-time, before eventually pulling the pin on policing for a change of career. 'After about three years' duration [working part-time] Cameron decided that he was going to leave the police force, and he decided he wanted to study law as he was unable to get into police prosecutions,' Jessica would later say.

> I supported his decision and he applied to the Victoria University to study law and did a four-year law course and then one year of articles before he graduated and qualified as a solicitor. During this five-year period that he was studying law, I paid for all his costs including schooling and living expenses and basically supported him throughout the entirety of his studies—as he had no income for the majority of his studies and only did occasional part-time work on a Saturday morning for a brief period.

Cook's foray into the legal profession saw him begin work as a criminal solicitor for Legal Aid Victoria. A posting in Morwell meant that he had to move out of the family home for about three months. 'But we still had a relationship, although we were having marriage difficulties,' Jessica explained. 'At one stage he stated that he wanted a divorce, to which I said yes, and then he stated that he wanted to take [our son] so I refused and we continued our relationship.'

The subject of divorce never really left the radar screen. Cook brought it up on a number of occasions in the five years before he would chain Jessica inside their family sedan and drive her into Port Phillip Bay. About three months before Cook enacted his death plan he left Legal Aid and started work with the Department of Infrastructure as a prosecuting solicitor. With a bolstered résumé behind him, his hope was to return to Victoria Police as a court prosecutor. By the time he began work at the Department of Infrastructure, he and Jessica had separate bedrooms and were scoring D-minus report cards at marriage counselling.

'The marriage had been increasingly going downhill … and I had basically had enough,' Jessica said in her police statement.

> I had recently changed jobs and I had just had enough of the marriage situation, as it did not appear very loving and the only friendship and companionship I seemed to be getting was at work and none at home from my husband … It just got to me that I no longer wanted my

> life to be like that any more. I had evaluated my life and decided that the marriage was going nowhere and was not working and I decided that there was no point continuing with it.

Jessica told Cook that her mind was made up: she wanted a divorce. She had fallen out of love. 'He seemed to flip out,' she would say in her police statement.

> Initially he was saying don't do this and that sort of stuff and appeared reluctant to cease the relationship and then over the following days he got very aggressive about it. During this period he was constantly arguing with me and being verbally aggressive and he was saying things like if I was on fire he wouldn't even piss on me to put me out. He also told me that if I ever got into another relationship with anybody or had kids to another man that he would hunt me down and kill me, kill the kid and kill everybody.

The following morning, after threatening Jessica, Cook appeared to have calmed down. He asked her to agree to further marriage counselling for twelve weeks. If it was not working by then, he said, she was free to leave the marriage. Jessica said there was no change after eight weeks of sessions.

'At the end of the last joint session, Cameron indicated to the counsellor that he didn't believe that I wanted a divorce and that I was just trying to hurt him … Cameron got really heated and told [the counsellor] to stop putting ideas in my head.'

A professional colleague named Tony was a close and trusted companion of Jessica's. 'During this time Tony and I began a sexual relationship, about a couple of months [before the pier incident],' Jessica told police. '[This was] after I initially told Cameron that I wanted a divorce and after I had re-evaluated my life and my marriage and decided that it was not working.'

On or around 6 September 2007, Jessica visited a family-law solicitor to seek advice about ending the marriage and having her will changed. Little did she know that Cook was aware of her new relationship—and had private detectives running surveillance on her.

'That evening, Cameron said to me that the worst thing that I could do to him was lie to him and I did not know what he was talking about.' Jessica thought Cook may have been referring to a sad walk she'd taken on the beach that afternoon to reflect on the death of her step-grandfather. Despite appearing somewhat of a distant relative on the family tree, that man had played a major part in her life since childhood.

'I was having a rough time and needed some time to think,' she said of her beach walk.

> I did not know what he was talking about because at the time I walked along the beach I was alone. He then asked me when we were sitting in the lounge room on the couch as to whether I was having an affair and I replied no ... I explained to him that I did not love him any more and that was the reason that I wanted the relationship to cease.

Cook believed otherwise, thanks to his private detectives.

The next day—7 September—Jessica was not required to go in to work so decided to spend the day making arrangements 'to move out and try to organise my life'. Cook left for work at about 8.30 am and, according to Supreme Court Justice Elizabeth Hollingworth: 'You telephoned one of the private investigators with details of your wife's proposed movements that morning and asked for surveillance to be carried out on her to see whether she met the person with whom you suspected she was having an affair.' Jessica dropped their seven-year-old son at school. At 10.45 am she returned to her solicitor's office to 'get my will and power of attorney changed to have Cameron removed from the will'. After that it was off to a real estate agency for a property viewing. She signed relevant paperwork to lease a home in the southern bayside suburb of Hampton. She next had lunch at a female friend's house, where her new friend and lover,

Tony, met her. They then left to look at property together, before Tony dropped Jessica back at her friend's house.

Hollingworth on Cook again:

> You remained in regular contact with the private investigators that day, at one stage ringing every fifteen minutes or so, seeking updates on the surveillance. At about 1.15 pm, one of the private investigators told you that he had seen a man and your wife kiss and have a long hug. He said you did not appear angry or agitated when given that news and you said to him, 'Good work. Keep on it.'

That afternoon, Cook went to an Aussie Disposals store and bought handcuffs and a hunting knife with a four-inch blade. At a Bunnings store he purchased padlocks and chains. Jessica, meanwhile, was picking up their son from school. Cook arrived at their Cheltenham home at about 6.30 pm. As Jessica cooked dinner he left, saying he had to meet a work associate about some closed-circuit TV footage. As Hollingworth described: 'You left the house again at 8 pm and met with the private investigators at a local supermarket. During this time you replayed, about three times, the footage showing your wife and the man kissing. You paid for the surveillance work.'

When Cook returned home he had a copy of the footage and a bottle of what he said were vitamin tablets. 'He did not appear angry or agitated,' Jessica would recall.

Jessica tucked their son in to bed at about 9 pm. Cook then went and said goodnight to the boy, slipping him a sleeping pill that he said was a vitamin C tablet. Cook then asked Jessica to his bedroom to watch a comedy show on the internet. 'He told me that he had just given [our son] another vitamin C tablet and I went, "argh", as I had already given him one.'

Jessica and Cook watched the comedy show on the computer, sitting on the bed with their backs against the wall. At 10.30 pm she said she was tired and wanted to go to bed.

'Cameron said that he had some sort of trick to do and he said, "Come here. I want to tie your hands behind your back,"' Jessica told police.

> Cameron was standing facing me. I was very unsure of what he was doing. I was nervous and did not feel comfortable with him tying my hands behind my back. I said, 'No thanks, I am just going to go to bed.' I then tried to get up and as I got to the edge of the bed Cameron approached me and punched me two or three times to the left side of my chest.

The assault left Jessica hurt and gasping for breath.

> I had no air and then he grabbed hold of me somehow and flipped me over and I felt his knees pinning my body onto the bed. He grabbed me by the hands and forced them behind my back and tied my hands with something, which I now know was grey gaffer tape. At the time I had my head forced into the bed and I was struggling as he was trying to tape up my hands.

As she struggled to free her hands, Jessica yelled: 'What are you doing? What on earth are you doing?' Cook ignored her, pushing gaffer tape across her mouth to silence her. He then moved to her feet and trussed her ankles with tape, before unleashing an angry flurry of punches. 'Cameron started punching me to the face whilst I was tied up on the bed seated with my head and back up against the wall. He punched me at least two times directly to the face, eyes and nose area. At the time I was unable to move or protect myself as I was backed up against the wall and tied up.

'I felt very dazed and was almost concussed from the power of the punches and I could feel blood coming from my nose and face. I had blood gushing out and coming in the back of my throat from my nose and I could hardly see.' Cook continued to punch her while asking 'Do you know how much you betrayed me?' Jessica said: 'He was calling me a whore and other stuff.'

When Cook unclenched his blood-stained fists, Jessica lay slumped on the bed with her eyes bashed shut. 'I was unable to open my eyes properly because of all the blood and immediate swelling to my face. I was crying but unable to scream out or say anything as I had my mouth taped over. I was in a lot of pain.'

Cook then upped the ante. Kneeling over the top of Jessica, he pulled the knife that he'd bought from the Aussie Disposals store and waved it in front of her eyes as she lay helpless on her back. Moving the blade to her breasts Cook seethed: 'This is one of the fucking sharpest knives in the world.' 'At the time I was freaking out,' Jessica said, 'and I thought that Cameron was going to stab me.'

In a moment of clarity, Cook seemed to calm down. Ice-cold intent washed across his white-hot rage. He peeled the tape from his wife's mouth and told her in quite simple terms that he would slit her throat if she said anything.

'At the time he was holding the knife, pressing the blade directly against the left side of my throat,' Jessica said. 'He then told me he had drugged our son … I was crying and sore but I was being co-operative as I did not want him to hurt [our son] or myself.'

Cook went on to explain that he had given the boy a sleeping tablet. 'Cameron then told me that he did not want [our son] to hear what was going on and said that he wanted to talk to me. He said, "I am sorry for doing this but it was your actions that brought me to this." Cameron told me that he wanted to talk about Tony.'

Cook then played the private detectives' surveillance footage to her.

Jessica: 'At the time I was placed seated up on the bed. I still had my hands taped behind my back and also my feet bound and secured so that I could not get away.' The secretly recorded footage showed her and Tony together. Cook looked across and said in a sarcastic tone: 'Look at these two in love … Have you been fucking him?'

The footage seemed to incense Cook. His anger rose again and he asked: 'Has he got a bigger dick than me?'

Jessica again: 'He asked me whether I was in love with this guy and I said, "Yes." He asked me how long I had been seeing him and I said a bit over a month.'

Much to Jessica's surprise, Cook began to wipe the blood from her face. Her clothes, too, were stained. She complained that the tape binding her wrists was too tight and that she had lost all feeling in her fingers. Cook cut the tape, helped her dress into clean clothes and then retaped her hands in front of her body.

> He did this by binding both of my forearms together. He then told me that he had a plan and that he wanted me to witness him killing himself by slitting his throat with the knife. He told me that that was all that was going to happen to me and that I was in no more danger.

Cook told Jessica that he was going to take her to a place in the beachside suburb of Mentone. 'He indicated that he wanted to kill himself there and he wanted me to watch.'

Cook pulled a box from beneath his bed. It contained three silver chains and padlocks. Cook wrapped one of the chains around Jessica's ankles and padlocked it so that her legs were tight together. He pushed another strip of tape against her mouth. Jessica was then ordered to carry her chain and hobble to the family car—a Magna sedan—in the driveway. 'I was placed in the back of the car and he put a blanket over me and he put a pillow against the side window and wanted me to shield my face so that the cars driving past would not see me.'

Cook wrapped a second chain around the front passenger seat and padlocked it to the chain shackling Jessica's ankles. 'Cameron then put my seatbelt on also,' she remembered. After going back inside, Cook returned to the car with the knife and the remaining chain and padlocks. 'He told me that the reason he restrained me within the car was that he did not want me to stop him [from killing himself with the knife] and believed that it would take him a while to bleed out.'

Cook drove to Mordialloc instead of Mentone. His change of plan sparked Jessica's worst fears. 'I started to get scared and panicked as he initially mentioned Mentone.

When I questioned him as to where he was going he said, "to Mordialloc to the place where I pray".'

Cook first drove to a road leading to a deep, cold waterway. A locked gate forced him to drive to a main car park where Port Phillip Bay enters Mordialloc creek. Jutting out into the bay is the pier. Cook cursed at the sight of fishermen as he did a lap and parked near a closed kiosk. Leaving Jessica restrained inside, he walked to a toilet block. Using Jessica's mobile phone he called his sister's home looking for his father. The time was about 3 am.

Neil Cook, a former member of the Australian Department of Defence, now retired, was naturally asleep at that hour. He and wife Helen, a former nurse, were staying at their daughter Nerrida's house that evening.

The Cooks had adopted Cameron in Port Moresby while engaged in their respective careers there. Neil Cook would tell detectives that 1966 was a 'great year' as it was the one in which he and Helen adopted Cameron and the year the St Kilda Australian Rules football team won its first premiership. 'Your birth mother was about sixteen when you were born, and died in an accident when you were five years old,' Justice Hollingworth said. 'You know nothing of your biological father.'

The Cooks brought Cameron back to Melbourne for a short while before moving in 1971 to Hong Kong, where Neil had a defence posting. Two years later the family returned to Melbourne, where Cook completed his secondary education as an above-average student before being accepted into the army at the Duntroon Military College. He left the army after six months and completed an arts/marketing degree. He then moved to Japan where he lived for nearly three years, studying martial arts and teaching English. Cook joined the Victoria Police force upon his return home in 1996. After meeting Jessica at the accident scene, he married her at the Victoria Police Academy chapel. They then bought their house and had their son.

Standing by the Mordialloc kiosk with his wife's mobile phone to his ear, Cook waited impatiently for somebody to answer. This conversation, he fully expected, would be the last he would have with his father. His sister answered.

'She told me it was Cameron,' Neil Cook said in his police statement, 'and that he didn't want to talk to her and wanted to talk to me.'

'Hello, mate, what's the problem?' Neil said. Cook explained his situation. Bewildered, Neil tried to talk his son out of his course of action.

NEIL: Jesus, Cameron, have you rung the police?'

COOK: No, and I'm not going to.

NEIL: Where the hell are you?

COOK: I'm not going to tell you. The police will find me quickly and by the time they find me I'll be dead too.

NEIL: Jesus, Cameron. Why?

COOK: I want you and mum to look after [my son] to make sure he grows up all right.

NEIL: We will.

COOK: I love you all, including Nerrida.

With that, Cook hung up.

'After the phone went dead, I was shattered,' Neil Cook said. 'So were Helen and Nerrida after I told them what Cameron had just said to me over the phone.' The family immediately headed to Cook's home to locate his son.

While Cook was on the phone, Jessica had managed to unclip her seatbelt. But the thirty-four-year-old was unable to work loose her chains. 'I didn't want to make him mad, so I just waited there, assuming that he was going to commit suicide and then I would be able to get free or attract someone's attention,' she said.

Upon his return, Cook told his wife that his relatives were on their way to collect their son. Cook asked how she was coping. 'I am scared, you dick!' she yelled through the tape. Cook smiled and chained himself to his seat before turning back to Jessica. 'I'm sorry,' he said, 'but I am taking you with me.' In vain she tried to break her bonds. 'I screamed through the tape and was in absolute terror,' she would remember.

Cook started the car, revved the engine hard and headed for the pier. A fisherman had to jump out of the way as the Magna sped past him. According to Hollingworth:

> Before entering the water, the car struck a steel gate which was flung off its hinges and flew at high speed in the direction of Stephanos Tsiatsios, who was fishing at Mordialloc Creek at the time. The gate deflected off the steel pole which Mr Tsiatsios was standing behind, before landing in the water.

Jessica rattled around in the back seat as the car hit several bumps at speed, having smashed through the gate.

> At the time I was trying to scream but my mouth was taped over. I was unable to move or unsecure the chains. I was getting thrown about all over the place. The car was going very fast. The next thing I knew there was a large crashing noise and the front of the car hit something and then immediately after there was a series of larger bumps where the car got airborne momentarily and then hit the ground again going at full speed … There was another large impact to the front wheels and then the car became airborne, and we hit something and the rear passenger side window smashed and blew out. Then there was a large splash.
>
> I was thrown forward into the seat and suddenly the car started filling with water, particularly through the broken window which was beside me, causing water to gush inside the vehicle all over me.

The black water was cold. Thoughts of her son flooded Jessica's mind. 'I was panicking and extremely scared,' she would admit. 'The car was completely filling with water and dropping down front-first.' Cook, sitting unmoved in what he hoped would become a submerged coffin, commented: 'Geez, isn't the water cold.' 'I was fighting against the chains and tape,' said Jessica. 'At the time I thought that I was going to die. I just kept thrashing about trying to get loose.'

During a press interview after Cook's court case, Jessica said she had a dual motivation to live. 'I was adamant I was going to get home to my son. I was also thinking, "How dare you try and do this to me. I'm not going to let you do this to me. I wasn't going to give Cameron the satisfaction.'

Jessica said a guardian angel may have been watching over her as one by one she broke from her bindings. First she managed to loosen the tape around her arms and get her hands free. 'My clothes were drenched and the tape had nothing to hold on to,' she said in her police statement. 'I was trying to keep my head above the water as the car was quickly filling.'

Jessica next ripped the tape from her mouth and, ignoring the pain, managed to twist her right ankle free from the chains. Her left leg remained chained, however, and the water was making any vigorous movement quite difficult. But she kept on fighting as the ocean sucked the car under. 'As I was thrashing about I kept yanking at the chains which were attached to the seat. Suddenly something broke and one of the chains from the seat managed to come loose. By this time the vehicle was engulfed with water and partially submerged.' The initial rush of water through the broken rear passenger-side window had eased. Jessica managed to swim her way through, with a broken chain still wrapped around her left ankle.

> I managed to get my head out of the water so that I could still breathe. I got my full body out of the car and the water was absolutely freezing and I was trying to rip the chain out of the floor. I was trying to climb onto the roof of the vehicle so that I would not drown and could keep my head above water. I kept yanking on the chain, which was still attached to my left foot and my left foot was still stuck through the window. The chain suddenly came free with my constant pulling.

Free from the sinking car, Jessica swam to shore. 'I saw some people on the pier and was screaming out for help, but nobody jumped in to the water to help me,' she told police.

> My clothing was becoming heavy and I still had chain secured around my foot. I could not kick my feet properly ... [but] I am a competent swimmer and this helped me get out of the vehicle and back to the land. As I approached the jetty and water's edge I was screaming out for help from some of the fishermen and anyone that may have been nearby. I saw a man suddenly run away and nobody would come to help me.

Jessica ran through the car park with chain in hand, exhausted, freezing and in shock. 'My feet were killing me and I just kept running because I was so scared. The adrenalin just kept me going.' She unsuccessfully tried to flag down two passing taxis and a four-wheel drive on Main Street. Resorting to drastic measures, she stepped in front of the next oncoming vehicle, giving it no option but to stop. It would have anyway; it was a police car.

With her swollen face crushed and bruised, Jessica collapsed into the arms of one of the officers. She explained that her husband had just tried to kill her by driving the car off the pier. She didn't know if he was dead or not. One of the cops covered her in a jacket as more police units and an ambulance arrived.

Police divers arrived at the pier and dragged a hypothermic Cook from the sinking Magna. Jessica was treated before being taken to the Alfred Hospital suffering injuries including a fractured nose and right eye socket, and two black and swollen eyes. According to one policeman she looked like she'd 'been hit by a Mack truck'.

Cook pleaded guilty to attempted murder, intentionally causing serious injury and reckless conduct endangering life. But he was still remorseless and continued to express disdain and hatred for his wife. On the morning of one of his court appearances a prison guard overhead him say: 'She's a fucking bitch and when I get out of here I will do the job properly.'

On 25 February 2010, Justice Hollingworth sentenced Cook to a maximum fifteen years' jail with a twelve-year minimum term. Cook, forty-four, had come from prison to court dressed in a daggy pair of tracksuit pants and a white T-shirt. He had shown no remorse for his crime and was showing no respect for the court.

'Around five feet tall, [your wife] only weighed about half as much as you,' Hollingworth said.

> You bound and gagged her—so that she was unable to defend herself, escape or call for help—before engaging in a cowardly, violent and unprovoked attack on her, causing her considerable pain and fear.
>
> Having restrained and shackled your already injured wife ... you attempted to drown her in what must have been a terrifying ordeal for her. It was only by sheer chance that she lived.
>
> Your record of interview is riddled with self-serving statements and outright lies, clearly intended to try to minimise your culpability. Your wife's fractured right eye socket and cheekbone had to be reconstructed with a titanium plate and her broken nose realigned. For about eight weeks she could not see properly and her balance and coordination suffered. The initial bruising was so bad that your son did not recognise his own mother, calling her a 'black-eyed freaky monster'—a comment which, quite understandably, caused her considerable distress.
>
> Your wife is still psychologically traumatised by what you did ... Unfortunately, the story of somebody who attacks or tries to kill their partner, out of jealousy and an inability to accept that the relationship is over, is all too common.

Outside court afterwards, Jessica said a few brief words to the assembled media. 'I'm just really relieved that it's over,' she said. 'It's been a two-and-a-half-year legal battle.'

Jessica said during her later interview with this author:

> There were so many times I could have died that night: when he had the knife out, the beating in the first place. He could have cut my throat in the car. The first gate was

> locked so he had to drive around. If that hadn't been locked he could have driven into deeper water.
>
> Someone was obviously looking out for me from up above. I'm not a religious person but my step-grandfather had died the previous day and we believe he had not fully crossed over and was looking over me.

Jessica said she hoped her story of survival could inspire other women—and men, for that matter—to have the courage to leave psychologically and physically abusive relationships. 'Getting out of that car in the water was easier than breaking free from that marriage,' she said.

10

Interview with a Killer

A cold-hearted bandit tells how he murdered an innocent man to assume his identity

'I stepped over him and shot him in the back of the head ... just to make certain.'

HARDCORE ARMED ROBBERS—the ones who stormed banks or held up money vans—were a brutal breed in days gone by. Before poker machine venues with little or no security became the preferred targets for bandits, the world of armed robbers was populated by ruthless urban terrorists prepared to pull a trigger to get away with cash. During the 1980s and '90s in particular, Victoria was synonymous with Australia's most vicious robbers, some of whom gravitated to murder. Some—like Russell Street bombers Stan Taylor and Craig Minogue, acquitted cop killer Victor Peirce and the likes of Frank Valastro, Graeme Jensen and Jedd Houghton—can be named. Others—like a serial bank robber who turned killer for Carl Williams during Melbourne's gangland war—cannot. Thanks to members of the former Victoria Police Armed Robbery Squad and their counterparts from the Special Operations Group, Victoria's most dangerous bandits are now either dead or in jail or they have scurried to other states and territories.

During the 'boom' time for bandits—in June 1997, to be exact—a prolific robber from Queensland found himself in one of the Victorian Armed Robbery Squad's interview rooms. A segment on the television program *Australia's Most Wanted* had prompted someone to inform police about his presence in Melbourne. One of the country's most notorious felons, he was wanted after escaping a Queensland prison nearly two years earlier and holding up several banks in three states. Crew 302 of the Armed Robbery Squad arrested the escapee on the Hume Highway at Fawkner, north of Melbourne. An itinerant fugitive, the forty-seven-year-old—who camped 'on and off' in the Millewa State Forest as part of his ploy to elude authorities—found himself sitting in a small bland room where even the staunchest of bandits had found reason to confess their sins. He, too, had confessions to make: startling confessions not even experienced detectives like Allan Birch and Michael Grainger could have expected. And so the marathon interrogation began. Birch stated:

> This is a tape-recorded interview between Detective Senior Constable Allan Birch and Ronald Joseph Williams of Ford Road, Shepparton, conducted at the offices of the Armed Robbery Squad on Thursday 26th day of June 1997. Also present is Detective Senior Constable Michael Grainger … Mr Williams, do you agree that the time is now 6.48 pm?

The man posing as Ronald Williams was escaped bandit Alexander Robert MacDonald, a man with a violent criminal history. In September 1995, with about three years to serve on a minimum stretch for armed robbery, he had escaped from the Borallon Correctional Centre at Ipswich, west of Brisbane.

Birch and Grainger were sure they had fugitive MacDonald in custody, yet MacDonald maintained he was forty-seven-year-old Ron Williams, born 14 May 1950. To confirm his true identity, Birch and Grainger needed fingerprints. The mention of prints caused a bead of sweat to break across MacDonald's forehead. At that stage Birch and Grainger had no idea where the name Ronald Williams had come from. There was no way they could have envisaged that Ron Williams—a battler from Melbourne conned and killed by MacDonald—was lying buried with two bullet holes in his head in a shallow grave on a remote West Australian beach. Ron Williams's life had meant nothing more to MacDonald than what his name and a few personal documents could offer: a chance to live life on the run with no scrutiny.

MacDonald told Birch he wanted to contact a lawyer and asked why his prints were necessary.

BIRCH: I suspect you of the offences of armed robbery and escape. In simple terms, Mr Williams, I believe you are actually Alexander MacDonald … And I have information that Alexander MacDonald is responsible for the commission of a number of armed robberies and has escaped a prison in the state of Queensland. You understand that?

MACDONALD: I do.

BIRCH: I believe that you have committed those offences.

MACDONALD: No, I'm sorry.

BIRCH: I'm not asking you whether you have or you haven't. I have reason to believe you have committed those offences. Therefore, using the law as applied in the state of Victoria, I'm asking you whether you'll supply your fingerprints voluntarily for identification purposes.

MACDONALD: I just don't understand how it can be done, that's why I'd like to speak to a legal …

BIRCH: It is a law … and, if you don't comply or you don't want to comply with that request, then I'll seek authorisation from my superior to take them forcefully from you. All right?

MACDONALD: And who would your superior be? The man who assaulted me earlier?

BIRCH: I don't know who you're talking about.

Detective Sergeant Denis Linehan entered and explained to MacDonald that a sergeant or above could authorise the use of force to take the prints. MacDonald was even shown the relevant 464K section of the Crimes Act. He knew the game was up. His charade had come to an end.

MacDONALD: Well, I see. So you're above the rank of a sergeant?

LINEHAN: I'm a sergeant.

MacDONALD: Well, it would seem that I have no option … But I don't do so voluntarily. I do it because I feel I'm being coerced.

At the resumption of the interview at 9.12 pm, MacDonald admitted his true identity, with his date of birth being 21 February 1950. What was to come next would truly shock both Birch and Grainger.

BIRCH: Now for what reason did you give the name [Ronald Williams] at the time you were arrested?

MacDONALD: Well, it's an identity I've assumed since being an escapee.

BIRCH: Right. Now how did you assume that identity?

MacDONALD: By taking the identity from the actual person.

BIRCH: Right. Who is Ron Williams?

MacDONALD: He's a guy from Melbourne.

BIRCH: Right. And do you know Ron Williams?

MacDONALD: Yes … I met him on the pretext of employing him.

BIRCH: Can you explain to me how you would assume the identity of a person who responds to an advert for employment?

MacDONALD: You kill them.

BIRCH: Did you kill Mr Williams?

MacDONALD: I did.

Birch cautioned MacDonald further, reading him his rights a second time before discussing the new offence. MacDonald said he understood and did not want to exercise any of his rights.

BIRCH: Can you approximate for me when that occurred?

MacDONALD: Early March 1996.

BIRCH: Right. And how did you kill Mr Williams? In as much detail as you wish, please.

MacDonald asked Birch for a cigarette and took drags as he explained: 'I needed an identity. I ran an advertisement in a newspaper … the *Herald Sun* … for someone to take up a position with a geological survey. My intention was to find a person of suitable age [and] background, with no close relatives, and assume his identity.'

Under the false name of Paul Jacobs, MacDonald placed the job advertisement in late January 1996 on behalf of Jacobs Associates—a fictitious family company that was said to carry out geological surveys for WA mining companies. The bogus job was for a field hand for two years' employment surveying expeditions in remote areas. The salary was $60,000 a year. MacDonald said about fifty men applied. He interviewed about fifteen from his fake office in his unit in the outer suburb of Greensborough.

'I interviewed a certain number of them, yes … To get as much background as possible on the individual and select the right one.' He was immediately interested in Ron Williams. 'He was quite drunk at the time [he rang] which was actually one of the factors that decided me to interview him further.'

Williams arrived for his first personal interview. '[He was] a guy of my build, roughly—maybe a little shorter,' MacDonald told the detectives.

> Obviously of the same age group … At that time I was 80 per cent certain that he was suitable, so I asked him back to a second interview perhaps a week later … at which time he could supply more personal details. Those details included educational background, family background and employment. [That was necessary] to give me the background story of the person.

MacDonald recapped Williams's life story. It was a bleak one. 'He's a person who was brought up largely in orphanages. Had no real close family ties. He has, or had, a mother—I don't know if she's still living.'

Williams told MacDonald that he had a sister named Mary Green and explained that he was once married but had divorced in 1982. MacDonald wrote down all of Williams's particulars.

BIRCH: At the times you were writing them down, what was your intention to do with Mr Williams?

MACDONALD: To kill him … in Western Australia.

BIRCH: Why Western Australia if the interviews took place in Victoria?

MACDONALD: 'Cos that's where the supposed employment was to occur … I told Williams the position was his.

According to all accounts, Ron Williams could not believe his luck when told the 'good' news. Finally, after kicking around a tin-can job at an auto-wrecking yard for years on end, he was now about to see the other side of Australia—while being paid. Or so he thought. Guys like Ron Williams are never meant to cop a break. To use a somewhat crude Aussie saying, he was the sort of guy who, if he fell into a box of tits, would come up sucking his thumb.

MacDonald explained: 'He signed a contract for the interim period between our agreement on his employment and his actual start of work, so that he would not seek or take up any alternative positions. That was purely and simply because the guy was a little unstable … and I wanted to have him locked into the program.'

By that stage MacDonald had borrowed Williams's driver's licence, birth certificate and other personal papers and used them set up two bank accounts in Williams's name. He also successfully lodged an application for his own copy of Williams's birth certificate from the Registrar of Births, Deaths and Marriages.

BIRCH: Did you alter the licence in any way when you used it to open bank accounts?

MACDONALD: No, I believe not … I guess there was vague similarity facially.

BIRCH: For what reason did you open those accounts?

MACDONALD: So that I'd be able to channel money into them and have them on call.

BIRCH: What money did you intend to channel into those accounts?

MacDONALD: Money from armed robberies.

According to his family, Williams was a new man when he got the job. 'He came to see us and he was just so happy,' his niece, Deborah Tylee, would recall. 'He wanted to come back and buy a house. He came to see us and, after a winning flutter on the pokies that night, I remember him saying to me as he was counting his money, "I haven't been so lucky for a long time. Everything is great and I've got this new job."'

His sister, Mary Green, said he had hopes of returning from WA to buy a home for himself and a 'little flat' for her. 'He was a quiet sort of bloke who never wanted to be without work. He could never sit still. This was the reason he took that job. I said to him the job didn't sound too good but he said it was all legitimate.'

MacDonald paid Williams a $500 a week retainer to keep him hooked until they left for Western Australia in early March 1996. Williams arrived at the Greensborough unit with his meagre possessions. 'Personal possessions, clothing, some fishing gear. That was it,' MacDonald said.

The two then drove the four-day journey in MacDonald's Toyota Land Cruiser, stopping on the first night at Port Augusta in South Australia. 'Perhaps there were two overnight stops on the crossing of the Nullarbor,' MacDonald said. 'And I know we did stay overnight at Norseman at the far end of the Nullarbor.'

At 9.50 pm in the stark Armed Robbery Squad interview room, Birch and Grainger suspended the recorded interview. There was some homework to be done to confirm aspects of MacDonald's confession. Missing persons reports needed to be checked in relation to a Ronald Joseph Williams.

BIRCH: Do you want another coffee?

MacDONALD: Coffee would be good, yes.

Ron Williams epitomised the true Aussie battler. A keen fisherman fond of a drink, he'd been employed at a bayside auto wrecker's yard—ironically called Come Back Auto Wreckers—for eight years on a $350 weekly wage. His former name was Runa Chomszczak, which he changed to Ron Williams when he married in 1981. It proved to be a short marriage. The couple had one child, whom he hardly ever saw. He spent a lot of his spare time alone fishing off piers in Port Phillip Bay. For a man who often looked for the golden side of life, rust had settled on his existence. Those who knew him described him as a jack-of-all-trades who devoted his time to his work and any odd jobs he could find. He loved to stay busy and to help people in the process.

'Ronnie was the best worker I've ever seen,' close mate Dennis Patterson would say. 'He had two speeds. Flat out and stop.' According to a former neighbour: 'He was a great little worker who used to go like hell. We used to call him the blue-arsed fly because he worked so hard.'

At 10.03 pm Birch and Grainger recommenced the interview. The detectives concentrated on the murder and picked for detail. MacDonald was reminded of his rights and the fact that anything he did or said could be used in evidence against him.

BIRCH: You previously stated that you caused the death of Mr Williams, is that correct?

MACDONALD: That's correct.

BIRCH: How did you cause the death of Mr Williams?

MACDONALD: I shot him.

BIRCH: And what did you shoot Mr Williams with?

MACDONALD: With a sawn-off .22 [semiautomatic] rifle.

The killing took place at Cheyne Beach, about fifty kilometres east of Albury. MacDonald had driven Williams there on the pretence of some good dusk fishing. After pulling in to a car park leading to the secluded beach, the men took their fishing gear from the rear of the vehicle and made the walk to the sand. MacDonald carried his sawn-off .22 rifle in his fishing bag. He said he chose Cheyne Beach because it was an isolated area. The two were standing at the water's edge. It may have been the prettiest sunset Williams had ever seen. It was to be his last.

'We fished for perhaps an hour and then I shot him,' MacDonald said coldly. 'I extracted the rifle from the bag, faced Mr Williams and shot him once in the forehead … He fell forward and was prone on the ground. I stepped over him and shot him in the back of the head … just to make certain.'

BIRCH: And when you shot him, did he have a fishing rod in his hand?

MacDONALD: No, no, no.

BIRCH: What was he doing?

MacDONALD: I believe he was just standing there. We were talking about something or other.

BIRCH: Do you recall what [were] the last words spoken by Mr Williams prior to you shooting him?

MacDONALD: No, I do not.

GRAINGER: What time of the day or night was it?

MacDONALD: Approximately 8 pm … We had torches.

GRAINGER: So how was it that you were able to distinguish him and kill him in the dark?

MacDONALD: I have reasonably good night vision.

After checking for a pulse to confirm Williams was dead, MacDonald lugged the body up into the sand dunes. He said he carried Williams over his shoulder and dug a metre-deep shallow grave using a small shovel. '[He had] a small hole in the forehead,' MacDonald said. 'And a similar hole in the back of the head.'

GRAINGER: Prior to the killing, what were you feeling at that time?

MacDONALD: In what way?

GRAINGER: Well, you say your intention was to kill him—were you apprehensive or were you just … you had a job at hand and you were doing that job?

MacDONALD: It was a job at hand.

GRAINGER: And the reason for doing that was to assume his identity to protect yourself. Is that true?

MacDONALD: That's correct.

GRAINGER: All right. How did you feel after the killing? Apprehension at all? Nervousness?

MacDONALD: No.

GRAINGER: You're a good shot, are you?

MacDONALD: I am.

MacDonald told the detectives he'd had 'quite some experience with weaponry' while a soldier with the Australian Army. He said he'd joined up in 1968 and served for five years, during which time he did a tour of duty in Vietnam. 'I was a gunner with the artillery,' he said. '[I was trained] with the SLR—a 7.62 self-loading rifle. F1 submachine gun. M16 assault weapon. M60 machine gun. M79 grenade launcher. M203 grenade launcher. I served in Vietnam for a period of some eighteen months.'

BIRCH: What were your duties to perform or that you performed in Vietnam? What did you do there?

MacDONALD: I'd rather not go into that.

BIRCH: Did you cause a death of any persons in Vietnam, by way of shooting them with a rifle?

MacDONALD: I'd rather not discuss that.

MacDonald's discretion did not extend to his description of Williams's unceremonious burial face up in the sand dunes. 'I dug a hole, placed the body in it, covered it by hand, smoothed out the area and put branches and shrubbery over it,' he said.

He kept Williams's clothing and his watch and wallet. 'I placed [his clothing] in a garbage bag, put them in the back of the ute and disposed of them … by pulling up in various spots [along the highway] and putting [them] in the undergrowth.'

The only items he kept were Williams's driver's licence and credit cards. He then drove up through Perth to Carnarvon, where he camped for two days and dumped his vehicle and rifle—a weapon stolen from a farmhouse after his prison escape. MacDonald hitchhiked back to Perth and then all the way back to Victoria. 'I remember getting a lift with a truck to

Perth and mainly private vehicles from there … I really don't like using public transport,' he said.

BIRCH: Did you use that firearm in the commission of any other offences?

MACDONALD: I used that weapon in two armed robberies in Queensland.

GRAINGER: Did you test-fire it anywhere?

MACDONALD: I had test-fired it.

GRAINGER: Where had you test-fired it?

MACDONALD: At a bush camp in Queensland.

GRAINGER: Where is that bush camp located?

MACDONALD: It's near the town of Gympie on the Mary River.

The interview was suspended at 10.45 pm as investigations continued elsewhere. At 11.19 pm it was up and running again. Birch and Grainger were interested in MacDonald's state of mind when he executed Williams.

MACDONALD: Just switched off, I guess … I guess it's part of military training that sometimes you need to switch off your emotions.

BIRCH: What is the intended purpose for which you switch off your emotions?

MACDONALD: To be able to perform anything that needs to be done.

BIRCH: And why would you need to switch off your emotions to perform those things?

MACDONALD: Because you perform much better.

BIRCH: What sort of things would you perform and in doing so would need to switch off your emotions?

MACDONALD: Anything which involves a degree of danger … a threat to your life.

BIRCH: Was there a threat to your life at the time or prior to you shooting Mr Williams dead?

MACDONALD: No.

BIRCH: Was he a threat to you at all?

MACDONALD: No.

Not long after arriving back at his Greensborough unit, MacDonald assumed Ron Williams's complete identity—with full identification to support his charade. He even started paying Williams' debts in an AGC personal loan account and deposited money into the dead man's bank account. MacDonald then moved to Shepparton in country Victoria. 'It seemed like a reasonably quiet type of area.' In May 1996, he applied for and obtained an Australian passport in Ronald Williams's name. He even sponsored a child with the Christian Children's Fund.

Western Australian prosecutor Patti Chong would later say: 'When interviewed about that [by WA detectives], he stated that it was not done for identification purposes. He simply wanted to sponsor a child.'

BIRCH: And from that day until now, have you used identification of Ronald Williams?

MacDONALD: I have.

GRAINGER: Why is it that you're telling us all this?

MacDONALD: Well, it's a foregone conclusion that you would've found this all out anyway.

By that stage Birch and Grainger had been provided with the Ron Williams missing persons case file. They showed MacDonald a photograph. 'It's very similar,' MacDonald said of the photo, while beckoning for another of Birch's cigarettes. Grainger handed him one from the pack. 'Go for it. Pretty happy in giving away other people's cigarettes, aren't I,' Grainger quipped.

MacDonald told the detectives that a psychiatrist at Fremantle Prison had once treated him for a personality disorder. When asked what effect that disorder had, he replied:

> It's difficult for me to say. Perhaps I don't share the same emotions that other people do. The disorder which I have probably means that my idea of right and wrong would be different from your idea of right and wrong ... If you look at my past history, that's my whole life.

GRAINGER: Do you know that killing someone's wrong?

MacDONALD: I know that many people consider it to be, yes.

GRAINGER: Do you consider it to be wrong?

MacDONALD: Depending on the circumstances, no.

GRAINGER: Did you consider the killing of Ron Williams to be wrong?

MacDONALD: No.

GRAINGER: Why?

MacDONALD: To me it seemed appropriate.

GRAINGER: Is what you're saying—his death was a means to you to assuming a new identity?

MacDONALD: That's correct.

GRAINGER: And you found it necessary to assume that identity to avoid further incarceration?

MacDONALD: That's correct.

BIRCH: When you say you believe that your killing of Mr Williams is not wrong in your mind, do you believe it to be wrong at law in Australia—to kill another person? Like shooting them with a rifle?

MacDONALD: I know in the eyes of the law that is a crime.

BIRCH: Right. Do you believe it is acceptable conduct by members of the community in Australia to shoot another person dead with a rifle?

MacDONALD: In many circumstances, yes.

BIRCH: What circumstances exist in Australia where it is deemed acceptable by society to shoot people dead with a .22 rifle on a beach in WA?

MacDONALD: Well, perhaps society doesn't accept that as being right.

BIRCH: You said under many circumstances. Can you name some of those circumstances where you believe it could be right, as judged by society, to shoot another person dead with a .22 rifle?

MacDONALD: Some person who had injured a member of your family.

BIRCH: Did that exist in this instance with Mr Williams?

MacDONALD: No.

BIRCH: Have you found yourself in other circumstances where you've found it necessary to kill someone?

MACDONALD: Yes.

BIRCH: When?

MACDONALD: In Vietnam.

Talk turned from Vietnam to Somerville, near Tyabb on Victoria's Mornington Peninsula, where MacDonald owned a thirty-four-foot motor sailer called *Sea Venture*. It was permanently moored at the Yaringa Marina. A man who had 'worked trawlers' in the early 1970s, MacDonald had bought the vessel for $23,000 cash in June 1996 through *Boat Mart Magazine*.

BIRCH: And where did that cash come from?

MACDONALD: From armed robbery.

At 11.56 pm it was time to suspend the interview again. Everyone needed fresh air and a break.

BIRCH: What we might do ... if you don't mind 'cos we're losing track of a couple of our questions, we might just suspend for five minutes. Get you a cup of coffee.

MACDONALD: That's fine.

BIRCH: And maybe have one ourselves.

MACDONALD: Yep.

GRAINGER: How do you have it again?

MACDONALD: Just black for me, thanks.

At 12.27 am the interview recommenced. As was done at the start of each session, Birch read MacDonald his rights and told him that he was not obliged to say or do anything, but that anything he did say might be given in evidence.

'I understand that,' MacDonald answered.

Birch went back to the beginning, and asked MacDonald about his escape from Queensland's Borallon Correctional Centre.

'I was working on an outside gardening detail and ... I walked away,' MacDonald told him. 'I guess I just couldn't see the end of [my sentence].'

The nearest town was Lowood, about ten kilometres away. 'But I didn't go in to Lowood. I went past Lowood and skirted around the general Brisbane area.' MacDonald said he walked 'a couple of hundred Ks' in the week that followed. 'I went up near Gympie, north of Brisbane for some time. Camped in the bush.' That was when he stole the rifle, he said.

BIRCH: After camping in the bush for two to three weeks, what happened then?

MacDONALD: I committed an armed robbery.

MacDonald said he robbed the Westpac branch at Cooroy in October 1995 after riding into the rural Queensland town on a stolen pushbike. 'I was shown into the manager's office and I produced the firearm. I explained the situation to him … just that it was a holdup and to get his head teller to put the money in the bag.' According to MacDonald's confession, he left the bank with the bank manager 'to ensure that the staff wouldn't sound alarms or anything of that nature until he got back'. 'I got on the pushbike and rode off along some back roads into the scrub.' He said it took him two nights to get back to his camp near Gympie.

Birch suggested he stole about $15,000. 'That would be about right … I used that for buying clothing and setting myself up with camping gear, et cetera.'

BIRCH: Okay. I have further information before me which suggests that the Westpac Bank at Airlie Beach was robbed on the 15th of December of the same year — 1995. Can you tell me anything about that?'

MacDONALD: Yes, I did that.

BIRCH: How was it that you came to be in Airlie Beach?

MacDonald began to answer, but broke into a coughing fit.

MacDONALD: Pardon me. While I was in prison in Stuart Creek, a chap there had told me how he robbed the bank in Airlie Beach. I'd been to Airlie Beach many years beforehand and I remembered what the terrain was like around there. It was suitable for what I wanted.

BIRCH: So, how was it that you travelled to Airlie Beach?
MACDONALD: I walked a lot of the way and hitch-hiked too.
MacDonald began coughing again.
BIRCH: You okay? Got a bit of a dry throat?
MACDONALD: I think it's the blasted cigarettes, actually.
BIRCH: They'll kill you, they say.
MACDONALD: So they say.

MacDonald said that, after grabbing about $83,000 and walking a female teller out of the Airlie Beach bank branch as a hostage, he camped for three or four days before heading to Melbourne for the first time. 'I wanted to get away from the Queensland area … to avoid apprehension. I hitch-hiked some of the way down to Mackay … then came by public transport.'

BIRCH: And what did you do when you got to Melbourne?

MACDONALD: I ferreted around. Got myself a unit out in Greensborough.

He also bought himself a Toyota utility through the *Trading Post* for $7500 cash.

BIRCH: By that time, had you placed any of the money that you'd stolen from the previous holdups into any bank accounts at all?

MACDONALD: No, I hadn't.

BIRCH: So you kept that on your person?

MACDONALD: That's right.

BIRCH: And it was at that time that you established a plan to assume the identity of another person. Is that correct?

MACDONALD: It was around that time that I first contemplated that, yes.

Soon afterwards, MacDonald recruited Williams and drove him across Australia and murdered him. He said that while living in Victoria he then embarked on several bank raids—in Western Australia, New South Wales and Queensland—sometimes for money and other times to confuse police. MacDonald admitted to robbing the Commonwealth Bank at Yepoon, near Rockhampton in

Queensland, on 10 May 1996. He said he drove there in an old Land Rover.

BIRCH: Why go up to Yeppoon when you could drive to Tocumwal or to Geelong? Why is it that you went north?

MACDONALD: Well, to hopefully convince the police in Queensland that I was still in that area.

MacDonald scored about $107,000 in the Yepoon heist. He went on to buy and fit out his motor yacht *Sea Venture*, on which, he said, he planned to take his own life.

BIRCH: For what purpose were you refitting the boat?

MACDONALD: It was my intention to sail it to the Solomon Islands.

BIRCH: Would that be in an endeavour to flee Australia?

MACDONALD: No. In fact, it was … I don't quite know how to phrase this—a terminal effort, shall we say.

BIRCH: This is a little bit confusing to me. You intended to kill yourself in the Solomon Islands?

MACDONALD: That's correct.

BIRCH: Why is that?

MACDONALD: Because I couldn't see any future.

BIRCH: Right. Why would it be necessary to kill yourself in the Solomon Islands?

MACDONALD: More pleasant surroundings.

The detectives redirected talk back to MacDonald's holdups: 'Have you been involved in the commission of other armed robberies, aside from those we've spoken about?'

'There was an armed robbery in Western Australia,' MacDonald said. 'And two in New South Wales. And one attempted armed robbery in North Queensland, and one armed robbery in North Queensland.' Of the WA robbery, MacDonald said he hid a motorbike in scrub near a beach in Busselton, then drove his vehicle to Bunbury and left it there before catching a coach back to Busselton the following day. He walked a bank staff member as a hostage to his getaway bike, which he rode to a beach and dumped before walking forty-odd kilometres back to Bunbury to collect his car.

BIRCH: How long did it take you to walk that distance?

MACDONALD: Overnight … [On the way back to Victoria] I stopped at several places and camped out.

BIRCH: If I suggest to you [the amount stolen] was in the vicinity of $19,800?

MACDONALD: That would be about right.

MacDonald spoke about a holdup he had committed at an ANZ branch in Laurieton, near Port Macquarie in New South Wales, about six months before his arrest. He also admitted to a Commonwealth Bank stick-up in Coonabarabran, during which he used a motorbike as a getaway vehicle. MacDonald said that this robbery was not committed for the money. He was flush at that stage but still trying to confuse police who may have been on his trail. With his successes came failure in Port Douglas. He said he drove to Cairns with a $300 black-market shotgun in a Land Cruiser he had bought for about $6000. Grainger asked him why he picked Port Douglas.

MACDONALD: It just seemed well north. A long way from Melbourne.

GRAINGER: Right. How long did it take you to drive up there?

MACDONALD: I'd say about four days.

MacDonald said he left his four-wheel drive in Cairns and caught a bus to Port Douglas, where he camped on the beach for about a week while doing his reconnaissance.

> I decided on this occasion that I would abduct one of the staff members and instruct the remainder to deliver money to a certain spot. I studied the area and decided upon a way that I could get away from the area and it didn't pan out the way I figured it would.

He took a male staff member hostage in a car park and walked him to the bank entrance. There he handed a female employee instructions stating money had to be delivered to the banks of a river about eight kilometres away. He said he forced his hostage to drive there. 'He seemed remarkably calm.'

According to MacDonald, a fisherman wandered into the plot and he had to be taken hostage—or 'in tow so to speak'—as well.

'When it became apparent that things were not going according to plan, I sent those two people on their way and I left the area myself,' he said. Grainger asked him what it was that indicated things weren't going according to plan.

MacDONALD: A procession of police cars proceeding down the highway.

BIRCH: How far from you were these police vehicles?

MacDONALD: As they went by? Thirty metres.

MacDonald said he immediately headed back to Airlie Beach and the Westpac branch there. Grainger asked: 'Was that the same bank that you'd previously robbed?' MacDonald replied: 'That's correct.'

GRAINGER: How much money did you steal on that occasion? Do you remember?

MacDONALD: No. I think it was about $40,000, thereabouts.

BIRCH: If I said to you the offence that you say you committed in Airlie Beach—that is, the armed robbery on the Westpac bank which you committed on the 6th of June 1997—was some week after the offence had been committed at Port Douglas?

MacDONALD: Yeah, that would be right.

BIRCH: I'm not making a statement to you. I'm merely asking you a question.

MacDONALD: Yeah. That's 'cos I had to actually walk from Port Douglas to Cairns.

BIRCH: How far is that?

MacDONALD: It's about 60 Ks.

BIRCH: And how long did that take you?

MacDONALD: Two nights.

BIRCH: What did you do in the daytime?

MacDONALD: Just kept to the scrub.

BIRCH: Did you walk at all any distance in the daytime?

MacDONALD: No.

BIRCH: Why is that?

MACDONALD: Very difficult for people to see you at night.

BIRCH: How do you not get lost?

MACDONALD: I can't explain that. I guess some people just have the feel for it.

MacDonald later returned to his boat in Victoria, one of the few states in which he says he never committed a criminal offence. When asked why, he replied: 'As they say: "Don't crap in your own backyard."'

GRAINGER: Right. You attempted to maintain your anonymity in Victoria, is that right?

MACDONALD: That's right.

The interview finally ended at 2.49 am. Later that day, the sketches of where MacDonald had buried Williams were sent to the WA Homicide Squad. WA prosecutor Patti Chong would say in court:

> Utilising the sketch provided by the offender, on Friday 27 June 1997 detectives from the Homicide Squad travelled to Albany and, in company with forensic staff and Dr Clive Cooke, state pathologist, there located the skeletal remains of a person believed to be Ronald Joseph Williams in a grave in the sand dunes of Cheyne Beach.
>
> The skeletal remains were excavated and returned to Perth for post-mortem examination, which revealed that the deceased's death was consistent with gunshot wounds to the head.
>
> The coroner, on 24 July 1997, was satisfied … that the body in question was Ronald Joseph Williams—date of birth 14 May 1950, formerly of Victoria—as a result of DNA profiling, dental records and the information received from the offender.

MacDonald was extradited back to Western Australia, where he was interviewed and charged. About seven months later, on 2 February 1998, he appeared in the Supreme Court of Western Australia, where he pleaded guilty to wilfully murdering Ronald Williams and charges relating to the Busselton bank holdup. A twenty-year minimum sentence was mooted. His barrister had no option but to label the murder as 'one of the most carefully planned that probably we have seen'. He told Justice Robert Anderson:

> In reality, there is probably no appropriate sentence before the court other than strict life imprisonment and I don't actually intend to waste either my energy or your time trying to convince you otherwise. From Mr MacDonald's point of view, he is himself convinced that he is not going to make the twenty years anyhow. He is convinced that he will die in custody one way or the other.

MacDonald's only straw of mitigation was the speed with which he killed Williams.

His barrister again:

> It appears … that he [MacDonald] simply bent over, picked the gun up, turned around and fired it. The movement was so quick and fast that apparently Mr Williams didn't even have the opportunity to change his expression. So basically, there was no kind of delay. There was no kind of torture … It was just flash, and it was done.
>
> One acknowledges, of course, that killing someone, no matter whether you do it quickly or whether you do it slowly—that person is just as dead. However, I would submit that [given] the speed with which this was done, at least the victim was not put to any further terror or horror as a result of the incident.

Justice Anderson was told that MacDonald did not hate people or society but did what he felt he had to do because he was an escapee. 'Having done it, he does not then, if you will pardon the expression—if I can use Mr MacDonald's own words—"cry in his own beer about it",' his barrister said.

Patti Chong said the murder was chilling and cold-blooded.

> It was not a frenzied killing nor a crime of passion that could easily be explained by human emotions. Neither was it a killing that could be explained by alcohol or substance abuse. It was not a killing by a person suffering some mental or psychiatric disorder. The offender was, by his own admission, calm and devoid of emotions, having switched his emotions off. He was, in the Crown's submission, stone-cold sober.
>
> The only redeeming features are his plea of guilty, thus saving the community the expense of a trial, and his full confession, without which perhaps the full story of what he did may not have been known. However, the offender, in the Crown's submission, is incapable of feeling any remorse.

Anderson sentenced MacDonald, forty-seven, to life imprisonment with a twenty-five-year minimum term.

Back in Melbourne, Mary Green still cries herself to sleep in the knowledge that her brother Ron will never again come knocking on her door for a chat or a cup of tea. 'Before Ron left he kissed and hugged me,' she says, holding back tears. 'I asked him not to go. He said, "I've got to get some money but I'm not going far. I'm just going around the corner. Please look after mum." I never heard from him again after that.'

11

Critical Incident

The police shooting of Tyler Cassidy

'It seemed to me like he was being a hero.
Like if the police shot him he was going to become
a hero or famous like a suicide bomber.'

ARMED WITH KNIVES AND standing in a face-off with police, teenager Tyler Cassidy appeared to have reached the point of no return. He looked 'full of rage', according to one witness at the inquest into his death, like he was 'on a mission to kill'. It was the end of a mini-rampage designed to attract police attention, during which the fifteen-year-old had stolen knives from Kmart, stabbed a Coke machine, attacked a passing car and told people to call the cops because there was a madman on the loose. His threats and demands had led to several 000 calls. Tyler had even made one himself, yelling about a mad 'psychopath' that police should shoot dead on arrival. It was about 9.30 pm on 11 December 2008 when four police officers surrounded Tyler in the All Nations skate park next to

Northcote Plaza. The troubled teenager had copped a face full of capsicum foam, but was still on his feet.

'He's resistant to the OC foam at the moment,' Senior Constable Richard Blundell puffed into his radio, catching his breath after a foot chase. 'He's still armed with the knives though and he's trying to get … ah … members to shoot him.'

Standing in an arc around Tyler were Senior Constable Blundell, Leading Senior Constable Colin Dods and constables Nicole De Propertis and Antonia Ferrante.

'Just shoot me! C'mon, shoot me!' Tyler was heard to scream at them.

The police ordered Tyler to drop the weapons. Keeping the blue shirts at bay, the teen put his mobile phone to his ear and spoke briefly to his brother Blake. 'The cops are here now and someone's going to die,' Dods believed he heard Tyler say.

What followed was a tragedy for all involved.

Tyler Cassidy liked to pretend he was a pirate, according to his mates. They called him 'Skinhead Superstar' because of his shaved head. He spent his last day drinking Bundaberg Rum with friends, some of whom had ties to a right-wing nationalist youth group called the Southern Cross Soldiers. On his head he wore a bandana emblazoned with a skull and crossbones.

'I spoke to Tyler [during the day] and we made plans to catch up on the weekend as Tyler wanted to build a "pirate bar" downstairs at his house,' friend Jarrod Felicetti would say in a police statement. 'Tyler loved pirates.'

According to Fiona Ellis, counsel assisting State Coroner Jennifer Coate during the 2010 inquest, Tyler's family and friends believed he was, 'well beyond his periodically troubled educational and mental health history'. While Tyler's personal history prior to December 2004 has been suppressed, his subsequent medical and educational antecedents can be revealed. He was first referred to the Austin Health Child and Adolescent Mental Health Service (CAMHS) on 22 December 2004, when he was eleven. Only three weeks earlier his dad Ian had passed away after a short battle with cancer.

'Tyler was deeply affected by his dad's illness and death,' his mother Shani Cassidy said in a statement to the Coroner's Court. 'Ian was Tyler's hero and inspiration.'

Two weeks after his father's death, Tyler had run from school and lain down on a road, causing cars to swerve around him. He had also threatened to harm others. 'He was referred [to CAMHS] for increasingly disturbed behaviour, angry outbursts and self-harm in the context of the death of his father,' his mental health case manager Victor Sant said in a statement to the court. 'Tyler was difficult to engage, with a dislike for medical staff and clinical settings.'

Sant would see Tyler eighteen times between 2004 and 2008. 'As an eleven-year-old, Tyler presented as a small, fair-headed thin boy who made verbal threats when frightened,' Sant said. 'He often appeared angry or scared rather than depressed although, at times around the death of his father, he had expressed wishes to die and threats to kill if he felt he was being forced to do something against his will.

'He did not report hallucinations and there was no evidence of thought disorder.'

Tyler was admitted to the child mental health inpatient unit at Austin Health for more comprehensive assessment and treatment. According to Sant: 'On admission to the unit … two knives were found during a bag search. When asked by staff as to why he had done this he stated that this was in order to "threaten the nurses".'

When Tyler was discharged from the unit Sant became his outpatient case manager.

Life chugged along until April 2006, when Tyler was asked to leave Fitzroy Secondary College after an 'aggressive incident with another pupil'. 'It was reported that he tried to strangle another male student, apparently unprovoked,' Sant stated.

About two months later he enrolled at Kamaruka private school. Sant said Tyler's behaviour appeared to be 'more settled' for a while, until incidents with other students in August 2007 led Shani to request individual counselling for her son. Kamaruka also requested intervention before allowing Tyler back. According to a December 2007 school report, '[Tyler's] impulsive outbursts with accompanying swearing continued into second semester. He has not demonstrated the necessary control for him to transition back into a mainstream setting. The impatience and insolence he exhibited towards new staff members during his enrolment at Kamaruka suggests that he would not cope in a larger school setting with many more teachers and varying personalities … He becomes very emotional when he mistakenly perceives [himself] to be unfairly treated.'

Sant said: 'Tyler reluctantly agreed to see me although only attended for nine sessions because he did not like intense involvement. Our therapeutic work involved an attempt to address his anger management and his school and family relationships. Whilst these issues had improved over the previous years, Tyler continued to be guarded and protective of his inner grief and fears.'

At the start of 2008 Tyler moved schools again. He joined his then girlfriend and a long-time male friend at Templestowe Secondary College, where he behaved himself for about six months. Sant said: 'Another stable six-month period ended in August 2008, following an incident with teachers and peers and resulting in expulsion from Templestowe Secondary College … At my last session with Tyler in late August 2008 he had settled a lot since the previous session. He wanted to "start new", and agreed to my suggestion that he explore The Island [the work education and training unit of Collingwood College]. Following discussions with the Education Department, he agreed to attend this alternative, trade-oriented school which had been his long-term wish.'

Shani said Tyler was in a good place at The Island. 'He was really enjoying it. He liked wearing overalls and safety boots to school.'

Leading teacher at The Island Rowena Bailey told police that Tyler was well behaved during his brief time there. 'He had completed his three-week trial period without incident and he was fitting in very well,' Bailey stated. 'He seemed very happy at the school. He was making friends and had formed a good relationship with his teachers. I remember that we awarded a certificate to Tyler for outstanding performance for a course he had completed about "You and the Law". He seemed particularly pleased to receive this award.'

Of a maturing Tyler, Sant said:

> As an older boy Tyler revealed strong signs of loyalty towards his friends, was strongly attached to his 'group' and was prepared to strongly defend or protect them—especially the girls and members of his family … His occasional aggression was generally towards peer males who had teased him or threatened his friends. On one occasion he agreed that he could put on a frightening face in order to compensate for his relatively small build. He agreed that he might brood over perceived threats but did not always follow through with violence … He was keen to be 'normal' and not be involved with support services.
>
> Whilst there were early expressions of wanting to die following the death of his father, he later always expressed a sense of future life; a desire for a career in hospitality or in a trade. He had a strong wish to have a girlfriend and be married with a 'house and kids' and be supportive to his mother … In my understanding he had no history of hurting peer females or animals and seemed kind to smaller children. Loyalty and justice were strong values for him, with a vulnerability regarding humiliation.
>
> His inability to discuss his father showed much unresolved grief.

In the months before his death Tyler was introduced to the ranks of the Southern Cross Soldiers. 'He was just looking for a group to belong with,' Shani said in her police statement. Bailey said she was surprised to hear of Tyler's involvement with the group. 'We never saw any evidence of this at The Island and Tyler mixed very well with all of the students who were from a variety of ethnic and racial backgrounds. We never saw any evidence of Tyler having any racist attitudes or tendencies.'

According to Shani, before his death Tyler was looking forward to the future, planning a career in hospitality. 'Tyler had told me … he wanted to be a cook in part because of a teacher from The Island.' He had considerable interest in cooking. 'Tyler had always wanted to learn to be a good cook and practice making interesting dishes,' Shani said. 'He would always want to know what was for dinner before I started cooking.'

In her statement she also said her son was looking forward to the more immediate future. 'Tyler was excited because he had been given two shifts as a kitchen hand at the Leinster Arms [Hotel]. He was thrilled because it was nearly Christmas so he would have money for Christmas shopping. Tyler had told me he was looking forward to the family Christmas party at home on the afternoon of Sunday 14 December 2008 … He had told me that he'd be in charge of the barbecue at the party.'

After the party Tyler was heading to Queensland on a family holiday. 'Tyler was looking forward to going to Queensland and visiting "the Worlds"—MovieWorld, SeaWorld, Dreamworld and other theme parks,' Shani said.

Despite his anger management issues, in his mother's eyes Tyler was a typical teenager. Like his friends he was a regular on the internet, communicating via chat sites and other social networks. Tyler was particularly close to his female friends. 'Sometimes we would go out for dinner in Lygon Street and Tyler would take absolutely ages to get ready just in case he saw any of the girls he knew,' Shani said in her court statement. 'He'd be constantly looking out for his friends, wanting to look cool. He was quite popular with the girls. They would confide in him and he'd be their counsellor.'

One sixteen-year-old friend of Tyler's was a particular favourite because she was pregnant. According to Shani, 'She was going to be on her own and Tyler was hugely supportive of her. He generally didn't like her getting the train by herself at night. He was quite chivalrous and protective of his female friends. She was about six months' pregnant and he told me that he could help her with babysitting after she gave birth. She ended up having the baby after Tyler died and named it Tyler.'

About eight-and-a-half hours before his death Tyler met up with mate Rory Jones, a part-time Coles employee some four years older. In his police statement Jones said: 'When I first met Tyler I thought he was a pretty smart kid and a responsible kid. He was also quiet and shy … Tyler loved punk music and I'm pretty positive he wanted to start a band with us.' Jones reckoned, for some reason, that Tyler had a size complex. 'I think he just felt he was small.'

The two mates met in Eltham and bought a slab of Bundaberg Rum cans. Tyler also purchased a 50 ml bottle of rum. He and Jones then travelled by train to nearby Diamond Creek. The anniversary of Tyler's dad's death had passed only the week before. 'Tyler [once] told me how much he loved his dad,' Jones told police. 'I knew that his dad had passed away as he had shown me a picture of him. He never told me how his dad had died and I never asked … Tyler was always a pretty happy kid. He was very active, always roaming about and making people laugh. It would tire us out just watching him go.'

At Diamond Creek, Tyler and Jones hooked up with mutual friends Aaron McGenniskin and a girl whose name has been suppressed—we'll call her 'Josie'. As the group made their way to Aaron's family home, Tyler temporarily split off and headed to the local McDonald's, where Aaron's sister, Emily, met him. 'I could tell he had been drinking, and he had a can of Bundaberg Rum in his hand,' Emily McGenniskin said in her police statement. 'He told me he had drunk nine cans of rum but I think he was exaggerating as he was talking to a group of girls.'

Tyler and Emily were close. 'We would speak to each other every day on the phone, through MSN and texting,' she told police. 'Every night we would talk for an hour or more on the phone. I got to know Tyler very well through these calls and he would tell me things he wouldn't tell anyone else.'

She said she was aware that Tyler would drink often, and that he loved drinking 'Bundy', but that he was anti drugs. According to Emily, the death of his father was plaguing Tyler more so than in the past. 'Recently Tyler had told me that he was finding this year harder to deal with his dad's death than previous years. He messaged me on the anniversary of his dad's death—which was the first of December. He said, "I fucken hate cematerys".'

While at McDonald's Tyler received a text and told Emily it made him angry. The message had something to do with an ex-girlfriend who was dating one of his friends. During the fifteen-minute walk back to the McGenniskin home, Emily saved Tyler from being hit by a car by pulling him off the road as he tried to cross. 'I think this may have been because he had been drinking,' she said.

When they arrived at the McGenniskin house at about 5.20 pm, Aaron, 'Josie' and Rory Jones were all there. 'He came out the back with us and we just chilled, had a couple of drinks,' Aaron told police. 'Tyler had one or two Bundies in a can.'

Tyler, Aaron, Jones and Felicetti all were or had been members of the Southern Cross Soldiers. 'It's really just a place to meet with people of any race that are proud to be Australian,' Aaron told police. 'It's nothing to do with white supremacy.' During the gathering Tyler gave his prized Southern Cross Soldiers jumper to Emily, and a sentimental bracelet to 'Josie'. Aaron would later tell police that he had thought that was strange. Emily said, 'I know this jumper meant everything to him.'

The group decided to walk to a nearby pizza shop before Tyler and 'Josie' caught a train home. Before they left the McGenniskin house, the inquest heard, Tyler skolled the 50 ml bottle of rum. 'Tyler appeared to be drunk after leaving our place and was more out of control,' Emily said in her statement, recounting that Tyler climbed onto the roof of a taxi on the way to the pizza shop and stood and yelled something. 'This behaviour was out of character for Tyler and it's why I told him I liked him better when he wasn't drinking,' she said.

The group sat outside the pizza shop and ate a couple of slices. According to Jones, Tyler was buzzing like a hornet. 'Tyler was running around and we were just doing our best to keep him under control. He was just hyperactive.' Emily peeled off from the group, which ended up sitting on the Diamond Creek railway station platform while Tyler and 'Josie' waited for a train.

Jarrod Felicetti joined the group, noticing Tyler was a 'little tipsy but in control of himself'. They spoke about the holidays and meeting up on the weekend to build the pirate bar. The inquest heard that it was through Felicetti that Tyler had first become interested in joining the Southern Cross Soldiers. 'SCS is a group of people or an association of people who hang out and share the same views and are proud of who we are,' Felicetti said in his police statement. 'When I first met Tyler I was a skinhead but I moved out of those circles and towards SCS instead. I wanted to steer Tyler away from the skinheads and to SCS as well to get him away from the violence. Tyler had wanted to meet some of my old skinhead friends but I wouldn't let him as they just make people angrier … I hadn't seen him be violent towards anyone.'

Tyler and 'Josie' caught a city-bound train at 7.07 pm. 'Tyler seemed happy and didn't mention to me that he had any problems,' Felicetti said.

The inquest heard Tyler spoke to 'Josie' about personal issues—mainly his dad—while on the train, before getting off at Heidelberg. According to the evidence, he met two female friends there at about 7.30 pm before later catching a train to Alphington. The inquest was told that at some point he realised he had left his bag at the McGenniskin house. It is estimated that at about 8 pm he sent the first of four text messages to Emily. It read: 'Worst mood ever, LOL.' Emily replied, asking Tyler to call her.

'He wanted to come back, drink rum and have a good time and wanted me to tell my brother,' Emily told police. 'I then rang my brother and told him Tyler wanted to come back but he said he couldn't as he had to work the next day. I messaged Tyler saying that he couldn't come back as the others had to work tomorrow and that he could come and get his bag the next day.' Tyler texted Emily a reply: 'FINE :('

Aaron rang Tyler, who asked if he could return. 'I said no because I was working.'

Jones told police that Felicetti thought Tyler had 'had too much to drink'. After Tyler sent Emily a rambling text about his forgotten bag ending with the words 'ive fucken lost it', she replied by suggesting he 'relax and chill out'. His final message to Emily was: 'I can't.'

Tyler's brother Blake was working his cooking shift at the Leinster Arms Hotel in Collingwood. At 7.58 pm he received a text from Tyler asking 'R u at home?' Blake replied 'no, why' to which Tyler texted back 'dw' (don't worry). Blake fired off another text, asking his little brother if he could work at the pub on the upcoming Friday and Saturday nights. Tyler replied 'ye'.

Peter Chen and wife Jing Lin were working in their milk bar, opposite Alphington railway station, when a person Chen described as a 'young boy' matching Tyler's description walked in. The teenager asked for water. 'He looked especially menacing with an angry expression on his face,' Chen said in his statement. 'My wife told me to get water for him.'

Chen handed over a bottle. The teenager gulped down three or four mouthfuls and handed the bottle back, pointing at Chen and saying something that sounded like 'I let you live'. 'I took it to mean that if I did not give him the water he would have killed me,' Chen told police. Chen replied 'No worries', and walked to the door to usher the teenager out.

'As I walked past him the hairs on my hands stood on end and I got goosebumps as well,' Chen said. The inquest was told the teenager crossed the road to a bus stop, where he began shouting and kicking a glass panel. 'The yelling he was doing was like a martial artist would yell when they punch or kick,' Chen told police.

Bus driver Peter Pecovski says he picked up the teenager at the Alphington station bus terminal. 'When I opened the doors to let him on he told me he had no money,' Pecovski said in his statement. 'I told the male he could jump on. He looked like he was unsettled, like he had just been running or something.' When Pecovski dropped Tyler at the Merri Creek bus stop he appeared to kick or punch the back door. Pecovski then watched as the teen attacked and jumped on a fence 'like a monkey': 'After trying to pull the fencing down he kicked and punched the fence a couple of times ... I thought, "Is this guy trying to act tough or something", but when he kept punching and kicking I thought, "This guy's got a problem." I watched him attack the fence for around thirty seconds to a minute.'

Lydia Firanyi was waiting at a bus stop in Arthurton Road, Northcote, at about 8.45 pm when she saw Tyler damage the fence. 'I could hear him swearing and yelling. He was saying "fuck" over and over again. He appeared agitated and pretty aggro about something.' Firanyi lost sight of Tyler as he disappeared through a gap in the fence. When she got home she called the police.

Shani Cassidy estimated that Tyler arrived home 'very upset and angry' some time after 8.40 pm. He rang the bell incessantly until stepdad Greg Taylor opened the door. Tyler yelled at the family dog, Bella. 'It was extremely unusual for Tyler to shout at the dog,' Shani said in her statement to the court. 'Tyler then entered the house, said "I'm angry" and went upstairs towards his bedroom. I went up to see him and Tyler said, "I'm angry, go away. Go away".'

In her police statement she described Tyler as 'boiling and furious'. 'His jugular veins were popping out of his neck and his face was bright red. He kept saying, "I'm messed up. My brain's fucked".'

According to Fiona Ellis, in Greg Taylor's first police statement—which he later changed amid claims it was made under duress—he said that Tyler told his mum 'he was going to kill someone or that someone was going to kill him'. In his second statement Taylor said Tyler 'only said he was angry and he never said he was going to kill himself or the police—just that the police were after him'.

Shani stated that she saw Tyler change his shirt. 'I saw dried blood and scratches on his knuckles and his elbow and cuts on his back and I asked him what had happened to him. He wouldn't answer. He just kept telling me that he was angry and to go away. I had never seen him as upset before. Normally Tyler would tell me why he was upset or angry, but this time was different. I was quite shocked when I saw Tyler's condition because his shirt was shredded and I felt that perhaps he'd been bashed or attacked.

'Also, Tyler's face was very red as if he was really angry and upset. It seemed to me that something had really rattled him, like he'd been in a fight.'

According to Emily a 'group of people' were after Tyler around that time. 'They were of a different background but I don't know what nationality they were ... I have since heard third-hand, through some people who are part of the SCS, that Tyler may have run into some of these people on the way home that night. I have no direct knowledge of this—it is only a rumour I have heard but if it had happened it would have made Tyler angry.'

After grabbing two knives from the kitchen, Tyler sat at his computer in his bedroom and chatted with mate Daniel Chowne via MSN. 'Since being introduced to Tyler we would be online and chat all the time,' Chowne later told police. 'We would generally chat online two to three times per week, usually for about half an hour. When he came online his name would appear as Tyler and in a box "Skinhead Superstar". That's what his mates called him when he got his head shaved.'

Tyler asked Chowne to meet him at the skate park behind Northcote Plaza.

At about 9.05 pm, with less than thirty minutes left on Tyler's clock, Shani rang eldest son Blake. He had finished his shift at the pub and was on his way to a mate's place. 'She told me to come home and see Tyler,' Blake said in his statement. 'She told me that he wasn't talking to her and he was in his room with a knife. She told me that Tyler had come home pissed … and that he had cuts on his arms. I told her that I would be home in about twenty minutes or half an hour. Mum asked me to come home because I get along well with Tyler and can generally calm him down.

'In the last ten years I would say that he had knives with him on about four or five occasions when he got upset. He would just have the knives in his room next to him or under his bed.'

While Tyler was still sitting at his computer, the inquest heard, Shani managed to take the knives away from him. He then briefly sought refuge on the rooftop. 'I remember that Tyler's fists were clenched,' Shani said, 'and he just said words to the effect that, "I'm angry mum, go away. Go away. I'm angry, mum".'

Tyler asked her where the baseball bat was before leaving the house empty-handed.

Ellis told the Coroner's Court:

> Tyler, according to Mr Taylor's first statement, 'stomped off out the front door with Shani chasing him … screaming that he was either going to kill someone or be killed by the police. Shani was pleading with him to come back but he stormed off.' In Mr Taylor's second statement, he states that Tyler often went for a walk to cool down.

According to Shani her son simply said he was going for a walk. It will never be known whether Tyler had already decided on his ultimate course of action and knew he wouldn't be coming home.

Blake heard from his little brother via a text at 9.07 pm. Tyler's message was: 'im sick of it'.

Judge Coate was told that at this time Tyler was marching to Northcote Plaza with what one witness described as a 'thousand-mile stare'.

Caterina Gallo and Tara Kohte were heading to the plaza for some late-night shopping when they heard a young man screaming. 'I couldn't see much because it was dark but he was on a phone,' Gallo told police. 'I then heard the same male yell out words to the effect of, "I am at Northcote Plaza. Kill, kill, come and get me." When he said this he was yelling really loudly. He was in a rage.'

At around 9.12 pm Tyler sent Blake another text. Blake later said of that message: 'I believe he meant that he thought people saw him as an angry kid, but he wasn't.' Blake tried unsuccessfully to call Tyler. He texted him, pleading for him to call, and then sent his little brother another message: 'U have so much 2 live 4.'

'When I sent him this message, I was concerned about what he was going to do,' Blake told police. 'I thought he was going to kill himself.'

At 9.18 pm Tyler upped the stakes. He called 000 and shouted: 'He's got a gun ... He's a psychopath ... and he's gone crazy ... Shoot him fucking dead!' The call was given a priority-one dispatch to Northcote 303—officers Dods and Blundell—at 9.23 pm. Details were also forwarded to constables Nicole De Propertis and Antonia Ferrante in the divisional van with call sign Preston 303. A Northcote sergeant, Scott Gevaux, was also informed of the 000 call.

In the meantime Blake had rung his friend James Wendt and told him how Tyler had run away from home and was apparently threatening to kill himself. 'Blake sounded upset,' Wendt would tell police. 'I was then asked by Blake if I could go and look for him. I immediately got out of bed and jumped in my car.'

Inside Northcote Plaza, Mitchell Papas was working front of store at Kmart. At about 9.20 pm Tyler walked in and asked Papas where the biggest knives were kept. 'Do you mean kitchen knives?' Papas asked, somewhat quizzically.

'No. Just the biggest knives,' Tyler replied.

Papas pointed the kid in the flannelette shirt to the kitchen section. 'He stormed off towards that section,' Papas told police. 'He seemed to be on a mission to get the knives. He was walking quickly, with a vigour or purpose.'

As Papas stood at the counter informing his manager Michael Petidis about what had happened, Tyler marched out of the store with a 30 cm long kitchen knife in each hand. Petidis told police he saw the faces of his staff 'light up with fear'.

'We had all scattered to safety. The male was wearing a blue long-sleeved chequered shirt and possibly dark denim pants. He was a skinhead, possibly blond, about five-feet-nine-inches tall, skinny build and was white skinned. He looked young.'

Outside Kmart, Tyler is said to have hacked at a stand containing boxes of chocolates. Petidis called 000 at 9.24 pm. That call was also assigned a priority-one classification and dispatched to De Propertis and Ferrante. Back at Northcote police station, Senior Constable Leemara Fairgrieve and Sergeant Julie Anne Goldrick overheard the radio dispatch. Dods and Blundell also heard the broadcast. The divisional vans were now well on their way to the plaza.

Tyler passed directly by Caterina Gallo as he marched from Kmart. 'He was holding the knives out towards the front of him,' Gallo told police. 'The male was screaming out constantly. I couldn't understand anything he was saying ... I could hear him hitting things with the knives. This male was very angry. I can best describe this person as being full of rage. He looked like he was on a mission to kill someone.'

Tara Kohte said she saw Tyler walk up to a Coke machine and stab it before attacking a set of doors while 'screaming and carrying on'.

Leaving Kmart behind, Tyler continued on towards an adjacent Liquorland store. On the way he passed Coles night manager Angelo Mascetti and night-fill manager Jay Westaway-Shaw. The two were having a coffee break outside. Westaway-Shaw said he heard Tyler say as he passed by, 'Oi, you two. You had better call the cops because I am about to kill someone because no one is taking me seriously.'

Mascetti remembered it differently: he thought an 'emotionless'-looking Tyler muttered, 'Call the fucking police. Someone is going to die. They won't listen to me. They might listen to you. That's it. Go call them.' Mascetti would later tell police, 'He seemed like he knew that he wanted police there and then. He kept walking at the steady pace.'

Mascetti ran straight to a phone and called 000, telling police he was considering shutting down the plaza.

Inside the Liquorland store, Tyler had a forceful chat with employees Daniel Gregory and Nick Skordos as customer Jill Birney watched from the other side of the counter. Skordos recalled:

> He came and stood next to register one and said, 'You better call the cops. Someone's going to die tonight or I'm going to kill someone.' The guy appeared agitated and was pretty aggressive. I judged this by his tone of voice and by the way he was moving very confidently.
>
> I was thinking that this guy was going to swing the knives at one of us and I just wanted to move away as I didn't want to get stabbed or slashed.

Daniel Gregory also described Tyler as acting aggressively. 'I was staring at the knives and he started talking to me in an aggressive voice. He said, "You better call the cops now because there is a madman in the plaza with two knives and he is going to kill someone." I could see he was talking about himself … He held the knives out more in front of him in a threatening manner.'

With his message delivered, Tyler turned and walked out. According to Gregory: 'As he was walking away he turned around and said something like, "Someone's going to die if you don't call the cops now. I'm serious." I was worried if I said the wrong thing he might have taken a swipe at me with the knives.'

Gregory grabbed the phone. It was 9.26 pm—less than five minutes before Tyler's last stand. 'I thought he was asking for help,' Jill Birney would later say in her police statement. 'I thought he wanted attention.'

Outside Liquorland Tyler stopped, knives still in hand, to pat a dog being walked by owners Kathryn Fradd and Kim Model. 'Chewie walked up to the boy wagging his tail,' Fradd would tell police. As he was patting the retriever Tyler told the two women, 'Better watch out. Your dog likes crazy people.'

'He was carrying two knives, one in each hand,' Model said. 'The knives looked like chef's chopping knives ... He bent down towards my dog and patted him whilst still holding the knives. I wasn't too concerned at that stage because I really thought that he probably worked in a restaurant.

'He looked quite intense—it was almost like he was upset and craved attention. I just laughed [his comment] off, thinking the guy was just kidding but it did kind of make me nervous. I think at that point it started to sink in that maybe he didn't work at a restaurant and that maybe something wasn't quite right.'

Dog squad member Senior Constable Con Matsamakis, with Alsatian Ace on board, was dispatched to Northcote Plaza's Liquorland at 9.28 pm. He and his dog were in nearby Fairfield. Northcote 303 was nearly at Liquorland by that stage, and received an updated message about staff reporting 'a male wearing a blue chequered shirt with a shaved head carrying two large knives'. Constables De Propertis and Ferrante advised that they would attend at Liquorland as back up to Dods and Blundell. Sergeant Gevaux broadcast a radio request to D-24 asking if they could 'get as many [units] as you can down there'.

Daniel Gregory walked out of Liquorland and told Dods and Blundell that the armed teenager had headed towards the skate park. Dods requested assistance from the police helicopter. Three men who had encountered Tyler in the car park stopped Preston 303 and told De Propertis and Ferrante that the teen had tried to stab them through the vehicle's window.

'He stabbed the window and the blade of the knife ran down it,' passenger Peter Afendoulides said.

Daniel Chowne, sitting at the skate ramp as arranged, saw the incident involving the vehicle. 'It stopped when Tyler had jumped in front of it,' Chowne would tell police. 'Tyler was yelling and he appeared to be agitated like something had happened beforehand.'

Tyler walked over to the skate ramp, placed his knives on the ground and greeted his mate with a handshake. 'G'day, how you going?' Tyler asked.

'I asked him what the knives were for and he didn't really answer me and dodged around the question,' Chowne later told police. 'I told him to put the knives away and throw them in the bush but he didn't. I only asked him the once but he just went back to the knives and picked them up.'

Tyler then saw the two police vans. At 9.29 pm Northcote 303 sent a broadcast: 'If Preston could take the north side of All Nations at Dennis Street … standby, we got the bloke in sight.' Sergeant Gevaux came on the air, asking how far away a canine unit was. When told four to five minutes, he then broadcast: 'The members in there just cordon and contain at the moment. Just wait for the canine.' If it had arrived on time, the police dog may have had a chance of ending the situation by bringing Tyler to the ground. Fiona Ellis, assisting the coroner, told the inquest: 'After coming to a stop, Leading Senior Constable Dods estimates that the male was standing approximately twenty feet away in the middle of the road and in what he would describe as an aggressive stance.'

Both male officers alighted from their van—Dods with an OC foam spray canister in hand and Blundell with his gun drawn. De Propertis and Ferrante were behind them. Ellis said: 'After asking the male to show his hands they saw that he had two large knives.' Judge Coate was told that Dods yelled at Tyler 'in his loudest voice' to drop the knives, to which the teen responded, 'You are going to have to kill me … you are going to have to shoot me … I'll hurt you. I'll fucking kill you.'

As Tyler advanced to within an estimated three metres of Dods, the officer employed the foam. Witness Sally Grey, out walking her dog, saw this initial confrontation. '[Tyler] was standing facing one of the police officers [who] had a real "stance" about him,' Grey would tell police. 'From the way the police officer was standing, it looked pretty serious … The spray reflected in the lights of the police car and seemed to travel quite a long distance.'

Daniel Gregory saw Tyler try to block the foam with his arm. 'It was quite a lot of spray and it definitely connected with the male's face,' he told police. 'After being sprayed, [Tyler] turned around and ran towards the skate park. I then saw two police officers start to chase him and another two police followed the first two.'

Chowne, who had moved down onto a gravel path, watched as Tyler stopped on a grass area and turned to face his pursuers. The inquest was told that police formed an arc formation around him at a distance of about five metres as he held his knives pointing towards the sky. Blundell then made his radio report about Tyler being resistant to the foam and trying to get members to shoot him.

Tyler managed a quick phone conversation with his brother. Still with OC canister in hand, Dods is said to have moved in and fired off the rest of the foam before backing away and barking: 'Put the knives down or I will shoot you.'

Tyler is said to have yelled back: 'Just shoot me! I want to die anyway.'

'I heard Tyler say this to the officers twice,' Chowne said in his statement.

Local man Daniel Holden now walked into the drama, and witnessed the second foaming. 'The policeman then backed away to the same location he had initially been in and again said, "Put the weapon down". I then heard the same police voice scream, "Put the knife down or I will shoot you" … When [he] sprayed [Tyler] he was very close to him, and the way I understand it he probably did what he was trained to do—but to me he was that close that he could have disarmed him.'

The inquest heard that the foam had no effect and Tyler began to move towards Dods at a 'steady marching tempo'. Ellis told Judge Coate: 'According to Dods, he drew his firearm from the holster and put it on target … [Ferrante] says that the male continued to sound angry and desperate and she drew her firearm as he was not complying with demands and was behaving in a threatening manner.'

Chowne watched as Tyler kept advancing. He told police later: 'He was walking towards the officer who had used the foam. He was walking real slow, like a few steps. He was still holding the knives the same way and the cops were telling him to put the knives down. I could hear Tyler saying, "Just shoot me. I want to die anyway."

'The officers crept back slowly trying to keep the same distance. As Tyler got closer the officers started moving back faster. The officers were still in, like, a semicircular line and they were all moving backwards away from Tyler.'

Holden, a student at the Victorian College of the Arts, described the incident as like watching a car crash. 'It seemed so obvious that if [Tyler] didn't put the weapon down they were going to shoot him ... It seemed to me like he was being a hero. Like if the police shot him he was going to become a hero or famous like a suicide bomber.'

While cross-examining Holden, Chris Dane, QC representing the Cassidy family, asked him to use his dramatic skills and think back to whether he heard a 'passive voice' saying anything like 'That's enough, let's everybody settle down' during the confrontation. Holden said there was no such voice. Ellis told the inquest that Dods retreated about seven to eight metres, walking backwards, being forced towards concrete stairs.

'Blundell ... says that Tyler closed the distance between himself and Dods to within a couple of metres,' Ellis said.

'De Propertis states that Dods ended up walking backwards up a flight of stairs and that there would probably have been five metres between him and [Tyler]. According to Dods he discharged a single shot into the ground as a warning ... [but] Tyler kept advancing and Dods states that he was extremely fearful for his [own] safety.'

Chowne said in his statement: 'I could see that all the police had their firearms [up] and they were pointed at Tyler … I couldn't tell who had fired but the fact that Tyler kept on walking towards the police after it made me think that it must have been a warning shot. Tyler was still yelling, "Kill me, I want to die anyway" and sometimes he was saying "Just shoot me!" I heard the police say "Put the knives down!" and "Keep away!"'

The inquest heard Dods believed he fired two rounds at Tyler's thighs at a distance of about four to five metres, as he stood at the top of the stairs 'with a small concrete flat area behind him'. In one of her statements De Propertis said: '[Tyler] turned slightly like he had been hit ... but he still continued towards Dods and he still had the knives pointed up in his hands.'

Judge Coate was told that Blundell, believing Dods's life was in danger, twice fired at Tyler's visible centre mass—but the teen continued on. De Propertis said the shots caused Tyler to slump before he straightened again and advanced. 'He was still moving normally, like he hadn't been injured,' she said in one of her statements. 'He still had both the knives in his hands and again began to approach Dods. That's when I discharged a round at [Tyler] to prevent him from attacking and in defence of Dods.'

Ellis said: 'According to Blundell, when Tyler reached the top of the stairs and due to the hazards of the skate park he remained in extreme fear that Dods's life was in danger. At this stage, according to Blundell, Tyler was approximately two metres above him and he again took aim and fired and was unaware as to whether or not the round had an impact.'

Ellis told Judge Coate of Dods's perceptions at that point:

> According to Dods there was a drop-off to the back of him and a ramp to the right. He heard about four to five shots from the vicinity of Blundell, De Propertis and Ferrante and this was the first time that he was aware of the presence of De Propertis and Ferrante and yelled out to watch the crossfire.
>
> According to Dods, as Tyler continued to advance he took aim at [Tyler's] chest area and kept firing until [Tyler] went to the ground.

Sergeant Goldrick and Senior Constable Fairgrieve were on their way to the skate park from the Northcote cop shop when Dods broadcast a message at 9.31 pm: 'Northcote 303. Can I get an ambulance here immediately? We have shot this male.'

In her statement Fairgrieve said, 'It all seemed to happen so fast.' The inquest heard that the time between Tyler's first engaging the police and the shots being fired was no more than three minutes. Tyler was hit five times—once in the right arm, once in the right knee and twice in the right thigh. The fatal wound was a gunshot wound to his chest. Pathologist Noel Woodford would later determine that Tyler's system was clean of illicit drugs and he had a blood alcohol reading of .09.

'No projectiles or projectile fragments remained in the deceased's body,' Dr Woodford said in his post-autopsy report.

In the immediate aftermath Sergeant Goldrick had the following conversation with the four officers involved:

GOLDRICK: What happened?

DODS: We foamed him twice. It was ineffective. He had [been] screaming to be shot. He had two knives and he ran at us. I fired a warning shot and he kept coming at us.

GOLDRICK: Who shot him?

DODS: I did at least three shots.

BLUNDELL: I did at least three shots.

DE PROPERTIS: I shot once.

FERRANTE: I didn't shoot because Dodsy was too close.

GOLDRICK: Where are the knives?

According to Fairgrieve, 'De Propertis indicated to two large kitchen knives that were on the ground to the south-west of the male.'

The inquest heard that ten shot were fired in total: Dods fired six, Blundell three, De Propertis one and Ferrante none. Tyler received five wounds.

Back at Northcote police station several officers had heard the shooting play out over the radio. One of them was Constable Stephen Jones on watch-house duties. He took a phone call from Shani Cassidy at 9.33 pm—about two minutes after her son was shot.

In the meantime, according to the evidence presented at the inquest, a message was being broadcast over the police channel: 'Just for the information of supervisors, we do have a sergeant present at the scene at the moment and … ah … all members can slow down. It would appear that … ah … the male is … ah … soon to be deceased.'

Unaware of Tyler's fate, a worried Shani told Constable Jones that her youngest son had come home covered in cuts and had possibly been 'beaten up or tortured'. According to Jones she said Tyler had tried to leave the house with two kitchen knives but she'd managed to stop him. 'Mrs Cassidy also said he had been on the roof of their three-storey home walking very close to the edge,' Constable Jones said in his statement. 'Mrs Cassidy was concerned about Tyler's state of mind. She said he had psychological issues but did not state what these were … She gave me a physical description of her son as being tall, a skinhead, had an eyebrow ring and he was wearing light-black jeans and a chequered shirt.'

In her statement Shani said: 'I told the police that he had left the house very upset and distressed and asked them to please bring him home.'

Jones realised straightaway that the description matched that of the male who had been shot—'But I did not give this information to Mrs Cassidy as it was unconfirmed.'

Blake Cassidy and mate James Wendt were still on their futile search mission. Blake was down near Merri Creek when Wendt, in his car near Northcote train station, saw an ambulance fly past and followed it to the skate park. Wendt told Blake about the apparent emergency at the skate park. Blake met up with his mother and Greg Taylor, who by that stage were also searching, and together they headed to the All Nations park. Inspector Therese Walsh had, meanwhile, arrived at the shooting scene. 'It was clear following the examination by paramedics that Cassidy had died,' Walsh documented in her statement:

> I recall Leading Senior Constable Dods looking absolutely distressed, raising his hands and placing them on the bonnet of one of the police vehicles. I observed him taking extremely deep breaths and shaking his head. After checking on the members' welfare, I set about establishing who had been involved … None [of the four] were physically injured but I observed that all were in a state of fear, shock and disbelief.

The four were then separated and assigned welfare officers. Shani was eventually separated from her family and placed in the back of a police car. Detective Senior Constable Cathy Sadler had the unenviable task of informing her of the situation. According to Sadler, she and Shani had the following conversation:

SADLER: There has obviously been a critical incident occur here tonight.

CASSIDY: Has he committed suicide?

SADLER: No he hasn't, but he is deceased. He has been shot by the police. As I understand it, he has threatened the police with two knives—and has been shot. He hasn't survived his injuries. I do have to say that we are not one hundred per cent sure that it is your son Tyler, but we believe that it is.

CASSIDY: Why did you have to kill him? Why couldn't you have just shot him in the leg? He's only fifteen years old. He's only a child.

SADLER: Other police are at the scene with Tyler. There will be a full investigation conducted by the Homicide Squad, and the police Ethical Standards Department and the Coroner's Office. That's done so all your questions about how and why he has died can be answered.

In her statement Shani said: 'The female officer was reasonable, patting me on the back … [but] at that moment it felt like they had destroyed me—my heart was ripped from my soul. I just went into shock. I had my hands on my head and was deeply distressed and was unable to stop crying.

'When I think about it now, I want to know why we couldn't have been all together when the tragic news was relayed to us … We were not offered any counsellors at all. No support was given to us.'

Back at home after hours spent at Preston police station, Shani was exhausted. 'I went and got all Tyler's clothes and put them in the bed to sleep on because I could smell him on his clothes. I slept with his clothes against my body and tried to sleep. I didn't really sleep. I have never cried as much as I did that night. My child was dead.'

Later that day she went to the Coroner's Court to identify Tyler's body. 'I wanted to touch him but I was told that I was not allowed.'

Shani said she would never recover. 'It gets worse every day,' she explained in her court statement. 'I now suffer from anxiety attacks. I can feel my heart muscles retracting. It feels like my heart is a rag and it's being twisted very, very tight. Tyler is constantly on my mind … I have a special place in my home for Tyler where I have this picture framed with three candles underneath. In the morning and afternoon I light the candles and in the evening I blow the candles out and give him a kiss goodnight.'

12

Hoddle Street — The Nightmare Continues

How Hoddle Street mass murderer Julian Knight haunts his victims to this day

'I can now understand why grandfathers don't tell their grandkids what happened at the war.'

ACCORDING TO POLICE AND survivors haunted by Hoddle Street mass murderer Julian Knight, the man is not worthy of the status of human being. An emaciated wretch suffering the effects of Crohn's disease, Knight has become a vexatious pest after being jailed—for life with a minimum of twenty-seven years—for a shocking gun rampage on the night of 9 August 1987. Due to a litany of legal challenges and actions he has brought before the courts since his incarceration, Knight was classed a vexatious litigant in October 2004. In the meantime his victims' nightmares continue: nightmares they openly described on the twentieth anniversary of the event still referred to quite simply as 'Hoddle Street'. It was one of Melbourne's worst ever shooting incidents, along with others commonly referred to by the streets in which they occurred: namely Queen Street and Walsh Street.

Despite the legacy Knight has left in the minds of those linked to his night of terror, he has, in more recent times, attempted to send a letter from prison to one of his victims. It is just another way Knight continues to haunt and badger his living victims and the loved ones of those he massacred. Knight said the letter was not a threat or a form of harassment. In a December 2009 judgement, Justice Peter Vickery explained:

> The letter was in handwritten form and consisted of four pages. It was dated 2 August 2005. He [Knight] said he did so after much thought and reflection and that it was a letter of apology and explanation. The 2 August letter was not sent directly through the authorised prison channels for correspondence. Mr Knight enclosed the letter in a [second] letter to a member of an organisation known as the Prison Fellowship. This was a one-page typewritten letter … [and] requested the recipient to determine whether the victim wished to receive Mr Knight's letter and, if so, to deliver it to him. The second letter also requested the member of the Prison Fellowship to read the letter intended for the victim before delivering it, and invited the member to express his views upon it. Both letters were intercepted by the prison authorities. They were opened and not sent to the member of the Prison Fellowship or the victim. They remain in the custody of Corrections Victoria.

The fact that Knight may not remain in custody for the rest of his life—and has the gall to mount a legal challenge to fight for the right to send letters to his victims—is a prospect that disturbs many. He will be eligible for parole on 8 May 2014. By then he will only be forty-six. That he will some day walk from prison is, apparently, justice for a man who, as a disaffected nineteen-year-old army reject, wreaked havoc on Melbourne with his guns. Knight killed seven and wounded nineteen. If he'd had his way—and more ammunition—he would have killed many more.

Julian Knight was $7000 in debt and having girlfriend trouble the night he went gun crazy from the cover of a line of trees and shrubs along Hoddle Street in Clifton Hill right on the border of the city. His car, a yellow SLR 5000 Torana which he'd planned to sell to pay off his debts, had blown up that day, and he'd gone to a pub and stewed in his own vindictive juices. The world had turned on him, so the Duntroon Military College misfit decided to turn on the world. At his disposal were a legally owned Ruger .22 semiautomatic rifle, a 12-gauge Mossberg pump-action shotgun and a .308 M-14 high-powered semiautomatic rifle. After collecting them from his mother's nearby home, where he also lived with his sister, Knight acted on his urge to kill. Men, women, citizens or police officers—it didn't matter to him. What he was about to embark upon just after 9.30 pm that cold winter night would be described in court as an 'orgy of deliberate shooting'.

'Julian at first always seemed to be talking about being a mercenary and had written to the South African embassy making enquiries,' a former girlfriend, Renee Cross, said in a police statement.

> From the first time I met Julian he always drank a lot. He used to get drunk on Wednesday nights after he had been to his Army Reserve meetings and come home and vomit. Sometimes when he got drunk he was very witty, and on other occasions he became very upset and cried. He cried a lot, more than any other male I know. Often on those occasions he would go on about being adopted and that he wasn't breastfed. On other occasions when he was drunk, Julian would get violent. It was usually a spontaneous act and he would strike out.

On the afternoon before his massacre, Knight celebrated his mum Pamela's birthday at a family lunch at his grandmother's house. After the party his car's gearbox blew up, and he went to his local pub to stew. He unsuccessfully hit on two barmaids, causing his mood to blacken further. He trudged home. 'Julian appeared to be in a weird sort of mood,' his younger sister, Sarah, said in a police statement. 'From the expression on his face, he didn't seem to be happy and he wasn't very talkative.' Knight collected his three longarms—the two rifles and the shotgun—and stepped out for mortal combat against a defenceless enemy. 'I walked out … into Hoddle Street and the first car I saw I started blasting away and I didn't stop,' he would say.

His first victims were lucky to escape with minor gunshot wounds and cuts. Rita Vitkos, a passenger in a car being driven by her husband, at first thought children were throwing stones at their vehicle. 'My window broke and the bullet actually went in front of my eyes, behind my husband's neck and out of the car,' Vitkos told this author on the twentieth anniversary. 'Pieces of the window went into my face and eyes. There was a lot of blood. I said to my husband, "I'm bleeding. I'm going to die." I was so scared.' Her husband was able to drive from the scene. He headed to the nearest hospital. The hospitals around the city would be kept busy by Knight's bullets that night. As the Vitkos couple sped to safety, Knight continued to fire away. In total he would shoot forty rounds from his .22, twenty-five shells from his shotgun and sixty rounds from the M-14.

Steve Wight saw the first murder—of Vesna Markovska—while working at the Collingwood Leisure Centre across from the Clifton Hill railway station. It was a cold, foggy night. Markovska, a twenty-four-year-old social worker, had been driving home from a party in her father's car. Her boyfriend, Zoran Trajceski, was following in her car. A well-placed bullet shattered Markovska's windscreen and she stopped to check the damage. As she stood, Knight calmly drew a bead and shot her in the head, shoulder and stomach. Trajceski was badly wounded by shotgun pellets. 'I looked out the window,' Wight remembered, 'and saw a gun flash and a woman being shot.'

Good Samaritans Robert Mitchell, a twenty-seven-year-old English company director, and Gina Papaioannou, a twenty-one-year-old university student driving home after a day spent with family, stopped to help Trajceski as he cradled his girlfriend near the gutter. As Mitchell and Papaioannou began to run across the road, a bullet burst through the Englishman's temple and his legs folded beneath him. He lay where he was felled, a gaping exit wound screaming from the side of his head. Before Papaioannou could draw breath, another shot rang out. Dying, but not yet dead, she collapsed wounded in the gutter.

Apprentice chef Andrew Hack, nineteen, was one of the next to come under fire. Knight set his sights on Hack's Cortina as he drove past with AC/DC's *Back in Black* blaring from his tape deck. 'As I got halfway down the hill I saw sparks fly from the car in front of me,' Hack told this author. 'Within a few seconds, in probably twenty to thirty metres, I heard an almighty bang and remember my whole body going numb. It felt like I ran over a bomb. Bullet fragments went through the door and hit me in the back, chest and shoulder.' In shock, he pulled over and saw people—a dead Markovska in the arms of Trajceski and a moaning Papaioannou—in the blood-filled gutter. Unable to help, but wanting to, Hack had no choice but to throw a U-turn across the median strip and head back towards Heidelberg Road and the restaurant where he worked. On the way he grabbed at a hole he felt in the side of his body.

The police radio airwaves quickly filled with sketchy reports about shots being fired in Hoddle Street, Clifton Hill. Any report of shots fired immediately raises a cop's heart rate, particularly if he or she is in a responding unit. A lot of the time, such reports turn out to be cars that have backfired or firecrackers, for example. But not on this occasion. The Collingwood 303 divisional van, containing constables Glen Sheluchin and Belinda Bourchier, was the first police vehicle on the scene. The seriousness of the situation was plainly evident, and gunshots began to pepper the police van. Sheluchin reversed to block the northbound lanes—so as to prevent other motorists driving into the death zone from the south. He and his partner took cover. A bleeding Trajceski ran towards them. He wanted a gun to shoot the man who had just killed his beloved Vesna.

Friends John Muscat, twenty-six, and Peter Curmi, twenty-two, were watching television at a house near the railway station when they heard what they thought were test charges exploding on the tracks. Back on Hoddle Street, Knight had just picked off CUB brewery employee Dusan Flajnik. On his way to start the night shift, the fifty-three-year-old forklift driver was now dead, sitting propped up by his seatbelt behind the wheel of his sedan. No doubt Flajnik never knew what had hit him. Muscat and Curmi ran to the roadway to see what was going on. Curmi said: 'I followed John up to Hoddle Street where we saw some bodies. There was one guy slouched in a car. We were standing under a lamp post. Then we saw someone shouting.' That person was Steve Wight, running from the Collingwood Leisure Centre as more shots rang out. Curmi, illuminated by the street light, was under fire. 'I was hit in the shoulder, but thought it was a piece of wood off the light pole,' he recalled.

Knight now had several fresh targets. They were on foot: easy prey. His trigger finger went nuts and innocent men fell. John Muscat copped it in the head and neck. 'I heard John scream,' Curmi would tell this author. 'He went down behind me. I looked up and then Steve Wight was down on the ground.'

At first Wight thought he had run into a tree. 'I put my hand over my head to stem the flow of blood and sat down,' Wight told this author. 'That's when I started coughing up blood. I looked down at my chest and saw all the blood and put my fingers over the hole.' He was forced to lie down out in the open. It was like a battlefield. If it had been a legitimate war zone, calls for medics would have been ringing to the heavens.

'People did start yelling out for help. I remember Peter Curmi yelling out that John wasn't moving. I said if John can't help himself then look after *your*self. I tried to crawl back to cover but couldn't get a breath.'

Curmi said he thought the gunman was going to pick him off. 'Poor John got shot in the head. Steve got it through the chest and took one across the top of his head. I was hit four times in a matter of microseconds.' With police sirens blaring in the distance, Curmi heroically covered John Muscat's body with his own.

About that time constables Michelle Young and Andrew Hiam arrived, taking cover behind trees next to the Leisure Centre. 'We had no idea where the gunman was,' Young recalled. 'The City West unit was yelling at us to take cover. As we looked across, there were people lying in the gutter. The most frustrating thing was our inability to reach victims.'

Efforts like that of a detective by the name of Rick McIntosh would be made to reach Gina Papaioannou, who was clearly still alive, her hand rising and falling in a weak plea for help. McIntosh managed to crawl to within metres of her, only to be forced back by bullets sparking off the asphalt. Back nearer the Leisure Centre, paramedics Noel Shiels and Peter Collins, along with police officers Sheluchin and Hiam and Garry Maddern and Phil Bradley, would crawl heroically across the ground to pull Steve Wight and Peter Curmi—as well as John Muscat's body—clear from the line of fire. 'They dragged victims back like rag dolls,' Young recalled with admiration. 'That's probably one image that sticks in my mind.'

Kevin Skinner, with wife Tracey and toddler son Adam in the front seat of their Datsun 180B, unknowingly motored into the kill zone. As Skinner drove his little car towards the railway station, he began to notice bodies and shot-up cars. Then one of the car doors seemed to explode. 'I yelled out to Tracey to get down,' Skinner said in his police statement. 'I felt her head hit my knee, and I thought she had done as I said. The first shot was followed by about four or five more. After I heard the first shot I tried to accelerate, but the car coughed and spluttered and nearly stalled.' Knight had shot Tracey, twenty-three, through her face, her blood spraying across Skinner and his little boy, who was in his mum's lap. 'She had no face left,' Skinner would tell police. 'Adam was sitting against the door just staring at her.' With head down below the level of his dashboard, peering up every few seconds, Skinner drove to an adjacent Mobil service station. 'I just wanted to get myself and Adam out of there,' Skinner told *Sunday Herald Sun* reporter Shelley Hadfield in August 2002.

The service station had by then started to resemble a makeshift hospital complete with ambulance and paramedics. Servo attendant Keith Halge had first been approached by a guy with blood splattered over him, saying, 'There's a guy shooting! There's a guy shooting!' as others began to flock there. 'I got everyone inside and told them to stay down and called the Collingwood police,' Halge would tell *The Sunday Age*. Skinner told Hadfield: '[It was] a room full of people; everyone terrified.'

Nurse Jackie Megens and partner Michael Smith were on their way home to St Kilda from Fairfield Hospital when they saw the Collingwood police van parked across the opposite lanes. Megens remembered telling Smith not to speed. 'No sooner had I said that than the windscreen shattered,' the good-natured nurse told this author. 'Michael had shrapnel wounds to his face. I looked out my side window and there were two bodies on the footpath. Every car coming down the off-ramp was consecutively being shot until the guy on the motorbike came down. He was very clearly shot.'

The 'guy on the motorbike' was Kenneth Stanton, a twenty-six-year-old mail centre officer on his way to the city to work a night shift. Knight skittled Stanton with a couple of gleeful shots but did not kill him straight away. Stanton screamed in agony, a pool of blood spreading around him, as two courageous policemen—Constable Simon Black and Senior Constable Stephen Aylward—crawled to him under gunfire. Despite their efforts, the brave coppers could not save Stanton. Knight shot the motorcyclist several times as he lay on the roadway pinned by his bike.

'I hit him and he started screaming out and he hit the ground and he was still screaming,' Knight would later tell police. 'I didn't want to keep him in any more agony, so I let off other rounds until he stopped screaming … It was better to be dead than badly wounded.' Megens recalled: 'You could see Stanton's body jerking as more and more bullets went into him. Michael asked me if I was injured. I could feel a hole in my jumper in the shoulder. From the street light I could see blood all over my hands.'

Megens and Smith noticed the ambulance at the service station and headed in that direction, driving past Flajnik, dead in his car, and Papaioannou and the bodies of Markovska and Mitchell. 'As soon as Knight realised that he hadn't killed us, he put a few more shots into the car, which missed us,' Megens said.

The police helicopter—call sign Air 490—had been up scouring the area with its powerful spotlight. Knight didn't like the idea of being lit up like a Christmas tree for the jacks, so he brought the chopper down with a couple of shots aimed at its underbelly. 'There was a bang and a huge bloody thump in the floor as though somebody had hit us with a sledgehammer from underneath,' said Darryl Jones, an officer on the chopper that night. 'I saw a few sparks fly out from under the helicopter.' Shots had hit the fuel tank, and the chopper was forced to land at a nearby athletics track. 'The bullet missed cutting the fuel bladder and piercing wiring,' Jones said. 'We missed becoming a ball of flame in the sky by about two millimetres.'

Knight continued to draw a bead on police and opened fire. As he waded across Merri Creek, he shot and wounded Constable Colin Chambers, who was in the open trying to prevent others from entering the line of fire. Every copper had their fingers on triggers, peering through the foggy glow for any sign of the bastard shooter. Charles Machen, then an acting sergeant from the Fitzroy police station, had cover behind a rubbish skip with his .38 searching for any movement. Shots were echoing out. Screams. Everyone's adrenaline was up. 'I'll never forget, as long as I live, the sheer terror in everyone's voice,' he told *The Sunday Age* on the ten-year anniversary.

> I knew we had to cordon him. The shots were ringing out. They were very close. The chopper was overhead.

> The radio just went berserk with members reporting in. I heard the chopper crew say they'd been hit and they were going down to land, and that certainly put a wave of panic through me.

Machen heard footsteps running towards him. It was an unidentifiable man carrying something that looked like rifles. There was a dog with him. Machen shouted, 'Stop!' The man was not Julian Knight but a local resident out collecting firewood when the shooting had started. Machen, with trigger finger tightening, approached the running man. Police training kicked in. He knew he had to identify the target before opening fire. Machen placed the barrel of his .38 revolver against the man's forehead. 'Police! Get down!' the cop ordered. 'He stopped and he threw the pieces of wood up in the air,' Machen told *The Sunday Age*. 'I reckon they're still cartwheeling to this day … I've never been able to track the man down, just to tell him how close he was [to being shot].'

Railway signalman Wayne Monohan was working alone in signal box B under the Hoddle Street overpass when a deafening volley of shots exploded above him. At the same time a train rumbled its way into the station. With no thought for himself, Monohan ran from the signal box, about fifty metres east of the station, to prevent the approaching train from entering the firing line. 'I grabbed the lantern and went towards the Hurstbridge train on the bridge over the Merri Creek,' Monohan told *Herald Sun* reporter Peter Mickelburough. 'I red-lighted the train and walked up to the driver, Tom Harris. We both looked around and saw Knight walking towards us near the signal box.'

Megens remembered reaching the service station as Knight moved with stealth, shooting at police to the north. 'We were covered in blood. There was a father [Kevin Skinner] with his young child. The kid had shrapnel wounds to the neck. It wasn't until the father turned around and said "That prick just killed my wife" that the enormity of it set in.' Sergeant Peter Butts, a plain clothes officer from the Prahran District Support

Group, had arrived and could not stand by watching Gina Papaioannou lying helpless any longer. He and his crew used their cars as cover to get to her. 'We just laid in the gutter with her,' Butts would later tell this author 'Her injuries looked like a shark attack.' Butts said he and Papaioannou promised to have a drink together once the drama was over and she had healed. That drink would never eventuate.

Constables John Delahunty and Ralph Lockman tracked Knight from Queens Parade into McKean Street and cornered him in an alleyway. Knight opened fire from close range, wounding Delahunty. 'I was just starting to open the door of the police vehicle when I heard gunshots,' Delahunty would say in his statement. 'There was a flash and I felt an impact against the side of my head.' In an interview the *Herald Sun*, Delahunty said: 'Ralph bailed out his side.'

Delahunty aimed his .38 service revolver and fired a single round. His muzzle flash lit the darkness. And then there was quiet. 'After a moment I heard a voice yelling, "Don't shoot! I'm unarmed",' he told this author. 'He'd actually thrown his gun out.' Delahunty remembered Knight standing with hands in the air. 'I think he said something like, "I surrender".'

Before he set out with his arsenal that evening, Knight had tucked a bullet in his jacket pocket for when *his* time came. He said he intended to kill himself at the end of his rampage—but could not find the bullet. 'I fired off my last rounds at the two police officers near me, then frantically searched for the round I had reserved for myself, but it had dropped out of my pocket,' Knight would later say. 'I realised the situation was hopeless and gave up without a fight. There is no doubt in my mind that I would have used that last bullet if I had found it. I would have killed myself. I wish I had.' So do many other Victorians.

With hands up, Knight knelt on the ground. 'When I first took hold of him and dragged him over to the car he just seemed like a skinny pathetic coward,' Delahunty said. 'He was crying for us not to hurt him … It was the most terrifying and exhilarating thing I've ever experienced.'

About forty-six minutes after the first shot rang out, Delahunty made a radio message to say the carnage was over. It was 10.15 pm and the gunman was in custody.

FITZROY 213: The offender has a weapon.

D24: Roger. You have the offender?

FITZROY 213: There's been a shot. There's a bloody automatic weapon. We've got one offender and one weapon.

D24: Roger Fitzroy 213. Has a member been shot or has the offender been shot?

FITZROY 213: I've got blood on me. I don't know where it's from.

Between 10.23 pm and 10.30 pm, as police took control of the scene, officers scouring the war zone found Knight's two other dumped guns. Homicide Squad detective Graham Kent arrived at Hoddle Street. The kill zone was shrouded in the ghostlike fog. The Reaper had run his scythe across Melbourne. 'It was a really eerie, surreal situation,' Kent would say. 'It was fairly quiet. You could see something really frightening had happened there. You were almost in a theatre that had been set up, but you couldn't imagine someone with a mind to set something up like that—other than perhaps Quentin Tarantino.'

Kent walked a remorseless and somewhat excited Knight through the scene for a re-enactment. 'What is clear is the chilling way he clinically described what had happened,' Kent told reporter Shelley Hadfield. 'Of one of the deceased, he said he put a couple of extra shots into him—in his words—to put him out of his misery.'

Kent conducted Knight's record of interview. The mass killer took delight in reliving the rampage, saying he had desired to kill and experience combat. 'He was very happy and actually wanted to tell the story,' Kent recalled on the twentieth anniversary. 'He actually sort of revelled in that storytelling. [It was like] this was his fifteen minutes of fame and he had the bragging rights, and he wanted to say how well he'd done. For him, it was an adventure.'

For Kent, professionalism was paramount when conducting

records of interview with suspects. The last thing a lead investigator wants is the integrity of an interview questioned on the basis of intimidation or improper behaviour. With Knight it was all about suppressing any feelings of animosity. 'My feelings were only about staying focused on the job. It was critical to record what this guy had to say in a way that would be admissible in court.'

In April 1988, the Melbourne Magistrates' Court was told that when Knight was sixteen he was keen to go to battle in Central America, Afghanistan and the Middle East, and had tried to join the South African army. His barrister, Robert Richter, QC, said the weapons he used at Hoddle Street were all legally obtained and registered. He said violence was glamorised in movies, and idolised. He said it was hypocritical of society to glorify movie killers, given the public's loathing of violence, and that society failed to recognise and guard against 'walking time bombs' while making violent celluloid heroes rich and famous.

'This society puts a premium on, and pays a fortune to, people who portray mass killers who act like Rambo,' Richter said. Six months later the Supreme Court was told that Knight, a wannabe mercenary who once asked a schoolteacher if he could use the magazine *Soldier of Fortune* as reference material for a project, had plotted his rampage as he drank alone at his local bar. It was told that Knight had longed to see what it felt like to kill someone and be killed himself in battle. Mr Richter said Knight's IQ ranked in the top 3 per cent of the population but he had the emotional development of a child. After his first shot, Knight had 'clicked into military mode'. According to Richter, Knight was trained to kill and kept shooting until he ran out of ammunition.

'Having run out of ammunition and being called on to surrender, he did what soldiers are taught to do [by surrendering],' Richter said. The judge heard that other prisoners regarded Knight as 'filth' for what he had done.

In the end, Knight pleaded guilty to seven counts of murder and forty-six charges of attempted murder. Justice George Hampel told him he had been responsible for 'one of the worst massacres in Australian history'. 'Many more were fortunate to escape death or injury as you indiscriminately fired over one hundred rounds of ammunition from three weapons at passing motorists and at the police as they tried to apprehend you,' Hampel said upon sentence.

> The answers to what you did lie in your background, your fragile and disordered personality, and ultimately in your inability to cope with the accumulation of pressures and stresses which operated on you. Your fantasy life was built around heroic killing in battle situations, ending up in victory or your own death in the so-called 'last man' stance.

Hampel sentenced Knight to life imprisonment with a twenty-seven-year minimum term, saying there were mitigating factors, including Knight's age, the absence of prior convictions, his abnormal mental state and his guilty plea.

The Herald journalist Keith Moor tagged along with Knight's family for a prison visit and gained an exclusive interview with the mass killer. Knight was quick to stress that he was not like mass murderer Frank Vitkovic, who shot dead eight people during a gun rampage in the Australia Post building in Queen Street in Melbourne's CBD on 8 December 1987. After his spree, Vitkovic threw himself out of an eleventh-storey window.

'He was mad and I'm not,' Knight told Moor. 'His was a premeditated act. Mine was spontaneous.' Knight blamed the army. 'They trained me to kill, and I killed.'

Knight had grown up under a military influence, thanks to his adoptive father's army career and postings in places like Malaysia, Singapore and Hong Kong. 'I was proficient in the use of arms before I was fourteen,' he told Moor.

> I was trained on the M60 machine gun at the age of sixteen. I had done a survival training course and been trained in ambush and counter-ambush situations before my seventeenth birthday. Among the other weapons I trained, shot and qualified on were an F1 submachine gun, M79 grenade launcher, M26 hand grenade, M14 and M16 mines,

> 84-millimetre medium-range anti-armour weapon, L1A2 automatic rifle and nine millimetre pistol.

It was fair to say the guy was a fanatic. To Keith Moor he went on:

> I did assault courses, survival courses and terrorist exercises. I was able to kill and wound so many in Hoddle Street because the army had trained me so well. Something snapped. I went into automatic pilot mode. Everyone bar me was the enemy that night, and you kill the enemy. I was trained 'Target up, fire, shoot to kill. Duck, weave, take cover. See a target, shoot to kill. Don't hurt. Shoot to kill.' They trained me to kill and I killed by the textbook.
>
> It still amazes me that I was able to wander around shooting at random for about forty-eight minutes. Where was the Special Operations Group? Where were the police crackshots?

Knight told Moor he had thought about killing from the age of about sixteen. 'It stands to reason that if you spend long enough training to kill people, that you are going to want to put that training to the test. That's all I did. It's like you training to write a story and never actually writing one.'

By the time the Hoddle Street twentieth anniversary had come around, Andrew Hack was running a successful painting business. He admitted to having staved off suicidal thoughts after his physical recovery. 'I'm embarrassed about it [the thoughts of suicide], but that's how I got help,' he admitted. 'I saw a psychologist for two years on and off. It was hard. When you're a young kid you think you're invincible.' The Christian church had taken Peter Curmi to an interstate seaside town where he was living with his wife and family. 'I still love Melbourne,' he said.

Jackie Megens admitted she was still a bit jumpy. 'If I go through a red light camera now [and it goes off], the first thing I do is duck. It scares the absolute shit out of me.'

Kevin Skinner told reporter Hadfield that he turned to the bottle for a couple of years. 'I just couldn't face anything. Couldn't face any of my friends, couldn't face any of my family. To walk into a room and know everyone's feeling sorry for you … to solve that I got drunk a lot. I still think about it.'

Graham Kent said he reflects on the tragic events every time he drives along Hoddle Street. 'I think what an enormous waste and tragedy, all because of an immature, selfish young man. Whilst there were seven who died, it was extremely fortunate there weren't more, including a number of police officers. There were tremendously heroic things done that night.'

Peter Butts, now a retired policeman, said Gina Papaioannou's death in hospital eleven days after Knight's massacre hit him hard. He had bonded with her in the blood-soaked gutter, while never knowing if he and his heroic colleagues were going to be shot next.

> I was pretty sad about Gina's passing. We struck up a friendship over what seemed like a lifetime—even though we only spent about an hour and a half together in that Hoddle Street gutter. If I can avoid going past there, I do. This is the incident that probably affected me more as an individual than a policeman. I can now understand why grandfathers don't tell their grandkids what happened at the war.

Relatives of the Hoddle Street victims joined survivors in calling for Knight to be made to serve out his life sentence. Christos Papaioannou, father of young Gina, said on the twentieth anniversary that he was angry that Knight could ever be released. 'The best way to keep this Julian Knight in jail is to give me the keys,' he said. 'He should be kept in jail forever. When I think about my Gina, I lose the ground under my feet. Keep him in jail forever. He should die in jail.'

Retired tram driver Phillip Muscat, who survived the war in Malta only to see son John killed in a Melbourne war zone said: 'He should stay inside. Justice is not much good in Australia.' The hero cops agreed. 'I am not convinced that anyone who committed a massacre like that can be rehabilitated,' Peter Butts said. John Delahunty added: 'What he did was not combat: it was just the slaughter of innocent people going about their lives. Perhaps it's time for the community and the government to seriously consider whether Knight should ever be eligible to apply for parole.'

Surviving victims urged authorities to throw away the key. 'I don't believe he can contribute to society in any way,' Steve Wight said. 'He's never shown any remorse and he's constantly flouted the law. He studied military strategies and some other courses while in prison. What's the likelihood of him coming out and wanting to do the same thing again? My biggest fear is that it could happen again.'

Peter Curmi put it in the simplest of terms. 'There was no sympathy and no remorse. He just went out and shot us like animals.'